Collections for Young Scholars ™

FRAMEWORK FOR EFFECTIVE TEACHING ™

Grade 1: Thinking and Learning About Print

TEACHER'S GUIDE, PART B

PROGRAM AUTHORS
Marilyn Jager Adams
Carl Bereiter
Jan Hirshberg
Valerie Anderson
S. A. Bernier

CONSULTING AUTHORS
Michael Pressley
Marsha Roit
Iva Carruthers
Bill Pinkney

OPEN COURT PUBLISHING COMPANY
Chicago and Peru, Illinois

CHAIRMAN
M. Blouke Carus

PRESIDENT
André W. Carus

EDUCATION DIRECTOR
Carl Bereiter

CONCEPT
Barbara Conteh

SENIOR EXECUTIVE EDITOR
Sheelagh McGurn

EXECUTIVE EDITOR
Shirley Graudin

SENIOR PROJECT EDITORS
Linda Cave
Nancy H. Johnson

PROJECT EDITORS
Joseph Barron
Jennifer Johnson
Janette McKenna
Beth Niewijk
Karen Sapp
Ana Tiesman

ASSESSMENT
Learning in Motion

SUPERVISOR, EDITORIAL SERVICES
Janice Bryant

SENIOR COPYEDITOR
Lucille Alaka

ART DIRECTOR
John Grandits

DESIGN
Diane Hutchinson

VICE-PRESIDENT, PRODUCTION
AND MANUFACTURING
Chris Vancalbergh

COVER ARTISTS
Hilary Knight
Normand Chartier

Acknowledgments can be found
on page 384 of this book and
are hereby incorporated as part
of this copyright page.

Printed in the United States of America

ISBN 0-8126-1103-9   2 3 4 5 6 7 8 9 10

CONTENTS

APPENDIXES

INDEX

Using Open Court's Thinking and Learning About Print

Contents
for Using
Thinking and Learning About Print

A child's success in first-grade reading looks like the single best predictor—and, in fact, an awesomely powerful predictor—of her or his ultimate educational outcome, however you measure it.—Marilyn Jager Adams

A Program for the 21st Century

Getting Acquainted

Thinking and Learning About Print is a very special part of *Collections for Young Scholars.*™ In this part of the program, students gain access to the most important technology ever developed—written language. Our system of writing is the gateway to all the world's knowledge. By learning to read, people acquire enormous power to find things out, educate themselves, and gain control over their own fates and lives. Nothing they learn in school will be remotely as important as this step. And every future step, every increment of learning, depends on the success of this first step.

A step of such fundamental importance in people's lives demands to be taken seriously. It demands that we bring to bear all the knowledge that the sciences of the human mind and of language development have struggled for over the past decades. These sciences have taught us a great deal—and yet, reassuringly, they have also taught us that what great primary teachers have always done has been absolutely right:

- Teach the sounds and letters early, intensely, and quickly;
- Never let students lose sight of the purpose and goal (read aloud to them, talk to them about books, make literacy irresistibly exciting);
- Get students into real reading as quickly as possible (give them a sense of power);
- Allow them to gain fluency in writing, enabling them to use it as a tool of inquiry as well as communication; and,
- Give them as much responsibility for their own work, their own mental development, and their own paths of inquiry as possible

Senior Author Team

The goal is to let children in on the excitement of literacy—not just doing things they couldn't do before, but knowing things they never knew before, thinking about things they never thought about before, and understanding things they never understood before. —Marilyn Jager Adams

Marilyn Jager Adams is a Senior Scientist in the Psychology Department at Bolt Beranek and Newman, Inc., a research and development laboratory in Cambridge, Massachusetts. She is also a Senior Research Scientist at Brown University and has been affiliated with the Center for the Study of Reading at the University of Illinois since 1975. She is the author of *Beginning to Read: Thinking and Learning About Print* (MIT Press, 1990), written on behalf of the U.S. Secretary of Education as mandated by Congress. The book, the most comprehensive study of beginning reading undertaken to date, examines instructional practices from a historical perspective and critiques them in terms of theoretical and empirical research in education, psychology, and linguistics.

Carl Bereiter is Professor at the Centre for Applied Cognitive Science at the Ontario Institute for Studies in Education in Toronto and a member of the National Academy of Education. He has coauthored many curriculum projects, including Open Court's reading and mathematics programs. He is coauthor with Marlene Scardamalia of *The Psychology of Written Composition* (1987) and *Surpassing Ourselves: The Nature and Implications of Expertise* (1993); and he has published extensively on the nature of teaching and learning. Computer-supported intentional learning environments and collaborative knowledge building have been the subjects of his most recent classroom investigations and publications.

Beginning readers have a lot to learn about how written language works. But at the same time, they are fully-formed human beings who wonder, think, get absorbed by a good story, enjoy and make jokes. A good reading program will honor all these facts. This program, when taught in the right spirit, will do that. —Carl Bereiter

Jan Hirshberg holds an Ed.D. in reading, language, and learning disabilities from Harvard University. She has taught in elementary school classrooms and has also served as a school district reading consultant. At Harvard she was a teaching fellow, research assistant, instructor, and lecturer at the Graduate School of Education. Her reading specialities are in linguistics and early literacy. Her work has focused on how children learn to read and write and on the logistics of teaching reading and writing in the early elementary grades. She is an author of the kindergarten and grade-1 levels of Open Court's 1989 reading and writing program as well as *Collections for Young Scholars*.

In order for children to learn how to read, they have got to break the code. And by teaching them about how the sound structure of their language works, you're only making it that much easier for them to break the code. —Jan Hirshberg

Young children need to learn to do more than simply go through the motions of reading and writing. They need to learn to take an active role in the wondering, problem solving, and responsiveness that literate people engage in as they read and write. —Valerie Anderson

Valerie Anderson is Research Associate at the Centre for Applied Cognitive Science at the Ontario Institute for Studies in Education and is on the editorial advisory boards of *The Reading Teacher* and *The Journal of Reading Behavior*. Anderson has extensive experience both in designing curriculums and in training teachers. She has been coauthor of a number of curriculum projects, including *Thinking Games* (with Carl Bereiter), *The Reading Connection*, and *Catching On*. Her main professional focus is on training teachers how to apply the latest educational theories in their classrooms. Her most recent work with children has centered on helping them learn to use thinking strategies to become independent readers.

Consulting Authors

You've got to have a dream. And when you have a dream, you've got to find out what it takes to make that dream come true. Everything takes something. There's no free lunch. It's not just going to happen. You're going to have to do something. And, if you're willing to pay that price, you can make the dream a reality.—Bill Pinkney

Michael Pressley is Professor of Educational Psychology and Statistics at the State University of New York at Albany, as well as Principal Investigator for the National Reading Research Center, centralized at the Universities of Maryland and Georgia. He does both basic laboratory research on cognition and learning and applied work in educational settings. Memory development and reading comprehension strategies have received much of his attention.

Marsha Roit spends considerable time in classrooms working with children to develop and demonstrate reading and writing activities and training teachers and administrators. Her work has been published in a variety of education journals, including *Exceptional Children* and *Journal of Learning Disabilities*, and she has articles in press in *Educational Leadership* and *The Elementary School Journal*. She has presented her work at national and international conferences.

Iva E. Carruthers is Professor and former Chairperson of the Sociology Department of Northeastern Illinois University. She is also President of Nexus Unlimited, Inc., a human resources development and computer services consulting firm, and of Ed Tech, a computer software development company. In addition to developing educational software aids for teaching history and interdisciplinary subjects, she has produced fourteen study guides on African-American and African history.

Bill Pinkney is the first African American to sail solo around the world, traveling around the five great capes in his sailboat named *Commitment*. Only forty-one individuals have accomplished this feat. More than 30,000 students across the United States were able to share in his legendary voyage, thanks to advanced satellite and computer technologies. Not only did he give these students lessons in math, science, geography, and social studies, but Captain Pinkney also modeled for them the courage, perseverance, skill, and commitment required to realize one's dreams.

Charles Abate, Ed.D.
Elementary Principal
Orchard Elementary School
Ridgewood, New Jersey

Doris B. Ash, M.S.
Assistant Director
Fostering a Community of Learners Research Project
University of California, Berkeley

Mary Lamon, Ph.D.
Project Director
Middle School Curriculum Development Project
St. Louis Science Center
St. Louis, Missouri

Martha E. Rutherford, M.A.
Assistant Director
Fostering a Community of Learners Research Project
University of California, Berkeley

Barbara Appleberry, *Grade 1*
Mollison Elementary School
Chicago, Illinois

Marie Beacham, *Grade 1*
Ephraim Elementary School
Ephraim, Utah

Joyce Bell, *Grade 1*
Brown School
Newburyport, Massachusetts

Kim Carey, *Grade 6*
Crestmont Elementary School
Northport, Alabama

Peggy Clelland, *Grade 1*
Washington Terrace Elementary
   School
Ogden, Utah

Emmy Daniel, *Grade 1*
South Shores School
Decatur, Illinois

Tony Dillon, *Grade 1*
John Foster Dulles School
Chicago, Illinois

Dorothy Dorsey, *Grade 4*
Glenmount Elementary School
Baltimore, Maryland

Kay Ericksen, *Grade 5*
Ephraim Elementary School
Ephraim, Utah

Debra Evans, *Grade 3*
Goldblatt Elementary School
Chicago, Illinois

Margaret Ewing, *Grade 3*
Abraham Lincoln Elementary
   School
Palm Desert, California

Sr. Susan Faist, *Grade 2*
Christ the King School
Toledo, Ohio

Mary Fatsi, *Grade 1*
Brooklyn Elementary School
Brooklyn, Connecticut

Susan Fowler, *Grade 2*
Yaquina View Elementary
Newport, Oregon

Bonnie French, *Grade 6*
Carl Sundahl Elementary School
Folsom, California

Lena Gates, *Grade 1*
Crispus Attucks School, P. S. 21
Brooklyn, New York

Lila Gilchrist, *Grade 3*
The Orchard School
Ridgewood, New Jersey

Leticia Gonzalez, *Grade 4*
Saenz Elementary School
Alice, Texas

Lora Gordy, *Grade 5*
Buckingham Elementary School
Berlin, Maryland

Janice Green, *Grade 1*
Francis T. Bresnahan School
Newburyport, Massachusetts

Joyce Haffey, *Grade 4*
St. Therese School
Kansas City, Missouri

Jackie Herath, *Grade 3*
Sunderland Elementary School
Sunderland, Maryland

Dorothy Hines, *Grade 2*
Benefield Elementary School
Lawrenceville, Georgia

Karen Horace, *Grade 6*
Goldblatt Elementary School
Chicago, Illinois

Patricia Horst, *Grade 5*
Harding Elementary School
Clinton, Ohio

Hurtice Howard, *Grade 1*
Julia L. Armstrong Elementary
  School
Greenville, Mississippi

Nancy Hughes, *Grade 2*
Eleanor Roosevelt School
Vancouver, Washington

Celeste James, *Grade 1*
John Foster Dulles School
Chicago, Illinois

Christine Johnson, *Grade 1*
Kelley School
Newburyport, Massachusetts

Patricia Johnson, *Grade 3*
Crispus Attucks School, P. S. 21
Brooklyn, New York

Laurie Jones, *Grade 4*
Grantswood Community School
Birmingham, Alabama

Lisa Kane, *Grade 5*
Disney Magnet Elementary School
Chicago, Illinois

Charlotte Lewis, *Grade 1*
L. B. Weemes Elementary School
Los Angeles, California

Rhet Lickliter, *Grade 6*
Park Tudor School
Indianapolis, Indiana

Sandra Loose, *Grade 1*
Indian Lane Elementary School
Media, Pennsylvania

Frank Lopez, *Grade 5*
Parker Elementary School
Panama City, Florida

Kathryn Lopez, *Grade 1*
Millville Elementary School
Panama City, Florida

Mary Ann Luebbert, *Grade 6*
Russell Elementary School
Hazelwood, Missouri

Ruth MacGregor, *Grade 3*
Mildred M. Fox School
South Paris, Maine

Lynne Malone, *Grade 3*
Carver Elementary School
Dawson, Georgia

Pam Martin, *Grade 1*
L. B. Weemes Elementary School
Los Angeles, California

Melony Maughan, *Grade 1*
Grantswood Community School
Birmingham, Alabama

Ursula McClendon, *Grade 3*
George West Primary School
George West, Texas

Phyllis Miles, *Grade 4*
Our Lady of Mount Carmel
Carmel, Indiana

Sue Miller, *Grade 1*
The Valwood School
Valdosta, Georgia

Nancy Mitchell, *Grade 2*
Pleasant Ridge School
Grass Valley, California

Trudy Mockert, *Grade 1*
Nicolaus Copernicus School, P. S. 25
Jersey City, New Jersey

Anna Molina, *Grade 1*
Ezra Nolan School, P. S. 40
Jersey City, New Jersey

Roberta Montoya, *Grade 3*
Alamosa Elementary School
Albuquerque, New Mexico

Carol Neyman, *Grade 5*
Cotton Boll Elementary School
Peoria, Arizona

Margaret Nichols, *Grade 1*
Brown School
Newburyport, Massachusetts

Cindy Noland, *Grade 2*
Jefferson Elementary School
Parkersburg, West Virginia

Bettye Nunnery, *Grade 2*
Otken Primary School
McComb, Mississippi

Jane Offineer, *Grade 5*
Belden Elementary School
Canton, Ohio

Sara Oliveira, *Grade 5*
Portsmouth Elementary School
Portsmouth, Rhode Island

Kathleen Pabst, *Grade 3*
Charles Drew Elementary School
San Francisco, California

Judith Palermo, *Grade 1*
St. Helen's School
Chicago, Illinois

Terri Patterson, *Grade 4*
Paradise Elementary School
Las Vegas, Nevada

Becky Philips, *Grade 2*
Sunderland Elementary School
Sunderland, Maryland

Donna Powell, *Grade 2*
Melville School
Portsmouth, Rhode Island

Barbara Purcell, *Grade 3*
Education Service Center
Corpus Christi, Texas

Caron Reasor, *Grade 6*
La Quinta Middle School
La Quinta, California

Sharon Robinson, *Grade 2*
Flournoy Elementary School
Los Angeles, California

Judith Roy, *Grade 1*
Grantswood Community School
Birmingham, Alabama

Maxine Rushing, *Grade 4*
Plymouth Day School
Detroit, Michigan

Kathy Rodger-Sachs, *Grade 4*
The Orchard School
Ridgewood, New Jersey

Agnes Schutz, *Grade 1*
Alamosa Elementary School
Albuquerque, New Mexico

Donna Sedlacek, *Grade 3*
Bear Creek Elementary School
Lakewood, Colorado

Ruth Seiger, *Grade 1*
Francis T. Bresnahan School
Newburyport, Massachusetts

Cheryl Sheehan, *Grade 1*
Nicolaus Copernicus School,
    P. S. 25
Jersey City, New Jersey

Margaret Simmons, *Grade 6*
Corpus Christi Elementary School
San Francisco, California

Renee Singer, *Grade 1*
Grantswood Community School
Birmingham, Alabama

Jacqueline Smith, *Grade 1*
John Foster Dulles School
Chicago, Illinois

Patricia Terrell, *Grade 4*
Gatewood Elementary School
Oklahoma City, Oklahoma

Barbara Uhrin, *Grade 2*
Amos Hutchinson Elementary
    School
Greensburg, Pennsylvania

Celia Waddell, *Grade 5*
Grantswood Elementary School
Birmingham, Alabama

Laurie Walters, *Grade 1*
L. B. Weemes Elementary School
Los Angeles, California

Robin Wexler, *Grade 5*
Roosevelt Elementary School
River Edge, New Jersey

Intelligent Resources for Teaching

All components of *Collections for Young Scholars* are carefully focused on developing self-motivated students who take primary responsibility for their own learning.

Core Teacher Materials

Overview

Collections for Young Scholars for Grade 1 is accompanied by four separate volumes of the *Framework for Effective Teaching* for Grade 1:

- *Thinking and Learning About Print*, Part A (accompanies the first two Big Books, *Look Who's Reading!* and *Animals*)
- *Thinking and Learning About Print*, Part B (accompanies the third and fourth Big Books, *Captain Bill Pinkney's Journey* and *Machines in Our Garden*)
- *Framework for Effective Teaching*, Grade 1, Book 1 (accompanies *Collections for Young Scholars*, Volume 1, Book 1)
- *Framework for Effective Teaching*, Grade 1, Book 2 (accompanies *Collections for Young Scholars*, Volume 1, Book 2)

The first two volumes, *Thinking and Learning About Print*, Parts A and B, are designed to give students the basic reading skills they need to be able to read the uncontrolled text in the grade 1 student anthologies, *Collections for Young Scholars*, Volume 1, Books 1 and 2.

Framework for Effective Teaching: Thinking and Learning About Print
These two teacher's guides contain lesson-by-lesson suggestions for all aspects of the reading and language arts curriculum in the first half of grade 1, including reading, language arts, writing, spelling, and literature. Each lesson should correspond to about one day of teaching.

The lessons in this volume, Part B, contain:
- Introduction of sound spellings.
- Direct instruction in blending of sound spellings.
- Suggestions for reading of Big Books, Phonics Minibooks, and Step-by-Step Practice Stories (see pages 21F–22F).
- Dictation of words and sentences in every other lesson.
- Informal word-building activities.
- Experiments and demonstrations to accompany science concepts in *Machines in Our Garden*.
- A simple introduction to social studies concepts.

- Writing process suggestions; if these are not used, teachers are strongly encouraged to use whatever approach to early writing they feel comfortable with.
- Suggestions for Workshop, in which students work independently or in small groups, and the teacher is able to give attention to individual children.

Each of these parts is associated with a basic technique of the program; these techniques are described on pages 27F–30F of this guide. For easy reference, there is also a Learning Framework Card (see pages 18F–19F) describing each technique in more detail.

The Teacher Toolbox

Learning Framework Cards

A few basic techniques are repeated throughout the program. These Learning Frameworks provide predictable approaches to instruction that enable students to focus on actual learning without wasting time getting organized for learning. These clear and simple frameworks offer the students invaluable tools that they can easily apply to all new learning.

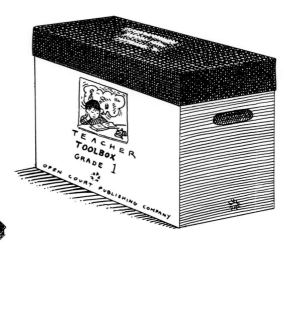

Outlined on convenient cards stored in the Teacher Toolbox, these Learning Frameworks consist of:

1. Phonemic Awareness
    1A. Oral Blending
2. Introducing the Sounds and Using the Sound/Spelling Cards
3. Blending
4. Dictation and Spelling
5. Reading Aloud
6. Reading Phonics Minibooks and Step-by-Step Practice Stories
7. Reading Big Books
8. Reading the Student Anthologies
9. Exploring Through Discussion
10. Writing
11. Workshop
12. Research
13. Sentence Lifting
14. Assessment and Monitoring

Each Learning Framework Card contains
- A statement of the purpose of the classroom technique
- An explanation of the recommended procedure
- Ways to utilize the technique
- Suggestions for applying each framework in other content areas
- Suggestions for assisting students who are not proficient in English

Teacher Tool Cards

The set of Teacher Tool Cards is an easy-to-use, practical resource designed to support opportunity-driven instruction. These cards
- Provide basic lessons that can be used to *meet the needs of your students at any time, not just during reading class*
- Provide on-the-spot instruction in skills and conventions that are applicable across the curriculum
- Help you meet students' needs during tutorial sessions
- Contain lessons in Writer's Craft/Reading; Grammar, Mechanics, and Usage; Spelling and Vocabulary; Study and Research; and Phonics
- Contain game instructions and suggestions for use in Workshop
- Provide classroom supports

Home/School Connection

The stronger the connection between the home and the school, the stronger the student's total educational environment will be. The Home/School Connection is designed to help the students communicate to their families what they are learning and to encourage those at home to become actively involved in their child's learning. The Home/School Connection includes

- Letters written in both English and Spanish explaining activities and materials
- Activities on which the students and their families can work cooperatively
- Bibliographies that include fine examples of children's literature for the children and their families to read and enjoy together

Reproducible Masters

The Reproducible Masters allow teachers and students to make choices. You can select the pages that will provide additional practice for students based on their individual needs. The Reproducible Masters include
- Activity sheets for use in Workshop
- Extension pages to be used in conjunction with lessons from the Teacher Tool Cards

Assessment

The assessment component of Open Court's first-grade program is based on the following principles:
- Students' progress and growth must be continually monitored, and
- Assessment is most meaningful when the teacher uses a variety of resources to measure growth and performance.

In the beginning, when students are not able to read or write, assessment by monitoring or teacher observation is embedded in the lesson activity. As students progress, a variety of assessments—including performance assessment, written assessment, and portfolio assessment as well as monitoring—are available. An assessment manual is provided in the Teacher Toolbox to give you an overview of the types of assessment and monitoring included in the program and to explain how to use the various assessment components. These components include
- Teacher's Observation Logs
- Performance Assessment rubrics
- Portfolio System
- Written assessment in the form of free responses or multiple-choice tests

Phonemic Awareness and Phonics Kit

Sound/Spelling Cards

The Sound/Spelling Cards are designed to provide powerful mnemonic support for children who are beginning to decode and to reinforce the multiple spellings for a given sound. They are displayed throughout the year and can be used by children on an as-needed basis to help them with both their reading and their spelling.

The picture on each card reminds children of the letter sound through the representation of an action that produces the sound. In addition, the picture name includes the letter sound at the beginning for consonants and

in the middle for short vowels. Each card is introduced with a brief, interactive story that focuses on the picture and involves the children in producing the letter sound. The bottom of each card contains spellings that represent the sound in words. The Sound/Spelling Cards are included in the first-grade Phonemic Awareness and Phonics Kit.

Letter Cards

Letter Cards provide students with a full set of alphabet cards to use as they learn the alphabet and as they learn to put letters together to form words. These Letter Cards may be used throughout the day as students participate in a variety of learning experiences designed to solidify their letter and sound knowledge.

Alphabet Flash Cards

Alphabet Flash Cards provide you with a convenient resource for working with the children on letter knowledge during regular class time and during Workshop.

Step-by-Step Practice Stories

The forty Step-by-Step Practice Stories provide students with a fun, engaging way to apply the phonic principles they are learning daily. Each Step-by-Step Practice Story focuses on a particular sound and spelling as it is introduced. These stories give students the opportunity to read short, enjoyable books independently. The children assemble these stories into books that they can color or decorate as they please. Students will enjoy taking these little stories home and sharing them with their families.

Core Student Materials

Big Books and Student Anthologies

Students using *Collections for Young Scholars*™ are introduced to a wide range of literature and nonfiction from the day they enter school. They start shared reading of authentic texts with the four colorful and engaging Big Books.

Look Who's Reading! contains traditional and contemporary rhymes, poems, and stories to lead students into basic concepts of print and literacy.

Animals introduces students to nonfiction through articles, photo essays, and picture essays about many different aspects of animal life.

Captain Bill Pinkney's Journey is the true story of Bill Pinkney's solo trip around the world on the sailboat *Commitment*.

Machines in Our Garden uses the familiar backdrop of a garden to introduce the children to the concept of simple machines and how they work.

In *Collections for Young Scholars*, Volume 1, Book 1, and Volume 1, Book 2, the students will experience literature that includes time-honored and contemporary classics as well as award-winning fiction and nonfiction. The reading selections are organized into learning units that are focused on important concepts and designed to encourage the students to think, raise questions, and build knowledge.

Phonics Minibooks

The eighteen Phonics Minibooks work with the Step-by-Step Practice Stories to consolidate the students' growing knowledge of the sound/spelling relationships in the English language. The sounds and spellings introduced to the children through their phonics lessons and Step-by-Step Practice Stories are presented in the Phonics Minibooks in fun, colorful stories that students can read on their own using their ever-increasing knowledge.

Whereas each Step-by-Step Practice Story is focused on a single sound/spelling combination, the Phonics Minibooks are cumulative in nature. Students acquire fluency in the sound/spellings they have learned by repeated reading of their practice materials.

Black-and-white, reproducible versions of the Phonics Minibooks are also available so that the children can take these stories home to share with their families.

Reading/Writing Connection

One of the goals of *Thinking and Learning About Print* is to make students aware of and completely comfortable with the connection between reading and writing. The Reading/Writing Connection is a resource for reinforcement of this connection. The Reading/Writing Connection provides

- A place for students to practice what they are learning about reading and writing
- A continuing record of their growing abilities

Getting Started

What Can You and Your Students Expect?

The transition from oral to written communication is one of the great moments in the history of humankind and in the history of a particular culture. It is also a critical moment in the life of an individual human being. Literacy does not displace oral communication; it supplements it and extends the range of human communication and inquiry. While it changes the nature of our thought, literacy also extends enormously the range of an individual person's ability to find things out. It makes the world much larger and richer.

Open Court's approach to this momentous transformation in the lives of students reflects the long and valuable experience of many teachers in classrooms across the country. It also reflects a generation of intense empirical research into the foundations of literacy and into the psychological mechanisms that lead to success in early reading. This research has been summarized in documents such as *Beginning to Read* by Marilyn Jager Adams. But research is often hard to apply to a curriculum. It is often difficult to balance all of the different findings and to set priorities. The approach in *Thinking and Learning About Print* puts together that research in a way you can pick up and use. It has been successful in many thousands of classrooms for three decades. It has been modified progressively by generations of teachers and students, but the basic core has not changed since the first publication of the program in the early 1960s.

This edition of Open Court's initial reading program, while retaining that basic core, has been completely rewritten, incorporating the experience of a new generation of teachers and the wisdom of several top educational researchers, including Marilyn Jager Adams, a leading proponent of balanced reading instruction. More than ever it is clear, in this approach, that phonics and whole-language instruction are not mutually exclusive but complementary. To find their way into the world of written language, students need *both* systematic instruction in phonics *and* rich experience with authentic literature.

The following principles give an idea of the kind of classroom environment you and your students can expect when you use *Thinking and Learning About Print*.

1 Explicit Phonics Instruction

Open Court's approach to initial reading relies on explicit teaching of sounds and on the blending of sounds into words. Written English is not perfectly regular, but it is alphabetic—that is, a more or less predictable association exists between the sounds of the spoken language and the letters in the written language. This alphabetic principle—associating sounds with letters in a predictable pattern—is one of the most powerful tools the

human race has ever invented. It permits us to represent thousands of words with just a few symbols.

The most urgent task of beginning reading instruction is to make written words and thoughts intelligible to students. The ability to read opens the door to just about everything else in a rich and productive life. The alphabetic principle gives them the key to that door.

2 No Unfounded Assumptions

For phonics instruction to work, it has to be systematic. It can't start somewhere in the middle. It can't assume that students will "pick it up somehow." And it can't take for granted that a student already knows all the letters or is able to distinguish individual sounds. It can't ever assume that children already have the idea that sounds and print have some relationship to each other.

Open Court therefore systematically teaches letter knowledge and phonemic awareness before and during the introduction of sound/spelling correspondences. The introduction of sound/spellings is systematic and is associated with pictures. The teaching of blending is embedded in a daily routine. The teaching of writing begins with dictation. All are used together in a series of predictable and recurring activities to teach the alphabetic principle and its connection with word meanings.

3 Authentic Literacy Experiences

We can't assume that students will keep the goals—real reading and writing—in view. They need to be reminded every day of why they are putting all this effort into learning the written code. They need to be reminded often that literacy is a powerful tool and that attaining it is the point of what they are doing. So along with the steady routines for learning the sounds, there is daily reading from Big Books or the Read-Aloud Anthology. There is also a writing strand that allows students to understand the uses of writing even as they are learning to write. These experiences help to reinforce the students' print awareness and their understanding of the structure and conventions of written language.

4 Lots of Practice—But Make It Relevant

The best way to practice reading is to read. So there is plenty of reading for students at each step along the way—even after they have learned only a few sounds, there are real books for them to read. These books are graded so that as students learn more sounds, they can read more books. Later, when sounds have been learned, fluency is practiced through authentic reading and writing, not through boring and artificial drills. The goals are always to use the students' and teacher's time as efficiently as possible and to waste no time on mindless repetition and seatwork.

5 Intentional Learning

Learning to read empowers students. Learning to learn enables students to use that power intelligently, to take charge of their own lives and their own learning process. Students should be encouraged to take responsibility for their learning as early as possible. In this program, self-correction is taught and reinforced through proofreading, which begins in the first few weeks and has an important role throughout. The focus is not on making things perfect but on making things better. Students learn how to monitor themselves rather than having to rely on the teacher's responses to guide their improvement. Workshop, which begins in Lesson 1, encourages students to work independently or in small groups, without the teacher's having to tell them what to do at every moment.

6 Support and Challenge for *All* Students

By making no assumptions, you ensure that no children fall through the cracks. And by making practice relevant and efficient, there is plenty of repetition for students who have a harder time catching on. Daily Workshop periods, in which students work independently, give the teacher a chance to focus attention on specific needs and deficits.

Whole-class instruction ensures that slower students learn from quicker ones; regular feedback through dictation, reading aloud, and other activities enables the teacher to monitor easily how each student is doing and where help might be needed.

Students who can already read are not held back. They, too, benefit from explicit instruction in phonics, which gives them the tools to read harder books than those normally given to first graders. In Workshop the teacher gives them, too, individual attention and encouragement and helps them to achieve all they are capable of.

7 High Expectations, Positive Evaluation

Students perform up to the level of expectations set by their surroundings. It is unfair to students not to expect the best of them. And that can't wait until the upper grades—it's in first grade that we're expecting them to learn to read; everything in later school years depends on this! So students need to know from day one that you will hold them to world-class standards. If you look at the reading materials in Open Court's *Collections for Young Scholars*,™ Volume 1, Books 1 and 2, you may be surprised at the level of reading expected of children by the end of first grade. Many teachers who have not used Open Court before are frankly incredulous; they refuse to believe that their students can read such materials at this level. But thousands of Open Court teachers have succeeded in helping their students read such material over the past thirty years and have enriched those students' lives as a result.

While expectations should be high, evaluation should be positive. Focus on what's right about what students are doing, not on what's wrong. And above all, focus on getting better. No matter where a student is, he or she can improve. It doesn't matter how many things are wrong on a student's paper; the main thing is to ensure that the student proofreads, corrects, and does a little better the next time. It's important to reinforce the things that students *do* get right, as specifically as possible, to reassure them, and to help them understand that there is a logic to the system they're learning.

The Basic Techniques

These principles are realized in *Thinking and Learning About Print* by way of a few basic techniques that recur frequently. The content is different each time, but the format is very similar from day to day. Thus the time spent setting up the activity is minimized, and the focus is on the content. Among these basic techniques, the following are the most important:

Phonemic Awareness

These activities teach students to distinguish individual sounds (phonemes). The ability to distinguish individual sounds within words is an essential prerequisite for associating those sounds with letters. Without phonemic awareness, phonics is difficult. These activities are purely oral and do not involve the teaching of any letter-sound associations. Sometimes writing is brought in; but writing is brought in only to make the point that sounds (phonemes) and writing (graphemes) can be associated and not to teach specific associations.

The phonemic awareness activities appear in different forms in three parts of the lesson. First, they appear in the Getting Started section. The phonemic awareness activities found in Getting Started will take the form of quick, fun reviews of activities learned previously. In the Reading section of the lesson, phonemic awareness activities are introduced, and students participate in carefully sequenced activities that will help ensure success as the year progresses. During Workshop, those children experiencing difficulty in distinguishing sounds will have the opportunity for further practice.

Oral Blending and Segmentation

There are two main formats for teaching phonemic awareness—oral blending and segmentation. The oral- blending and segmentation activities are brief, teacher-led activities whose main focus is on some form of word play: words are taken apart in various ways and put back together. Sometimes a puppet is used to repeat parts of words said by the teacher. Students are then encouraged to imitate or correct the puppet. The activities are carefully sequenced. Each series of exercises begins with a great deal of support for the students. As students progress, support is gradually removed and the exercises become more difficult.

Oral blending and segmentation (which continue through Lesson 30) overlap with the introduction of sound/spellings (which begin in Lesson 11). This can cause confusion, since oral blending and segmentation remain *purely oral* throughout *Thinking and Learning About Print*. In the oral-blending and segmentation exercises, all the sounds continue to be used, while in phonics (introducing sound/spellings and blending them together into words), only the sounds that have been introduced up to that point are used.

The phonemic awareness (oral blending and segmentation) material is set in red type. It is important to understand that the phonemic awareness parts of the lessons involve no instruction in sound/spellings. Their function is to teach children that speech can be broken down into smaller units—syllables and phonemes. These parts of the lesson do *not* teach phonics. That comes in later parts of the lesson, which involve the techniques of introducing sounds through sound/spelling cards and blending.

Introduction of Sounds Through Sound/Spelling Cards

Sounds are associated with spellings through Sound/Spelling Cards. These large wall cards associate sounds with spellings in two ways: first, the action pictured on each card generates a sound (for example, the Timer goes /t/ /t/ /t/); second, the object pictured begins with that same sound (Timer starts with the sound /t/). (Note: slash marks around letters [for example, /t/] mean that just the sound is being referred to, not the letter — the letter *t* makes the sound /t/.) Vowel sounds are treated somewhat differently: short vowel sounds have two clues, just as consonants do, but the target sound is *within* the word, not at the beginning (for example, the picture for /a/ [short *a*] is Lamb). And long vowels are just a picture of the "long" (tall) vowel, saying its name.

The Sound/Spellings are introduced one by one (usually one per day), by turning over the Sound/Spelling Card in question and telling an alliterative story about the pictured action, character, or object, using the new sound as often as possible. A great deal of practice in producing and listening for the sound follows.

This systematic introduction helps to reinforce the association of sound and spelling in students' minds. The double association of the picture on the Sound/Spelling Card fixes a reference point that will be used constantly by students when referring to the sound in future blending, dictation, and writing contexts.

Blending

Blending is the heart and soul of phonics instruction. It is the key strategy children must learn in order to apply the alphabetic principle and open up the world of written text.

In *Thinking and Learning About Print*, blending is a daily routine. As you write the spelling for each sound in a word, students will say the sound, relying on the associations fixed by the Sound/Spelling Cards. Then they will blend the sounds together into a word. To be sure they recognize the word in the string of sounds they've put together under your guidance, they are immediately asked to use the word in a sentence. The connection with word meaning is reinforced constantly, so that students recognize that what they've blended is indeed the word they know from spoken language.

Dictation

As students practice decoding through blending, they practice encoding through dictation. At first, dictation takes the informal shape of a "Word-Building game" played with individual Letter Cards. Then, students are asked to write words sound by sound, using the Sound/Spelling Cards for reference if necessary. By Lesson 19, whole words are dictated, and by Lesson 27, whole sentences. From that point on, dictation includes all three elements—sounds-in-sequence dictation, whole word dictation, and sentence dictation.

Dictation is not only a starting point for fluency in writing, it is also a springboard for self-correction through proofreading. At the same time, it provides important practice in fixing the all-important associations between sounds and spellings. It thus links reading with writing and powerfully reinforces both.

Workshop

This is the time when children work collaboratively in small groups or individually, with or without the teacher. This gives them a first experience of managing their own learning process and working on their own. For you, it is a time for giving individual attention to students.

All the basic techniques generate feedback from students that lets you observe exactly how well they are understanding what you teach. This informal "monitoring" is followed up during Workshop by working individually or in small groups with students having similar problems or demanding enrichment. Suggestions are given both within this guide and on Learning Framework Cards about strategies for giving extra help where needed, and providing additional stimulation for students racing ahead. Reproducible Activity Sheets are available for students who need them to reinforce concepts recently learned. Many students will prefer to read practice materials to partners or to continue with writing projects.

Practice (Phonics Minibooks and Step-by-Step Stories)

It is important to give students material to which they can apply what they have learned about sounds and spellings and to let them see that their power over written language is growing with each new sound/spelling they learn.

That has been done in *Thinking and Learning About Print* through two series of practice stories, the Phonics Minibooks and the Step-by-Step Practice Stories. (See pages 21F–22F for descriptions of these books.) These stories are used in whole-group reading, for reading aloud and class discussion, as well as for individual and partner reading. Partner reading with these practice materials after each whole-group reading session is strongly encouraged. Students gain fluency in word recognition from repeated reading.

While these practice materials are not literature, their function is very important. They provide the fluency and independence students need to unlock real literature on their own. Thus these materials play an important role in empowering children to read and explore without assistance from adults.

Print Awareness

To learn to read independently, children need to understand some basic things about the mechanics of literacy. Many of these things seem obvious to adults, but such things need to be learned: how words look on a page, the existence of spaces between words, the connection between pictures and words, the arrangement of printed text in lines, the left-to-right progression of letters in a word and words in a line, paragraphing, pages in a book—and much else.

These fundamentals are taught through whole-class reading and discussion of Big Book selections, through reading aloud, and through students' own writing and "publishing" of what they write. In all these ways, children also learn that books are sources of information, enjoyment, puzzlement, and laughter. Literacy becomes important, and its parameters become part of daily life.

1 Check Your Materials

You will need the following program materials for each student:

- *Captain Bill Pinkney's Journey* and *Machines in Our Garden*
- Step-by-Step Practice Stories
- Phonics Minibooks
- Reading/Writing Connection, *Thinking and Learning About Print*

In addition, you should have the following books and materials:

- *Framework for Effective Teaching: Thinking and Learning About Print,* Part B
- *Beginning to Read: Thinking and Learning About Print*
- Teacher Toolbox
- Phonemic Awareness and Phonics Kit

2 Become Acquainted with the Instructional Goals

Before you begin *Thinking and Learning About Print*, read *Beginning to Read: Thinking and Learning About Print* by Marilyn Jager Adams, *A Summary* (Center for the Study of Reading, The Reading Research and Education Center, University of Illinois at Urbana-Champaign 1990). This resource offers an overview of the goals and ideas that motivate the instructional design of the program.

Each lesson in this guide gives some background of its goals in the text describing each important step. A broader discussion of the goals of the major techniques (pages 27F–30F) can be found on the Learning Framework Card for each technique. Learning Framework Cards can be found in the Teacher Toolbox. Both the **Scope and Sequence Chart, page 378,** and the **Index, page 385,** can give a quick overview of the content in *Thinking and Learning About Print*.

3 Organize Your Teaching Materials

Teacher Toolbox The Teacher Toolbox serves as easily accessible storage for your instructional materials. In it you will find Teacher Tool Cards, Learning Framework Cards, the Home/School Connection, Reproducible Masters, Instructional Posters, and a set of dividers. Unpack the materials and use the dividers to organize the box. See pages 18F–19F for descriptions of these materials. You will find on each section divider a list of the cards contained in that section.

Step-by-Step Practice Stories As each new sound/spelling is introduced, the children will be able to read a new Step-by-Step Practice Story. Each Step-by-Step Practice Story requires some assembly. You may have the children do this, or if you have classroom help available, you might want to have this done in advance. Instructions and suggestions for making the books can be found at the front of the Step-by-Step Practice Story book.

4 Set Up Your Classroom

Sound/Spelling Cards Display the Sound/Spelling Cards from the Phonemic Awareness and Phonics Kit. Place the first twenty-six cards above the chalkboard or along a wall, with only the back of each card visible. These twenty-six cards will form a model alphabet for the children to use during the first lessons.

As sounds and spellings are introduced, you find out when to turn each card to display the picture side. Several cards have more than one spelling for a single sound. It is recommended that you cover all but the sound being introduced. You can do this with removable stick-on notes. Cards 27–43 will be introduced one at a time. You may display each card as it is introduced.

Phonics Minibooks Set up one or both of the Phonics Minibook display cases. As students progress through the program, they will read Phonics Minibooks. It is recommended that the books be on hand so that children can reread the books as many times as they please.

Workshop It is recommended that you select a shelf or an area of the classroom where Workshop materials can be kept. Let the children know that they will be able to choose activities from this area when they have completed their work. Choose an area that has enough space to expand as the year goes on. Allow material to remain available long enough for all children to have a chance to use it.

Selecting books to read can always be one Workshop option. If space is limited, your reading corner can be a shelf or a table with a collection of books that the children may take to their seats. Learning Framework Card 11 contains a complete discussion of establishing and conducting Workshop.

LESSON
31

Lesson Overview

New Learning

- /k/ spelled *ck*
- Adding *-ed* for past tense

Materials

- *Captain Bill Pinkney's Journey*, pages 4–5
- "My Trip," Step-by-Step Practice Story 13
- Puppet for each child
- Learning Framework Cards 2, 3, 4, 5, 11
- Reading/Writing Connection, pages 52–53
- Activity Sheet 31

GETTING STARTED

Choose one or both of the following activities to focus the children's attention and to review some of the concepts they have been learning.

Substituting the Sound /o/   To review the short *o* vowel sound, play a substitution game. Say the word *fix* and ask the children what sound they hear in the middle. Tell them that you are going to make up a new word by changing the short *i* sound to short *o*, then say the word *fox.* Invite the children to create their own new words by identifying the middle sound in words such as the following and then changing that sound to short *o*. Then have them use each word in a sentence.

pit	hit	map
pet	duck	hug
click		

I Pack My Bag   Begin by having the children sit in a circle and telling them that today they are going to play a game about journeys. Say to them, "I'm going on a journey, and in my bag I am packing something whose name starts with the sound /r/: a raincoat." Ask the children to suggest other things to pack that begin with /r/.

TEACHING TIP

If the children have difficulty thinking of things with names beginning with the /r/ sound to take on a journey, encourage them to include silly answers such as *rhinoceros, Red Riding Hood, wrapping paper.*

Review /ar/ Spelled *ar* Touch the Sound/Spelling Card 27, Armadillo, and ask the children what sound this card represents. Have them tell how they can use this card to remember the /ar/ sound. Write the letters *ar* on the chalkboard and have a child add one or more letters to make a word. When the child has finished, have the class read the word. Call on another child to change any letters except *ar* to make another word and then have everyone read the new word. Continue calling on different children to make words.

1 READING

PHONICS

* **Introduce /k/ Spelled *ck*** Point to Sound/Spelling Card 3, Camera, and ask how to spell the sound /k/. Then tell the children that there are other ways to spell /k/. Uncover the spelling *ck* on the card and tell the children that when the letters *c* and *k* come together, they make the sound /k/. Point to the green box in front of the *ck* and ask what this box means. The children should remember that the green box indicates that a short vowel always comes before the spelling.

Then tell the children that the *ck* spelling is found only at the end of a syllable or a word. On the board write *a* followed by *ck* and pronounce this phonogram. Ask the children to suggest words that end in *ack* and list their words under the letters. Continue with words ending in *ick* and *ock*.

Encourage the children to review the Camera card by having them tell you all they know about the card and how the picture will help them remember the sound. For example, the word *camera* starts with /k/, and a camera makes the sound /k/ when you take a picture. The sound /k/ is spelled *c*, *__ck*, and *k*, and the box before *ck* is a place holder for a short vowel.

A complete discussion of the introduction of sounds and spellings can be found on **Learning Framework Card 2, Introducing Sounds.**

* **Blending** Have the children blend the following words and sentences. For a complete discussion of the blending process, see **Learning Framework Card 3, Blending.**

Line 1:	sack sock sick stick
Line 2:	rock crack brick trick
Line 3:	back pack backpack
Line 4:	car cart carton
Sentence 1:	My mom packed the car for the trip.
Sentence 2:	Mack fixed a rip in my backpack.
Sentence 3:	Bart said, "My socks are tan."

TEACHING TIP

A new spelling of a familiar sound can be introduced in several ways. Use the method with which you are most comfortable:
- Cover each spelling with a piece of construction paper or cardboard, then uncover the new spelling as you introduce it.
- Leave all the spellings uncovered and use a pointer to focus the children's attention on the particular spelling that you are studying.

Words   As you write the words, be sure to write the *ck* spelling as a unit. As you sound and blend the words in line 1, ask the children, "How are the words the same? How are they different?"

Help the children blend the word *carton* in line 4 as follows: *car—ton, carton.* As they say the word, they should adjust their pronunciation.

Review the words by having one child name a word, then having other children erase words that rhyme with the given word.

Sentences   The past tense ending *-ed* is introduced in sentences 1 and 2. Before writing the sentences, contrast the present and past-tense forms of the following verbs. Say the sentences and write the verbs on the chalkboard.

Bob can fix the car today. *fix*
Bob fixed the car yesterday. *fixed*

I like to pick strawberries in the summer. *pick*
Last summer I picked two pails of strawberries. *picked*

Compare the two forms of the verb and tell the children that *-ed* at the end of a verb usually shows that the action happened in the past.

Introduce Outlaw Word *my*   Before writing sentence 1, write the word *my* on the board. Pronounce the word and have the children repeat it. Have the children use the word in oral sentences. Then write sentence 1 on the board and underline the outlaw words. Have the children blend the words and read the sentences. Write the other sentences and have the children read them. Remind the children not to blend *my* or the other outlaw words. Give help as needed.

In sentence 3, ask the children about the use of the quotation marks.

➤ Reading/Writing Connection, pages 52–53, reinforces the /k/ sound spelled *ck*. Have the children form as many words as they can on page 52 by combining the initial consonants and *ck* endings provided. When they have finished this page, you might invite the children to think of other words that end in *ck* but start with letters that are not given on this page.

For the top part of page 53, the children should choose the sentence that describes the picture and write the sentence in the blank.

Name

Lesson 31

Sounds and Spellings

C

■ck

Writing Words   (Student answers may vary.)

| s | st | p | r | sn | d | tr |

_ack   _ick   _ock

(sack)   (sick)   (sock)

(pack)   (pick)   (stock)

(snack)   (trick)   (rock)

(track)   (stick)   (dock)

Sounds and Spellings

52 R/WC   *Captain Bill Pinkney's Journey*

Name

Lesson 31

Reading and Writing Sentences

Rick has socks in the sack.
She picks a stick from the stack.

She picks a stick from
the stack.

Dictation and Spelling

_____   _____

_____   _____

_____   _____

_____   _____

_____   _____

                                          Decoding/Spelling

Captain Bill Pinkney's Journey   R/WC 53

Reading/Writing Connection, page 52   **Reading/Writing Connection, page 53**

✳ READING THE BIG BOOK

Captain Bill Pinkney's Journey
pages 4–5

About the Selection

What would it be like to circle the globe in a sailboat, all alone?
Captain Bill Pinkney accomplished that daring feat, and he describes it
in fascinating detail in *Captain Bill Pinkney's Journey*. In a voyage that
covers 32,000 miles and lasts 372 days, Captain Pinkney displays the
courage, perseverance, knowledge, skill, and—most important—the
commitment needed to realize his boyhood dream of sailing around the
world in his own boat. As they share Captain Pinkney's inspiring
account of his bold journey, the children will begin to understand that
they, too, can realize their own dreams, provided that they are willing to
pursue those dreams with determination and commitment.

Link to the Unit Concept

Captain Bill Pinkney's Journey gives the children a firsthand account
of the author's solo trip around the world and an understanding of his
commitment to a boyhood dream. As they follow the route of Captain

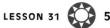

Pinkney's sailboat, *Commitment,* they learn more about the world and the people and animals that live in it. They also learn about the risks involved in committing oneself to such a bold adventure and the rewards that one may reap.

About the Author

Captain Bill Pinkney was the first African American to circumnavigate the globe alone. Thanks to advanced satellite and computer technologies, more than thirty thousand students across the United States followed the voyage of his sailboat, *Commitment.* Not only did Captain Pinkney give these students lessons in math, science, geography, and social studies, but he also modeled for them the character traits required to follow one's dreams. He has delivered his inspirational message to students at nearly six hundred schools and universities in the United States and abroad, and the story of his exploits has been read into the *Congressional Record.* In addition, he has told his story in *Captain Bill Pinkney's Journey,* written especially for Open Court Publishing Company's *Collections for Young Scholars.*™

Activating Prior Knowledge

Display the cover of *Captain Bill Pinkney's Journey* and read the title aloud, pointing to each word. Ask the children to tell about trips they may have taken with family members or friends. Make a list of places the children have visited to refer back to in Writing.

Recommendations for Reading

- Browse through the book and encourage comments and questions. You might point out the Sailing Calendar on page 3, the map on pages 8–9, and the Glossary on page 32, explaining that the calendar will provide helpful information about places and dates, that the map will help follow the trip, and that the Glossary contains definitions of sailing terms.
- Make a list of anything the children wonder or have questions about. These may include questions about people, places, unusual animals, maps, and instruments. Be sure to keep the queries you list for future reference throughout the reading of the book.
- Read aloud pages 4 and 5.

When I was a boy, I dreamed about boats, so I started reading about boats.

"I will grow up to be Captain Bill," I said, "and sail across wide oceans."

4

I made a commitment—that's a powerful promise—to sail around the world in my own boat.

When I grew up, I learned to sail. I read more about boats. I learned to use tools and fix equipment. I learned to use radios and radar. I studied geography and weather.

5

Responding

Invite the children to discuss Captain Bill's dream and his promise. Encourage them to comment on all that he had to learn. They may wonder about places they think Captain Bill will visit.

✳ READING A STEP-BY-STEP PRACTICE STORY

"My Trip"
Story 13

Getting Ready to Read

Browsing the Story   Have the children assemble Step-by-Step Practice Story 13, "My Trip." Invite a volunteer to read the title of the story. Remind the children that *my* is the outlaw word they learned earlier today and that they should not try to blend the word. Say "I want you to look through the story and to comment on anything you notice about the words or the pictures." Call on volunteers to share their observations with their classmates.

Recommendations

• Call on a different child to read each page of the story aloud. Discuss with the class anything of interest on the page and clarify any difficulties. Then have a second child reread the page before going on.

- Reread the story at least twice, calling on different children to read. Then have the entire group do a choral reading of the story.

Responding

- Invite the children to discuss any questions they have about "My Trip."
- To make sure that the children are paying attention to the words as well as the pictures, have them answer the following questions by pointing to and reading the words aloud:

   What did the woman eat?

   What did she pick?

   What was the spot like?

   What was missing from the woman's backpack?

   What did the fox have?
- Call on volunteers to point out any words they can read. Then invite volunteers to read entire sentences. Does anyone notice that many of the action words in the story end with -*ed*? Invite a volunteer to tell what the ending -*ed* usually shows.
- Have the children discuss what they liked best about the story. Ask whether they are still wondering about anything after having read the story. Respond to the children's wonderings or invite their classmates to do so if appropriate.

Have the children reread the story with a partner.

✱ READING ALOUD

A number of children's books tell about taking trips. You may want to share one or more of the following with the children:

Let's Go Traveling by Robin Rector Krupp
Stringbean's Trip to the Shining Sea by Vera Williams
The Most Delicious Camping Trip Ever by Alice Bach
The Wonderful Pumpkin by Lennart Hellsing

Ask the children what they have learned about trips.

See **Learning Framework Card 5** for suggestions for reading aloud.

TEACHING TIP

Set aside ten minutes for partner reading every day. During this time, you should read with individuals, recording their progress. Reading Assessment Sheets for Phonics Minibooks are available in *Assessment Masters, Grade 1*.

2 WRITING

✱ DICTATION AND SPELLING

Dictation provides the children with an opportunity to apply to their writing what they have been learning about sounds and spellings. Have the children turn to page 53 of their Reading/Writing Connection book and finish the bottom part of the page. Dictate the following words and sentence. A complete discussion of dictation appears on **Learning Framework Card 4**.

Line 1:	bar star
Line 2:	had hard
Sentence:	Dad will start the car.

In line 1, dictate the words sound by sound. In line 2, pronounce each word for the children to write on their own. Remind them that they may check the Sound/Spelling Cards if they are uncertain about how to spell a sound.

Read the entire sentence, then dictate it word by word. Encourage the children to ask for clarification if they do not understand a word. Repeat problem words sound by sound. Remind the children to think about what should be at the beginning of a sentence and what should be at the end.

Help the children proofread their work. A discussion of the proofreading procedure can be found on **Learning Framework Card 4.**

EXPLORING THE WRITER'S CRAFT

In *Captain Bill Pinkney's Journey,* Captain Bill Pinkney shares with the children his dream of sailing around the world. Talk with the children about their dreams—what they hope to become, where they would like to go, what they would like to do. These dreams may cover a wide range of ideas—from voyages through outer space to trips to the zoo, from being a doctor to being an explorer like Captain Bill.

The children may continue talking about places they have been. Refer to the list begun during Activating Prior Knowledge. Keep the list of these places on the board or on a large piece of paper for the children to refer to throughout the next series of writing lessons. Tell the children that during the next few lessons, they will be working on a class book of places they have visited or would like to visit.

Give the children some time to note some of these writing ideas in their journals. They may choose, instead, to write about their own hopes and dreams.

TEACHING TIP

Have the children date each of their writing projects. They will continue to keep their work in a folder as an ongoing record of their writing growth.

3 GUIDED AND INDEPENDENT EXPLORATION

WORKSHOP

Tell the children that it is time for Workshop, the time each day when they will work on projects and activities on their own or with one or more classmates. Remind them that during Workshop they can always select a book to read. They also may write in their journals.

For a review of information about establishing and conducting Workshop, see **Learning Framework Card 11.**

Work with the Teacher

- Review today's Blending exercise with small groups of children. Encourage them to read the words as whole units in addition to blending them sound by sound.
- Reread any Phonics Minibook to practice reading short-vowel words.

Independent Work

- Activity Sheet 31 reviews the sound /k/ spelled *ck*. Tell the children to choose words from the box to complete each sentence, then write the answers in the corresponding boxes of the crossword puzzle. Remind the children to use the arrows to help them write their answers correctly in the puzzle.
- Have the children write and illustrate one or more sentences containing words from today's Blending exercise. Also, challenge them to use an action word that ends with *-ed* in their sentences.
- Remind the children that Captain Bill Pinkney loves to travel by sailboat. Ask the children to think about some of the different ways to get from one place to another. Invite them to draw and label pictures of themselves using their favorite means of travel.
- Have the children prepare Letter Cards *a, b, c, g, k, t, u* for the Word-Building game in the next lesson.

Student Collaboration

- Have the children reread, with partners, Step-by-Step Practice Story 12, "Grab a Star." Remind them to follow the usual turn-taking procedure for reading in pairs. Encourage them to help each other blend difficult words.
- Have the children work in pairs to find *ck* words in Step-by-Step Practice Story 13 and to write new sentences with the words.

> **TEACHING TIP**
>
> Encourage the children to read to each other. You, too, should choose children to read with. As you read with each child, note his or her progress.

Home/School Connection

- Send home Step-by-Step Practice Story 12, "Grab a Star." Ask the children to read it to their families.

> **MONITORING BLENDING** In the next lessons, observe several children a day to determine whether they are able to blend words using the new spellings. Record your observations in Teacher's Observation Log 3.

Name

| snack | socks | stack | bricks |

→ 1. My __socks__ are soft and warm.

↓ 2. You can __snack__ on hot dogs.

→ 3. The __bricks__ are hard.

↓ 4. Can you __stack__ the blocks here?

Captain Bill Pinkney's Journey   Activity Sheet 31

Activity Sheet 31

LESSON
32

••• Lesson Overview

New Learning

- /u/ spelled *u*

Materials

- *Captain Bill Pinkney's Journey,* pages 6–15
- "The Bug," Step-by-Step Practice Story 14
- Sound/Spelling Card 21, Tugboat
- Learning Framework Cards 2, 3, 5, 11
- Reading/Writing Connection, pages 54–55
- Games and Songs Teacher Tool Card 4
- Letter Cards *a, b, c, g, k, t, u*
- Activity Sheet 32
- Home/School Connection 9

Prepare Ahead

- Outlaw Word Flash Cards (see page 21)
- Short *u* index cards, generic game boards, dice (see page 21)

GETTING STARTED

Choose one or both of the following activities to focus the children's attention and to review some of the concepts they have been learning.

Cool Consonants Game Play the Cool Consonants game with the children. Begin by dividing the class into small groups. Then point to Sound/Spelling Card 21, Tugboat, and ask the children what sound the spelling makes. Make up an alliterative phrase using the /b/ sound, for example, "Bob's berries." Then, add to the phrase: "Bob's basket of berries" and "Bob's basket of beautiful berries." Repeat the process using another sound that the children have learned, such as: "Pink pigs." This time, have each group of children add a word to the alliterative phrase you suggest. One by one, ask each group to use all the words said previously and include their own as well, making this a cumulative activity.

Review Sound/Spelling Cards Say a word and have the children name the Sound /Spelling Card and the spelling for the beginning sound. Use the following words:

cap	mitten	ox
button	needle	rain
ant	turkey	soup

/ik/, /ak/, or /ok/? Print *ick, ack,* and *ock* widely apart on the chalkboard. Ask the children to read each spelling as you point to it. Then say words that end in these sounds and ask the children to point to the spelling that belongs with the words. Write the word on the chalkboard under the appropriate category and draw the children's attention to the spelling *ck* at the end of each word. Use the following words:

stick	dock	brick
snack	sack	pick
rock	sick	back
crack	sock	pack
mock		

1 READING

PHONICS

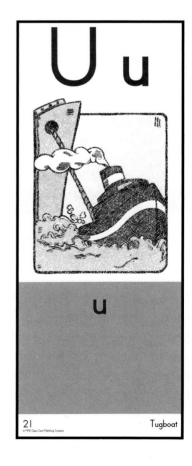

✱ **Introduce /u/ Spelled *u*** Turn Sound/Spelling Card 21, Tugboat, and discuss what kind of letter this is. Then ask what the green color on the card means. Make the point that vowels are special letters that can have many sounds. The green color indicates that this is the short sound of the vowel *u.*

Point to the picture and ask the children if they know what this special kind of boat is called. If necessary, explain that a tugboat is a small boat used to tow or push larger boats. Then read the Tugboat story.

You can find the procedure for introducing a new sound and spelling on **Learning Framework Card 2.**

Tubby the tugboat can huff and puff
And push and pull to move big stuff.
/u/ /u/ /u/ /u/ /u/ /u/: That's the sound of Tubby the Tug.

If a boat is stuck and will not budge,
Tubby the Tugboat can give it a nudge. /u/ /u/ /u/ /u/ /u/ /u/
It's Tubby the Trusty Tug.

If a ship is caught in mud and muck,
Tubby the Tugboat can get it unstuck. /u/ /u/ /u/ /u/ /u/ /u/
It's Tubby the Trusty Tug.

Can you help Tubby push and pull?
(Have the children join in) /u/ /u/ /u/ /u/ /u/ /u/!

Ask the children to listen to some words and to signal thumbs-up when they hear the /u/ sound. Read the following words:

up	under	ape
ugly	ice cream	umbrella
umpire	baby	us

Then ask the children to listen for words with the /u/ sound as you reread the Tugboat story. Because sounds in the middle of words tend to be more difficult for children to hear than those at the beginning or end, reread the story slowly. Tell them to pay careful attention to the sounds in the middle of words and have them raise thier hands when they hear the /u/ sound in a word. Finally, have the children summarize how they can use the Tugboat card to help them remember the sound.

✱ Blending Have the children blend the following words and sentences. For a complete discussion of the blending process, see **Learning Framework Card 3, Blending.**

Line 1:	up cup pup
Line 2:	fun run sun
Line 3:	hut cut nut
Line 4:	hug rug mug
Line 5:	button
Sentence 1:	What is in my mom's mug?
Sentence 2:	What is stuck in the rug?
Sentence 3:	Fran stamped in the mud.

Words As the children blend and read aloud the words in each line, invite them to point out any patterns they notice. Emphasize that being able to see patterns like these will help them in their reading.

In line 5, the children will adjust their pronunciation when they figure out what the word is.

Review the words in the word lines by pointing to them one at a time, in random order, and having the children read them. Have children erase each word that they read correctly.

Sentences Introduce the outlaw word *what* before writing the sentences. Write the word *what* on the board, pronounce it, and have the children repeat it. Have several children use the word in oral sentences. Then write the sentences and have the children read the sentences. Help them read the outlaw words if necessary.

For sentences 1 and 2, be sure to point out the question marks at the end of the sentences.

As the children sound and blend sentence 3, point out the ending *-ed* in the word *stamped*. Ask what the ending tells about when the action took place.

Reading/Writing Connection, page 54

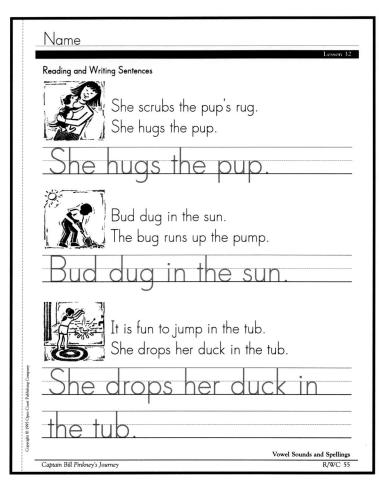

Reading/Writing Connection, page 55

➤ Reading/Writing Connection, pages 54–55, reinforces the /u/ sound spelled *u*. Have the children complete page 54 by blending and copying the words and sentences. For page 55, they should write the sentence that describes each picture on the blank provided.

✳ READING THE BIG BOOK

Captain Bill Pinkney's Journey
pages 6–15

Activating Prior Knowledge
Invite comments on anything the children remember from their browsing of *Captain Bill Pinkney's Journey* in the previous lesson.

Recommendations for Reading
• Tell the children that today you will begin reading the book to them. It is suggested that you continue reading the book through in two parts, in this and the next lesson, without calling attention to the pictures or the captions. Reading the story through once without interruptions may help the children understand the point of the book.

Explain to them that for this reading, they are to listen very carefully in order to understand Captain Pinkney's purpose in taking his journey and in writing his book for them and other students like them. Tell them that you will not stop to show pictures until the second reading.

• Children should be encouraged to ask questions. Stop and ask them to summarize from time to time.

Boston Harbor

I learned enough to be captain of my own boat. Today I leave from Boston to sail around the world!

I have said good-bye to dozens of Boston schoolchildren. They will talk with me by radio when I am at sea.

Captain Bill named his boat <u>Commitment</u> for his powerful promise.

6

7

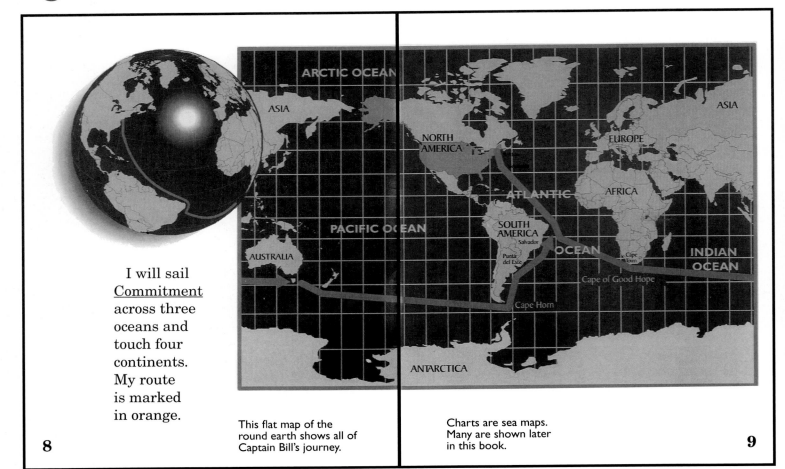

I will sail
<u>Commitment</u>
across three
oceans and
touch four
continents.
My route
is marked
in orange.

This flat map of the
round earth shows all of
Captain Bill's journey.

Charts are sea maps.
Many are shown later
in this book.

8

9

Captain Bill talks
to students by radio.

He cooks his meals
in the galley, the
kitchen of the boat.

On Wednesday nights
Captain Bill watches
videos.

Captain Bill sleeps
in his bunk.

<u>Commitment</u> is a snug home.
I do everything by myself.

Day and night it sails along,
even when I'm asleep.

10

11

On the way to Bermuda, I meet a pilot whale that is curious about <u>Commitment</u> and me.

Whales are not fish. They are big mammals that swim to the surface to breathe air.

12

SAILING DAY 3

Houses on Bermuda have special roofs that collect rain for drinking and washing.

After sailing for eight days, I see land. It is the island of Bermuda, far out in the Atlantic Ocean.

SAILING DAY 8

13

Hooray! I am crossing the equator, the imaginary line between the northern and southern halves of the earth. Sailors always have a party when they "cross the line."

Northern Hemisphere

Equator

Southern Hemisphere

14

SAILING DAY 47

Like Captain Bill, many sailors have had African ancestors.

Paul Cuffe was a ship owner in Marion, Massachusetts.

Absalom Boston was captain of a whaling ship. His sailors were African Americans, too.

Bill Pinkney was a U.S. Navy sailor for eight years.

Captain Michael Healy's ship patrolled the icy coast of Alaska.

15

Responding

Ask volunteers to tell what has happened so far and what they have learned about Captain Pinkney. Invite further questions and wonderings to add to the lists you have already made.

✳ **READING A STEP-BY-STEP PRACTICE STORY**

"The Bug"
Story 14

Getting Ready to Read

Browsing the Story   Have the children put together Step-by-Step Practice Story 14, "The Bug." Call on a volunteer to read the title of the story. Then ask the children to look through the story and to comment on anything they notice about the words or the pictures.

Recommendations

Call on a different child to read each page of the story aloud. Discuss with the class anything of interest on the page, and clarify any difficulties. Then have a second child reread the page before going on.

Reread the story at least twice, calling on pairs of children to read. One child should read what the anteater says, and the other should read what the bear says. Then have the entire group do a choral reading of the story.

Responding

- Encourage the children to comment on the story and to discuss any questions they may have about it. When the bug spoke, were the children as surprised as the anteater and the bear seem to be? Did anyone notice the tongue twisters? ("Is the bug in the bag big? It is a big bug bag.") Invite volunteers to read these two sentences as quickly as they can.
- To make sure the children are paying attention to the words as well as the pictures, have them answer the following questions by pointing to and reading the words aloud:

  What does the anteater ask the bear?
  What does the bear say?
  What does the anteater ask the bear?
  What does the bear ask the anteater?
  What does the bear say?
  What does the bug say?

- Call on volunteers to point out any words they can read. Then invite volunteers to read everything that is written in one speech balloon.
- Ask the children to tell what happened in the story and to discuss what they liked best about it. Is there anything about the story that still puzzles them? Discuss any questions the children may have.

Have the children reread the story with a partner.

TEACHING TIP

Remind the children to read each book twice. When they finish today's book, they should get one from a previous lesson. Reading Assessment Sheets for Phonics Minibooks are available in *Assessment Masters, Grade 1.*

Two books written by Berniece Freschet—*Bernard Sees the World* and *Little Black Bear Goes for a Walk*—fit in nicely with the theme of this unit. You may wish to share one or both of these books with the children.

See **Learning Framework Card 5** for suggestions for reading aloud.

2 WRITING

✳ DICTATION AND SPELLING

Word-Building Game Have the children take out Letter Cards *a, b, c, g, k, t, u.* Then play the Word-Building game by writing the word *bug* on the board and having the children make the word with their cards. Then have them make the words that follow. You should write each word on the board or overhead after allowing a few moments for the children to make it on their own.

bug

tug

tuck

tack

back

cab

cub

INDEPENDENT AND COLLABORATIVE WRITING

Children should recognize that not all trips need to be to far away places but to places in their more immediate environment. You may want to read one or more of the following books to the class to help them appreciate that some every day visits could be shared as trips. You may want to put some of these books in the literacy center for children to explore on their own.

Zachary Goes to the Zoo by Jill Krementz

Going to the Doctor by Fred Rogers

Visiting the Art Museum by L.K. Brown and M. Brown

Review the list that the children generated yesterday and add any new ideas to the list. Highlight the different places the children have visited or dream about visiting. Tell the children that today the class will start a book about their trips to different places. Remind the children that before they start writing they need to develop a plan for their work. The topic of the book is "Places we visited or dream about visiting." When they are all done, they will put their pages together and make a class book. If children prefer, they can write their own individual books.

Remind the children to think about what they want to include in their pieces. You may want to model this for the children, as in the example that follows.

I'm going to write about my trip to the beach. Let's see, I'd like to write about the ocean, the beautiful shells I found, and the fish I caught. I think I'll write a list of these things.

Have the children write down on a piece of paper the place they would like to include as their contribution to the class book. They may want to note what is special about this place, draw some ideas, or just write down any ideas about this place that come into their heads. Have children share their places. Remind the children to put this paper into their writing folder.

You might like to suggest that if the children have pictures of the places they have visited they may want to use them instead of illustrations when they write their page for the book. You can also suggest that children find pictures in magazines and other sources of places they might like to go.

Activity Sheet 32

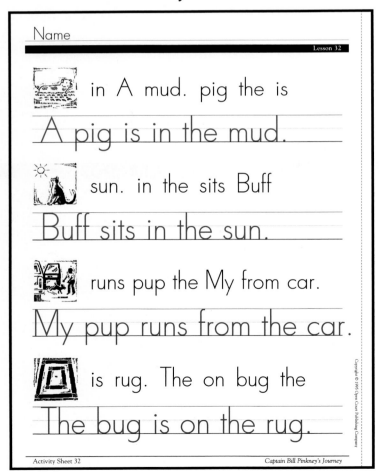

Activity Sheet 32   *Captain Bill Pinkney's Journey*

3 GUIDED AND INDEPENDENT EXPLORATION

WORKSHOP

Remind the children that they may use this time to work on projects independently or in small groups. Make sure all the children know what their options are for this time and how to proceed with any projects they choose. Suggestions for teacher-guided, collaborative, and independent activities follow.

For a review of information about establishing and conducting Workshop, see **Learning Framework Card 11.**

Work with the Teacher

• Review today's Blending exercise again with children who need practice with short vowels. You may wish to review Sound/Spelling Card 21 and reread the Tugboat story with these children, inviting them to join in each time the /u/ sound is repeated in the story.

• Listen to individual children reread Step-by-Step Practice Story 14, "The Bug."

Independent Work

• Activity Sheet 32 reviews the /u/ sound spelled *u*. Tell the children that each group of words on this sheet can be unscrambled to form a sentence that describes the picture. Some children might prefer to work in pairs to unscramble the words and write the sentences on the lines provided.

• After the children have completed Activity Sheet 32, challenge them to draw a picture of their own and to write a scrambled sentence below it. Tell them to save their work for an activity they will complete tomorrow.

• The children may fold a piece of paper in half twice. In each of the four boxes, they should draw a picture of something that has the /u/ sound spelled *u*. Encourage the children to try to label their pictures.

Student Collaboration

• Have the children work in pairs or small groups as they use Flash Cards to review the outlaw words introduced thus far.

• Before Workshop begins, copy the following words onto index cards: *hut, cat, rock, bug, hat, hit, stick, dart, big, bus, stuck, sack, fun, sick, duck, pack, bat, fin, smart, hum, back.*

Using generic game boards (see Games and Songs Teacher Tool Card 4), dice, and the index cards, small groups of children can play a board game to review short vowel spellings. The players take turns rolling the die, then turning over a card and reading aloud the word on the card. If a player reads his or her word correctly, he or she may advance as many squares as are indicated on the die. If the player is unable to read the word, he or she must stay on the same square. Save the cards for use in future Workshop sessions.

• Suggest that the children work with a partner to copy a sentence from today's Blending lesson and extend the sentence into a brief story. Encourage them to draw pictures to illustrate their stories.

Home/School Connection

• Distribute Home/School Connection 9. This letter provides the children's families with information about journeys in general and about Captain Bill Pinkney specifically, along with a list of books that the children and their families might want to read together.

• Send home Step-by-Step Practice Story 13 and encourage the children to read it to their families.

LESSON
33

Lesson Overview

New Learning

- /z/ spelled *z*

Materials

- *Captain Bill Pinkney's Journey*, pages 16–31
- "Zip on the Run," Step-by-Step Practice Story 15
- Sound/Spelling Card 26, Zipper
- Learning Framework Cards 2, 3, 4, 5, 11
- Reading/Writing Connection, pages 56–57
- Activity Sheet 33

GETTING STARTED

Choose one or more of the following activities to focus the children's attention and to review some of the concepts they have been learning.

The Short Vowel Song   Sing the short *u* verse of the short vowel song to the tune of "The Farmer in the Dell." Then sing all the verses.

The short *u* is in tug.
The short *u* is in tug.
/u/ /u/ /u/-/u/ /u/-/u/
The short *u* is in tug.

The short *a* is in lamb.
The short *a* is in lamb.
/a/ /a/ /a/-/a/ /a/-/a/
The short *a* is in lamb.

The short *i* is in pig.
The short *i* is in pig.
/i/ /i/ /i/-/i/ /i/-/i/
The short *i* is in pig.

The short **o** is in frog.
The short **o** is in frog.
/o/ /o/ /o/-/o/ /o/-/o/
The short **o** is in frog.

Short Vowel Discrimination   Ask the children to listen as you say pairs of words that are the same except for the short vowel and then have them identify the vowel sound they hear in each word by holding up the vowel cards from their individual Letter Cards. Suggested pairs include

zip   zap
spot   spit
luck   lick
disk   dusk
draft   drift

Middle Consonants   Have the children listen for the consonant sound in the middle of the word. Say the word and have the children repeat it and then give the sound in the middle. Then have them identify the Sound/Spelling Card that represents the middle sound in the word. Confirm the children's responses by saying the sound as you point to the Sound/Spelling card. For example, "That's right. You heard /m/ in *hammer."*

hammer   hoping   bunny
later   rabbit   pillow

1 READING

PHONICS

* **Introduce /z/ Spelled z**   Turn Sound/Spelling Card 26, Zipper, and ask the children what they see in the picture. Then read the zipper story that follows.

  A complete discussion of the procedure for introducing new sounds and spellings can be found on **Learning Framework Card 2.**

Zack's jacket has a big long zipper.
The zipper zips like this: /z/ /z/ /z/ /z/.

When little Zack goes out to play,
He zips the zipper up this way: /z/ /z/ /z/ /z/.
Later, when he comes back in,
Zack zips the zipper down again: /z/ /z/ /z/ /z/.

Can you help Zack zip his jacket zipper?
(Have the children join in) /z/ /z/ /z/ /z/.

Tell the children that you will say some words. Ask them to signal thumbs-up when they hear a word that begins with /z/. Use these words:

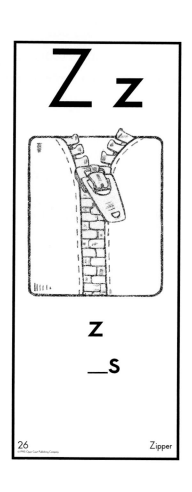

zinger	zoo	zigzag
zero	sofa	puppy
feather	zipper	zucchini

Then ask the children to name a /z/ word that:
- rhymes with *too*
- is the name of a number
- is a vegetable
- rhymes with *map*
- means to go back and forth

Have the children tell how they can use the Zipper card to help them remember the /z/ sound and spelling.

❯ Reading/Writing Connection, page 56, reinforces the sound /z/ spelled *z*. You might want to have the children complete the top part of the page at this time, saying the /z/ sound each time they write a letter.

✳ **Blending** Have the children blend the following words and sentences. For a complete discussion of the blending process, see **Learning Framework Card** 3.

MONITORING BLENDING Continue observing several children as they blend words with the new sound and spelling. Record your observations in Teacher's Observation Log 3.

Line 1:	zip zap zig zag
Line 2:	duck tuck truck
Line 3:	bump dump must dust
Line 4:	drum snug stump
Sentence 1:	Does Gus have a plum for a snack?
Sentence 2:	Bob's rabbit does not run too fast.
Sentence 3:	The rabbit is snug in his hut.

Words Help the children blend the words in each line. Be sure to have unfamiliar words used in sentences.

Review the words by asking the children to find and read pairs of words that rhyme.

Sentences Introduce the outlaw word *does* before writing the sentences. Write the word on the chalkboard and pronounce it. Use the word in an oral sentence, then call on children to use it in oral sentences of their own. Then write the sentences on the board and have the children read them.

Point out the question mark at the end of sentence 1 and ask what it means.

In sentence 2, ask who the rabbit belongs to. Point out that the apostrophe *s* in *Bob's* shows that the rabbit belongs to Bob.

In sentence 3, the *s* in *his* actually makes the /z/ sound, but the children should have no problem sounding out the word. If the children comment on this, remind them that *s* also makes this sound in plural words such as *pans* or *pigs.*

Reading/Writing Connection, page 56

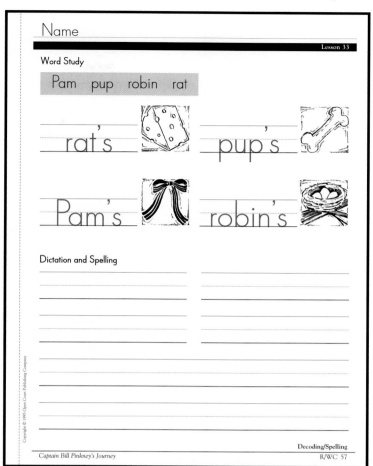

Reading/Writing Connection, page 57

▶ Reading/Writing Connection, pages 56–57, provides additional practice with the /z/ sound spelled *z*. Have the children read and copy the words and sentence on page 56. The top part of page 57 provides practice adding apostrophe *s* to show possession. Help the children choose the name of the person or animal to whom the pictured object belongs, and write that name in the blank, adding *'s*.

✳ READING THE BIG BOOK

Captain Bill Pinkney's Journey
pages 16–31

Activating Prior Knowledge

Point to the cover of *Captain Bill Pinkney's Journey* and ask if anyone remembers the title of the book. Ask a volunteer to read the title, pointing to the words while doing so. Have children retell anything they remember about the story so far.

Recommendations for Reading

Read the second half of the story (pages 16–31) as you did the first half. Stop to have children ask questions and to ask volunteers to summarize what has happened.

South America! In Salvador, Brazil, I meet children in a marching band, beating exciting rhythms on their drums.

RAIN FOREST

Salvador
BRAZIL

PACIFIC OCEAN

ATLANTIC OCEAN

Boston

BERMUDA

16   60°W 50°W 40°W 30°W 20°W   SAILING DAY 61

Macaws live high in the trees of the rain forest.

Caimans live in swamps and rivers.

The world's biggest rain forest is in South America.

17

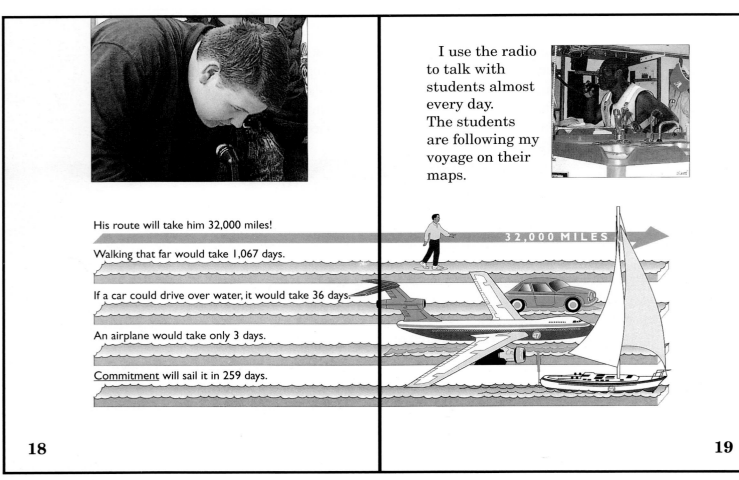

I use the radio to talk with students almost every day. The students are following my voyage on their maps.

His route will take him 32,000 miles!

Walking that far would take 1,067 days.

If a car could drive over water, it would take 36 days.

An airplane would take only 3 days.

Commitment will sail it in 259 days.

32,000 MILES

18   19

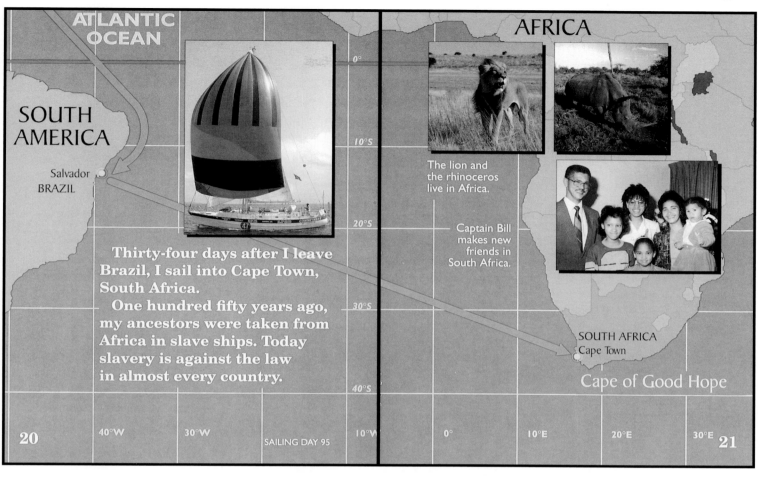

ATLANTIC OCEAN

SOUTH AMERICA

Salvador
BRAZIL

Thirty-four days after I leave Brazil, I sail into Cape Town, South Africa.

One hundred fifty years ago, my ancestors were taken from Africa in slave ships. Today slavery is against the law in almost every country.

20

40°W   30°W   SAILING DAY 95   10°W

AFRICA

The lion and the rhinoceros live in Africa.

Captain Bill makes new friends in South Africa.

SOUTH AFRICA
Cape Town

Cape of Good Hope

0°   10°E   20°E   30°E   21

0°
10°S
20°S
30°S
40°S

Storm! Only eight days away from Cape Town, <u>Commitment</u> is rolling and pitching in strong winds and waves.

This is no fun! The waves are as tall as apartment buildings. I hold on tight and hope the storm ends soon.

22   SAILING DAY 103   23

The storm is over! I sail on to Tasmania, a part of Australia.

The Tasmanian devil is small but fierce.

INDIAN OCEAN

AUSTRALIA

Tasmania • Hobart

24

SAILING DAY 51

The kangaroo bounces on its strong hind legs.

The koala lives in eucalyptus trees and almost never touches the ground.

The kookaburra's voice sounds like silly laughing.

The platypus has a duck bill and a beaver tail. It lays eggs like a bird.

NEW ZEALAND

PACIFIC OCEAN

25

I leave Australia for the longest part of my trip—fifty-two days without seeing land!

A bird rests on Commitment.

A hawksbill turtle swims by.

I check my charts and listen to weather reports. Animals that live far from land are my only company.

White sharks live under the waves.

26

SAILING DAY 185

27

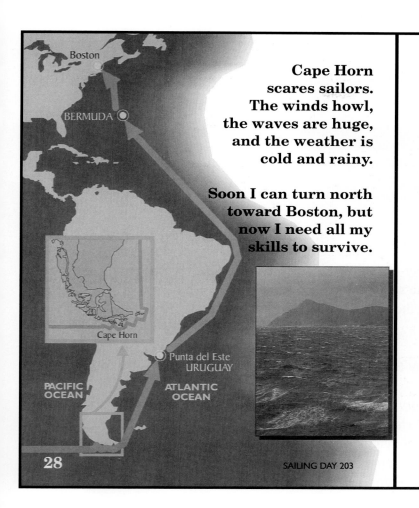

Cape Horn scares sailors. The winds howl, the waves are huge, and the weather is cold and rainy.

Soon I can turn north toward Boston, but now I need all my skills to survive.

28

SAILING DAY 203

To make this trip, Captain Bill had to study math, geography, and science. Reading, however, was his most important skill.

29

I made it! I have kept my promise. I have made my dream come true.

30

SAILING DAY 259

On the dock in Boston, some of the students who were my radio friends are waiting. I am so happy to be back. I have so many stories to share with them.

31

Responding

Invite comments and questions and add to the list begun in the first lesson during browsing. Encourage children to wonder about what happened on the trip.

✱ READING A STEP-BY-STEP PRACTICE STORY

"Zip on the Run"
Story 15

Getting Ready to Read

Browsing the Story   Have the children put together Step-by-Step Practice Story 15, "Zip on the Run." Call on a volunteer to read the title of the story. Then ask the children to look through the story and to comment on anything they notice about the words or the pictures.

Recommendations

Follow the standard procedure for reading a Step-by-Step Practice Story:

- Call on a different child to read each page of the story aloud. Discuss with the class anything of interest on the page and clarify any difficulties. Then have a second child reread the page before going on.
- Reread the story at least twice, calling on different children to read. Then have the entire group do a choral reading of the story.

Responding

- Ask the children if they have any questions about the story. Did they have trouble sounding and blending some of the words in the story? Did they understand the meanings of all the words? Allow the class to try to clear up any problem areas. Also encourage the children to simply comment on the story.
- To make sure the children are paying attention to the words as well as the pictures, have them answer the following questions by pointing to and reading the words aloud:

  What is the rabbit's name?
  What does Zip do as he works?
  What does Zip eat?
  What hits Zip?
  What does the bus do?
  What does Zip do at last?

- Call on volunteers to point out any words they can read. Then invite volunteers to read entire sentences.
- Ask the children to tell what happens in the story and to discuss what they liked best about it. Say: "Do you think *Zip* is a good name for the rabbit? Why or why not?" You may wish to ask the children what they do when they first get up in the morning.

Have the children reread the story with a partner.

TEACHING TIP

Set aside ten minutes for partner reading every day. During this time, you should read with individuals, recording their progress. Reading Assessment Sheets for Phonics Minibooks are available in *Assessment Masters, Grade 1*.

Be sure to set aside time for reading aloud. The children may enjoy hearing about how the main character in *Brave Baby Elephant* prepares for a trip. This book was written by Sesyle Joslin and illustrated by Leonard Weisgard.

See **Learning Framework Card 5** for suggestions for reading aloud.

2 WRITING

Have the children turn to page 57 of their Reading/Writing Connection book so that they can finish the bottom part of the page. Dictate the following words and sentence, using the suggestions for dictation that appear on **Learning Framework Card 4.**

Line 1:	hug bun
Line 2:	tuck stuck
Sentence:	The duck is in the mud.

Help the children proofread each line. Discuss what kind of letter should be at the beginning of a sentence and what should be at the end.

This lesson concludes the first reading of *Captain Bill Pinkney's Journey.* Take out the Big Book and leaf through the pages with the children. If you have the student versions, have small groups of children look through the pages. Ask the children to share their observations about the book. If children don't notice, tell them that Captain Bill's book has pictures of the places he visited and that under each picture is a description of what he saw. Some children may remember that captions were used in the Big Book, *Animals.*

Review with the children the places they talked about yesterday. If some of the children have brought in pictures, hold Seminar to share the pictures. Encourage children to extend sentences and to tell more about the place shown. Possible questions that may help children elaborate on their ideas include What else did you see? What was your favorite part? What made it so special? What do you remember best about it? Their replies may make good captions to put under their pictures.

If children did not bring in pictures, give them some time to draw scenes or things from where they have been or where they would like to go. Have the children share their pictures in Seminar. Children can draw these pictures before they start writing.

Have the children start writing about their trips. Hold conferences with those children who may be having trouble getting started. If there are children who feel they have never been on a trip, talk about every-day trips that we make—to the park, to the store, to the library, or to the homes of family and friends. What are the interesting things that the children see on the way? Is there a favorite person seen on the visit? Trips need not be to faraway places to be special. If children don't know what to write, suggest that they draw a picture and then write a caption under it.

Remind the children to be sure that their name and the date are on their work before putting it into their writing folders.

TEACHING TIP

Just as Captain Bill did, children may want to use more than one picture to tell about a place.

Activity Sheet 33

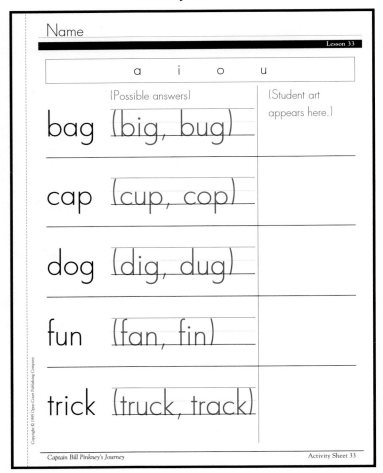

Name _____

Lesson 33

| a | i | o | u |

(Possible answers)   (Student art appears here.)

bag (big, bug)

cap (cup, cop)

dog (dig, dug)

fun (fan, fin)

trick (truck, track)

Captain Bill Pinkney's Journey   Activity Sheet 33

Copyright © 1995 Open Court Publishing Company

3 GUIDED AND INDEPENDENT EXPLORATION

WORKSHOP

Workshop is the time each day when the children can work on projects and activities on their own or with one or more classmates. Remind them that they can always select a book to read during Workshop. They also may write in their journals or work on other projects they have started.

For a review of information about establishing and conducting Workshop, see **Learning Framework Card 11.**

Work with the Teacher

- Review today's Blending exercise with a small group of children.
- Reread Step-by-Step Practice Story 15, "Zip on the Run," with children.
- Repeat the short vowel discrimination activity from today's Getting Started with children who had difficulty the first time around.

Independent Work

- Activity Sheet 33 reviews short vowel sounds and spellings. Tell the children to read each word, change the vowel to make a new word, and then draw a picture to illustrate the new word. Some children might benefit from working in pairs to complete the page.
- Challenge the children to write a sentence using two or more words from today's Blending lesson. They may then illustrate their sentences.
- Provide a selection of books for the children to read or browse. You may wish to include the books you read aloud to the class in this or the previous two lessons.
- Have the children take out Letter Cards *a, g, i, p, t, u, z* for the Word-Building game in the next lesson.

Student Collaboration

- Ask the children to take out the pictures they drew and the scrambled sentences they wrote during yesterday's Workshop session. Have them exchange papers with a partner and unscramble each other's sentences.
- The children may wish to play the Fish for a Sound game. From the deck of Letter Cards, find the ones for the sounds that the children have learned and place them in a jar in the middle of a group of children. Have them take turns "fishing" for a card and then saying a word that begins with that sound.
- Have children reread any previous Step-by-Step Practice stories with a partner.

TEACHING TIP

Encourage the children to read to each other. You, too, should choose children to read with. As you read with each child, note his or her progress.

Home/School Connection

Send home Step-by-Step Practice Story 14, "The Bug." Encourage the children to read it with their families. A letter to accompany this story can be found in the book of Step-by-Step Practice Stories.

LESSON
34

Lesson Overview

Materials

- *Captain Bill Pinkney's Journey*, page 3
- "Zack the One-Man Band," Step-by-Step Practice Story 16
- Learning Framework Cards 3, 5, 11
- Reading/Writing Connection, pages 58–59
- Letter Cards *a, g, i, p, t, u, z*
- Activity Sheet 34
- Short vowel sound word cards from Lesson 32

GETTING STARTED

Choose one or more of the following activities to focus the children's attention and to review some of the concepts they have been learning.

Review /z/ Spelled z   Reread the Zipper story aloud. Ask the children to pay special attention to the /z/ words and to try to remember as many as possible. As you read the story a second time, stop just before each word beginning with /z/ and ask the children to tell you what word they think comes next.

A Tisket, a Tasket   This version of A Tisket, a Tasket will give the children practice reading words with short vowel sounds. Have the children sit in a circle and invite a volunteer to pretend to be a traveler. Give the traveler a basket that contains the cards printed with short vowel sound words from the game the children played during Workshop in Lesson 32. The traveler should move around the circle and say

A tisket, a tasket
a green and yellow basket,
I took a word to my friend
and on the way I dropped it

On the last line, the traveler should stop in front of another child and drop one of the cards. That other child should pick up the card and read the word. That child then becomes the new traveler.

Dictate to the Teacher   Use this game to review the short vowel sounds /o/ and /u/. After writing the word *hot* on the chalkboard, point to the word and ask, "If this is the word *hot*, then how would you spell *hut*?" Have a volunteer dictate the spelling to you and add the new word to the board. Continue with this procedure, moving through the following sequence of words:

cot	cut	cut	cup	cup	cub
cub	rub	rub	rob	rob	rock
rock	dock	dock	duck		

1 READING

PHONICS

✽ Blending   Have the children blend the following words and sentences. For a complete discussion of the blending process, see **Learning Framework Card 3, Blending.**

Line 1:	**buzz fuzz fuss**
Line 2:	**cuff puff huff stuff**
Line 3:	**boss toss moss**
Line 4:	**pass grass brass**
Sentence 1:	**Do not sit on the rug.**
Sentence 2:	**Todd's pup can do six tricks.**
Sentence 3:	**Zack tossed the bag to Cass.**

Words   Use the first word, *buzz,* to help the children see that the double *z* at the end makes only one sound (/b/ /u/ /z/). Draw attention to the other double-consonant endings in the lines and explain that whenever two of the same consonant appear together, they make a single sound.

Have children use some of the words in sentences; invite other children to extend the sentences. Review the words by asking the children to point to and read the words you identify. Use clues such as
- something that grows in the yard
- a word that rhymes with *stuff*
- someone who is in charge
- a kind of metal

- what is at the end of a shirt sleeve
- the sound a bee makes

Sentences Introduce the outlaw word *do* before writing sentence 1. Write the word on the chalkboard, pronounce the word and use the word in an oral sentence. Have children use it in oral sentences of their own. Then write the sentences for the children to read.

When the children come to the word *Todd's* in sentence 2, point out the *'s* and ask what it tells about the next word. (It will be something that belongs to Todd.) Then blend the word *pup* to find out what belongs to Todd. Reinforce the children's answer by saying, "Yes, it is Todd's pup." In sentence 3, point out the *-ed* ending on the word *toss*.

▶ Reading/Writing Connection, pages 58–59, provide practice with double-consonant endings. Help the children choose the correct words to complete each sentence.

Reading/Writing Connection, page 58

Reading/Writing Connection, page 59

Captain Bill Pinkney's Journey
page 3

Activating Prior Knowledge

Invite children to retell what they remember about the author and the journey he took.

Recommendations for Reading

- Turn to page 3 and read the heading Sailing Calendar. Ask the children what they know about calendars.
- Point out that this is a special calendar that tells how long it took Captain Bill to sail from one place to another.
- The first leg of the journey took eight days. Point out that this is about a week. Discuss what the children do during a week.
- Relate the thirty-four days spent sailing from Brazil to South Africa to about a month of time.
- Discuss the other time periods spent sailing.

SAILING CALENDAR

Left	Sailing Days	Arrived
Boston, Massachusetts August 5, 1990	8	Bermuda August 13, 1990
Bermuda August 21, 1990	53	Salvador, Brazil October 13, 1990
Salvador, Brazil November 9, 1990	34	Cape Town, South Africa December 13, 1990
Cape Town, South Africa January 11, 1991	56	Hobart, Australia March 8, 1991

Captain Bill stayed in Hobart, waiting for Australia's summer before setting sail again.

Left	Sailing Days	Arrived
Hobart, Australia December 24, 1991	63	Punta del Este, Uruguay February 25, 1992
Punta del Este, Uruguay April 6, 1992	10	Salvador, Brazil April 16, 1992
Salvador, Brazil April 24, 1992	27	Bermuda May 21, 1992
Bermuda June 1, 1992	8	Boston, Massachusetts June 9, 1992

A ship's clock

3

Responding

Make the point that this journey took a long time. Discuss what kinds of plans he may have needed to make to be gone on a trip that long. Some points to consider are food, clothes, entertainment, maps.

This might be a good time to talk about how Captain Pinkney planned for such a long journey and what equipment he might have taken along. Add questions, comments, and wonderings to the list begun earlier.

TEACHING TIP

You may want to start a class calendar on which you note activities or learning experiences for each day.

✳ READING A STEP-BY-STEP PRACTICE STORY

"Zack the One-Man Band"
Story 16

Getting Ready to Read

Browsing the Story   Have the children put together Step-by-Step Practice Story 16, "Zack the One-Man Band." Read the title of the story aloud. Then ask the children to look through the story and to comment on anything they notice about the words or the pictures.

Recommendations

Follow the standard procedure for reading a Step-by-Step Practice Story:

- Call on a different child to read each page of the story aloud. Discuss with the class anything of interest on the page and clarify any difficulties. Then have a second child or a group of children reread the page before going on.
- Reread the story at least twice, calling on different children to read. Then have the entire group do a choral reading of the story.

Responding

- Encourage the children to comment on the story and to discuss any questions they may have about it. Did they have trouble sounding and blending some of the words in the story? Did they understand the meanings of the words? Answer the children's questions or allow their classmates to do so, if appropriate.
- To make sure the children are paying attention to the words as well as the pictures, have them answer the following questions by pointing to and reading the words aloud:

     What sounds do Gus and Cass hear?
     What do Gus and Cass see on the bus?
     What is the name of the man on the bus?
     What does the man say that Gus and Cass can do?
     What does Cass tell Zack?
  According to Zack, how can Gus and Cass start a band?

Call on volunteers to point out any words they can read. Then invite volunteers to read whole sentences.

- Ask the children to tell what happened in the story and to discuss what they like best about it. Is there anything about the story that still puzzles them? Discuss any questions the children may have.

Have the children reread the story with a partner.

TEACHING TIP

Remind the children to read each book twice. When they finish today's book they should get one from a previous lesson. Reading Assessment Sheets for Phonics Minibooks are available in *Assessment Masters, Grade 1.*

✳ READING ALOUD

Be sure to set aside time for reading aloud. After reading about Captain Pinkney's adventures, the children may enjoy hearing about a toy rabbit who has an adventure of his own. *There and Back Again* by Harold Jones describes the rabbit's adventure.

See **Learning Framework Card 5** for suggestions for reading aloud.

2 WRITING

✳ DICTATION AND SPELLING

Word-Building Game   Have the children take out Letter Cards *a, g, i, p, t, u, z* for the Word-Building game. Start with the word *tip*. Then have the children make the following words. You should write each word on the board with the children.

zip
zap
tap
tag
tug

INDEPENDENT AND COLLABORATIVE WRITING

Start this lesson with Seminar. Remind children that during Seminar they must listen carefully to the author. When the author is done, he or she will call on several students. These students should tell the author what they liked about the piece and then make comments or suggestions or ask questions about the piece. These comments should be related to the piece. Have some children share what they have written so far about their trips. If children do not ask questions or make comments, model appropriate inquiries by asking questions that encourage children to add information about the trip. If children have pictures, they may want to share them with the class as well. This becomes a good opportunity to help children extend their writing by noting details in the pictures they did not talk about. Ask questions such as, What else is in your picture? Tell us about that building in the corner. Why did you take this picture? What is special about this picture?

As children read their stories or talk about their pictures, write down the suggestions from the audience and share them with the author later.

Let children continue working on their contribution to the class book. As you hold conferences with individuals or small groups, remind the children about using the caret when they want to add something to their piece. They can also draw a line through anything they want to take out. Some children may want to start keeping a record in their journal of what they do each day, similar to Captain Bill's sailing calendar.

3 GUIDED AND INDEPENDENT EXPLORATION

WORKSHOP

Workshop is the time each day when the children can work on projects and activities on their own or with one or more classmates. Remind them that they can always select a book to read during Workshop. They also may write in their journals or work on other projects they have started.

For a review of information about establishing and conducting Workshop, see **Learning Framework Card 11.**

Work with the Teacher

- Repeat today's Blending exercise with children who seemed to have difficulty with it. Challenge them to extend the sentences and to use some of the words in new sentences.
- Ask some of the more fluent readers to read to you from books or magazines that they are reading for pleasure. Invite other children to listen.
- Listen to children read Step-by-Step Practice Story 16, "Zack the One-Man Band."

Independent Work

- Activity Sheet 34 provides practice with short vowel sounds and spellings. Tell the children to complete the sentences by writing in the correct words. They can then draw a picture of their favorite sentence in the box provided.
- Tell the children that today they will take home their copies of Step-by-Step Practice Story 15, "Zip on the Run," to share with their families. Suggest that they draw their own pictures of Zip to take home with the story. Have them write a sentence to tell what Zip is doing.

- Encourage children to read on their own. Provide a selection of books for them to choose from.

Student Collaboration

- Have the children reread a Phonics Minibook with a partner. Remind them to follow the usual turn-taking procedure for partner reading. Encourage them to help each other blend difficult words.
- Remind the children that as a boy, Captain Pinkney dreamed of sailing around the world in his own boat. Have the children discuss with a partner some of the things that they have dreamed about doing or becoming. The children may wish to draw a picture of themselves actually doing something that they have dreamed about. Encourage them to write one or two sentences to describe their pictures.

Home/School Connection

Send home Step-by-Step Practice Story 15, "Zip on the Run." Encourage the children to read it to their families.

Name

Lesson 34

cart drifts hot dog frogs nut

1. You can crack a nut.
2. A hot dog fits on a bun.
3. The man drifts on a raft.
4. Frogs hop in the pond.
5. Mom has six bags in the cart.

(Student art appears here.)

Activity Sheet 34 *Captain Bill Pinkney's Journey*

Activity Sheet 34

LESSON

35

Lesson Overview

New Learning

- /l/ spelled *l*
- Revising: Extending Sentences

Materials

- *Captain Bill Pinkney's Journey*, pages 4–7
- Phonics Minibook 6, *In the Pond*
- Sound/Spelling Card 12, Lion
- Learning Framework Cards 2, 3, 4, 5
- Reading/Writing Connection, pages 60–61
- Activity Sheet 35

GETTING STARTED

Choose one or both of the following activities to focus the children's attention and to review some of the concepts they have been learning.

Sound Card Review   Engage the children in a review of the Sound/Spelling Cards they have learned. Give several words that begin with the same sound and have the children identify the card, the spelling, and the sound represented. Some example words are

gum, gift, gold	umbrella, under, up
zoo, zebra, zoom	ox, opera, ostrich
funeral, fox, forest	brave, bowl, bedroom

Silly Sentences Game   To help the children become more aware of initial consonant sounds, make up a silly alliterative phrase, such as "silly Sammy seal." Ask the children what sound they hear at the beginning of all three words and what the spelling is for that sound. Then change the first sound of each word to make up another silly phrase, such as "tilly tammy teal." Again ask the children what sound they hear at the beginning of the words and what the spelling is. Invite the children to make up their own silly alliterative phrases based on your model and to ask one another what repeated sound they hear each time and how to spell it.

1 READING

PHONICS

* **Introduce /l/ Spelled l**   Turn Sound/Spelling Card 12, Lion, and ask the children what animal they see. Then read the Lion story to introduce the /l/ sound.

A discussion of the procedure for introducing a new sound can be found on **Learning Framework Card 2.**

Look! It's Leon the Lion.
Leon loves to lap water from lakes,
And this is the sound the lapping lion makes: /l/ /l/ /l/ /l/ /l/.

Let's join Leon. Quick!
Take a little lick: /l/ /l/ /l/ /l/ /l/.

Are you a thirsty lass or lad?
Then lap until you don't feel bad: /l/ /l/ /l/ /l/ /l/.

What sound do you make when you lap like Leon the Lion?
(Have the children say) /l/ /l/ /l/ /l/ /l/.

Have the children listen to some words and signal thumbs-up when they hear a word that begins with the /l/ sound. Use these words

lemon	**lunch**	**lollipop**
library	finger	**lady**
pumpkin	**licorice**	**lucky**

Ask the children to suggest other words that begin with /l/. Then have the children signal when they hear /l/ at the end of a word. Use these words

ball	**pail**	**snail**
skate	**buckle**	**school**
canal	tiger	**feel**

Finally have the children tell how they can use the Lion card to help them remember this sound and spelling.

➤ Reading/Writing Connection, page 60, reinforces the /l/ sound spelled *l*. Have the children complete the top part of this page at this time.

✱ **Blending**   Have the children blend the following words and sentences. For a complete discussion of the blending process, see **Learning Framework Card 3, Blending.**

Line 1:	log lap lock clock
Line 2:	land list lamp plant
Line 3:	hill fill pull full
Line 4:	all ball tall fall
Sentence 1:	Three small pigs hopped in the mud.
Sentence 2:	One pup and two cats sat on Dad's lap.
Sentence 3:	Bill dropped four cups and five glasses.

Words   As you sound and blend *lock* and *clock* in line 1, remind the children that *ck* is another way to spell the sound /k/. In line 2, point out that each word ends in a cluster, *nd, st, mp,* or *nt.*

In line 3, explain that *ll* makes the sound /l/. Even though there are two letters, they form only one sound. Note that the *u* in *pull* and *full* is not quite a short *u,* but the children should have no trouble adjusting their pronunciations when they blend the words.

In line 4, write the word *all* and tell the children what it says. Then write the other words and blend as follows: /b/ /all/, *ball* and /t/ /all/, *tall.* Tell the children that *all* is a special pattern found in many words.

Review the words by pointing to them in random order and asking the children to read them. The children should erase those words they read successfully.

Sentences   Introduce the outlaw words *one, two, three, four, five* by writing each on the board, reading it, and using it in a sentence. Have the children use the words in oral sentences. Then write the sentences to blend on the board.

Before you blend sentence 1, write *hop* and *hopped* on the chalkboard. Have the children use both words in sentences to illustrate the difference between the two. Then point out the double consonant in *hopped.* Explain that when a word has a short vowel we double the last consonant before adding the *-ed* to make the past tense. Repeat with *drop* and *dropped.* Then have the children read the sentences.

➤ Reading/Writing Connection, pages 60–61, provide additional practice with the /l/ sound spelled *l.* Work with the children to complete all of page 60 and the top of page 61.

TEACHING TIP

The number words *one, two, three, four,* and *five* will be used in Phonics Minibook 6 and are reviewed in the sentences. The children may wish to illustrate these sentences, using the number words as a guide.

Name _____

Lesson 35

Sounds and Spellings _____

l

L

L

Writing Words and Sentences

last   last   tickle   tickle

Bill slips in the puddle.

Bill slips in the puddle.

Consonant Sounds and Spellings

60 R/WC   Captain Bill Pinkney's Journey

Reading/Writing Connection, page 60

Name _____

Lesson 35

Reading and Writing Sentences

Lil fills the pickle jar.
Liz has lots of dolls.

Liz has lots of dolls.

Dictation and Spelling

_____   _____

Captain Bill Pinkney's Journey   Decoding/Spelling
                                                  R/WC 61

Reading/Writing Connection, page 61

✳ READING THE BIG BOOK

Captain Bill Pinkney's Journey
pages 4–7

Recommendations for Reading
- Display pages 4–7 of *Captain Bill Pinkney's Journey* and invite the children to comment on anything they notice about the pictures or the words.

Responding
Ask volunteers to comment on Captain Pinkney's dream and have them relate this to any dreams that they may have about things they want to do or to be.

Call attention to Captain Bill's commitment. Ask the children how he explained what a *commitment* is and encourage discussion of reasons for making "powerful promises" when we are young.

Invite comments about the pictures.

Add any questions and wonderings to the list begun earlier.

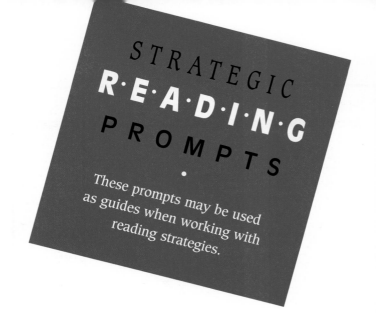

1 Model responding to unfamiliar words by say-ing, Commitment *is a hard word, but the writer tells us what it means in the same sentence.* Encourage questions about other word meanings on this spread. If the children do not question any words, wonder aloud about *oceans, radar,* and *geography. Oceans* and *radar* appear in the Glossary. *Geography* is the study of the earth.

When I was a boy, I dreamed about boats, so I started reading about boats.

"I will grow up to be Captain Bill," I said, "and sail across wide oceans."

I made a commitment—that's a powerful promise—to sail around the world in my own boat.

When I grew up, I learned to sail. I read more about boats. I learned to use tools and fix equipment. I learned to use radios and radar. I studied geography and weather.

4

5

Boston Harbor

Captain Bill named his boat <u>Commitment</u> for his powerful promise. ②

I learned enough to be captain of my own boat. Today I leave from Boston to sail around the world!

I have said good-bye to dozens of Boston schoolchildren. They will talk with me by radio when I am at sea.

6

7

② Discuss the picture of Captain Bill's boat. Children may comment on the sails and the size of the boat.

In the Pond
Phonics Minibook 6

Getting Ready to Read

Reading the Title   Invite a volunteer to read aloud the title on the cover of the book.

Browsing the Selection   Allow the children to look through the book, commenting on what they see in the pictures and what they think the story will tell them.

Recommendations

Follow the standard procedure for reading the Phonics Minibook:

- Call on a different child to read each page of the story aloud. Clarify any difficulties on each page, and then have a different child reread the page before going on.
- Reread the story at least twice, calling on different children to read.

ISBN 0-8126-1276-0

10 9 8 7 6 5 4 3 2 1

2

"It is hot," said five pigs.
"It is too hot!"

3

The pigs hopped in the pond.
Five pigs in the pond.

4

"It is hot," said four dogs.
"It is too hot!"

5

The dogs hopped in the pond.
Five pigs and
four dogs
in the pond.

6

"It is hot," said three cats.
"It is too hot!"

7

The cats hopped in the pond.
Five pigs,
four dogs, and
three cats
in the pond.

8

"It is hot," said two bats.
"It is too hot!"

9

The bats hopped in the pond.
Five pigs,
four dogs,
three cats, and
two bats
in the pond.

10

"It is hot," said one hippo.
"It is too hot!"

11

"Not in the pond!" said the five pigs.
"Not in the pond!" said the four dogs.

12

"Not in the pond!" said the three cats.
"Not in the pond!" said the two bats.

13

"It is hot," said the five pigs,
four dogs,
three cats, and
two bats.
"It is too hot!"

14

15

One hippo in the pond.

16

Responding

- Ask the children to talk about any hard words they came across in their reading, and to explain how they figured out those words.
- To make sure the children are focusing on the words and sentences in the story and not just the pictures, have them answer questions such as the ones that follow. Ask them to point to the words or sentences in the story that answer each question.

> What do the pigs say?
> What do the pigs do?
> Who is in the pond?
> What do the cats say?
> Who is in the pond?
> What do the animals say to the hippo?

Have the children reread the story with a partner.

✷ READING ALOUD

Be sure to set aside time for reading aloud. Another book related to the unit theme of journeys is *Warton and Morton* by Russell E. Erickson.
See Learning Framework Card 5 for suggestions for reading aloud.

TEACHING TIP

Set aside ten minutes for partner reading every day. During this time, you should read with individuals, recording their progress. Reading Assessment Sheets for Phonics Minibooks are available in *Assessment Masters, Grade 1*.

2 WRITING

✷ DICTATION AND SPELLING

Have the children turn to the bottom of page 61 of their Reading/Writing Connection book. Dictate the following words and sentence, using the suggestions for dictation that appear on **Learning Framework Card 4.**

 Line 1: zip   buzz

Line 2: rack   track

Sentence: Tom stops <u>the</u> car.

Help the children proofread each line. Tell the children that the /z/ sound of *buzz* is spelled *zz.* Explain that this sound is often spelled *zz* at the end of words.

Revising: Extending Sentences

In earlier lessons, children were informally introduced to the idea of revision as you made changes in class big books, inserting and deleting information. In this lesson, children will begin applying a technique they have been using in Blending to their writing—extending sentences. It is a natural and comfortable way for children to start revising.

Tell children that writers reread what they have written and often make changes in their stories. This rereading and making changes is called revising. One way to revise is to tell more about what you have already written to make the story more interesting.

Remind children of how they extend sentences in Blending by adding information that answers the questions *what, where, how,* and *when.* Model for the children how they can use the same technique in their own writing. Copy the following short story about the beach onto the board or a transparency. Read it to the class.

My Vacation

Last summer I went on a trip. I went swimming. I collected shells. I went fishing. It was sunny. I had a good time.

After reading the story, tell the students that the author could make it better by rewriting the story and telling us more about the trip. Reread the story sentence by sentence, stopping after each one and asking for suggestions from the children as to how to extend it. For example, after the first sentence, wonder with the children where you went on a trip and have someone answer the question. For example, a student might say, "Last summer I went to the beach." Using a caret, show where the information should go and write it above.

Continue reading and extending the remaining sentences. Have the children consider whether or not their proposed additions make the story clearer or more interesting before they make the additions or changes.

Have the children take out the pages about a trip that they are working on for the class book. Have several children read a sentence or two and talk about how these could be extended. Then have the children work in pairs to read and extend their sentences. Remind children that asking questions about *where, when, what,* and *how* can help them extend their sentences.

Hold conferences with pairs or groups and focus on extending sentences to add information.

3 GUIDED AND INDEPENDENT EXPLORATION

WORKSHOP

Workshop is the time each day when the children can work on projects and activities on their own or with one or more classmates. Remind them that they can always select a book to read during Workshop. They also may write in their journals or work on other projects they have started.

Work with the Teacher

- Reread recently introduced Sound/Spelling Cards and have children blend words using these sounds and spellings.
- Listen to individual children reread Phonics Minibook 6.
- If you have student versions of the book available, have children read *Captain Bill Pinkney's Journey* along with you. Have them find words they know and read them for you.

> **MONITORING BLENDING** You should be finishing your observations of individuals blending new words. Record your observations in Teacher's Observation Log 3.

Independent Work

- Activity Sheet 35 provides practice with short vowel sounds and spellings. Tell the children that they can help the lion find his way back to his cave by coloring in the pictures that go with the words at the bottom of the page. To get the children started, have them blend the first word and color in its corresponding picture.

- Challenge the children to extend a sentence from the Blending exercise by answering a question such as *when, where,* or *why.* Ask them to print and illustrate their extended sentences.
- Suggest that the children revisit Big Book 3, *Captain Bill Pinkney's Journey,* in their small copies.
- Have the children prepare Letter Cards *e, i, l, n, s, t* for the Word-Building game in the next lesson.

Student Collaboration

- Have pairs of children reread Phonics Minibook 6, *In the Pond.* Remind them to follow the usual turn-taking procedure. Encourage them to help each other blend difficult words.
- Suggest that groups of children may want to go to the learning center to find books about boats to share with the class.
- Have children work in pairs to write sentences using words from Blending. Challenge them to use more than one word in a sentence.

Home/School Connection

Send home Step-by-Step Practice Story 16, "Zack the One-Man Band," and encourage the children to read it to their families at home.

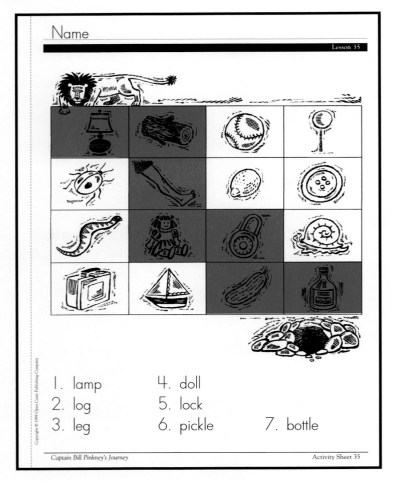

Name

Lesson 35

1. lamp
2. log
3. leg
4. doll
5. lock
6. pickle
7. bottle

Captain Bill Pinkney's Journey

Activity Sheet 35

Activity Sheet 35

LESSON 36

Lesson Overview

New Learning

- /e/ spelled *e*

Materials

- *Captain Bill Pinkney's Journey*, pages 8–9
- "Meg's Sled," Step-by-Step Practice Story 17
- Sound/Spelling Card 5, Hen
- Learning Framework Cards 2, 3, 5
- Reading/Writing Connection, pages 62–63
- Letter Cards *e, i, l, n, s, t*
- Outlaw Word Flash Cards
- Activity Sheet 36
- Home/School Connection 10

Prepare Ahead

- Scrambled Sentences Game (see page 64 and Games and Songs Teacher Tool Card 8)

GETTING STARTED

Choose one or both of the following activities to focus the children's attention and to review some of the concepts they have been learning.

Find a Word Game   Write words on the chalkboard that contain various short vowel sounds and some of the consonants that the children have recently learned. Name a short vowel Sound/Spelling Card and ask a child to point to a word on the board that contains that sound. Have the group read the word aloud. The child should identify the spelling used in the word and then erase the word. You might want to use some of the following words:

fluff	box	lock	brick	spill
frog	buzz	slip	pass	black
full	lump	truck	flag	lost
drill	miss			

Short Vowel Sounds   Have the children take out the *i, o, u,* cards from their set of Letter Cards. Tell them you will say a word and they should hold up the letter that spells the vowel sound. Use these words:

ox	in	up
itch	odd	us
big	dot	bug

1 READING

PHONICS

Some of your students will not yet have mastered the sounds that have been introduced and may be having difficulty blending them with other sounds. This is normal. It is very important that you not wait for mastery of each sound before going on to the next. Students will gradually learn the sounds through repetition and practice.

* **Introduce /e/ Spelled *e***   Turn Sound/Spelling Card 5, Hen, and ask the children what kind of letter this is. Discuss what the green color means about this vowel sound. If necessary, explain that the green color means a short vowel sound. Then tell the children to listen as you read the Hen story.

A discussion of the procedure for introducing a new sound can be found on **Learning Framework Card 2.**

5   Hen

Jem's pet hen likes to peck, peck, peck.
She pecks at a speck on the new red deck.
This is how her pecking sounds: /e/ /e/ /e/ /e/ /e/.

Jem's pet hen pecks at corn in her pen.
She pecks ten kernels, then pecks again.
This is how her pecking sounds: /e/ /e/ /e/ /e/ /e/.

Jem's hen pecks at a cracked egg shell.
She's helping a chick get out, alive and well.
This is how her pecking sounds: /e/ /e/ /e/ /e/ /e/.

Can you help Jem's hen peck?
(Have children say) /e/ /e/ /e/ /e/ /e/.

Ask the children to listen to some words and to signal thumbs-up when they hear a word that has the /e/ sound at the beginning. Use these words

ever	**every**	flavor
etch	hand	**echo**

Then have the children signal when they hear /e/ in the middle of a word. Use these words

hen	wet	bed
tape	desk	next
pest	bike	feather

➤ Reading/Writing Connection, page 62, reinforces the /e/ sound spelled *e*. You might want to have the children complete the top part of the page at this time, saying the /e/ sound each time they write a letter.

✱ **Blending** Have the children blend the following words and sentences. For a complete discussion of the blending process, see **Learning Framework Card 3, Blending.**

Line 1:   tell fell sell bell

Line 2:   red let men deck

Line 3:   next tent help send

Line 4:   exit carpet ticket puppet

Sentence 1:   Meg and Bess <u>would</u> send <u>me</u> a present.

Sentence 2:   <u>She</u> fell and lost <u>the</u> red mittens.

Sentence 3:   Ted pulled his sled up <u>the</u> big hill.

Words Help the children blend the words in each line. Have children use some of the words, such as *carpet, ticket,* and *exit,* in oral sentences.

Review the words by giving clues such as the following. The children should erase each word they read. Encourage the children to give each other clues for other words.

- rhymes with *sell* but starts with /t/
- a color
- the opposite of *enter*
- another name for a rug
- you sleep in this outside

Sentences Before writing the sentences, introduce the outlaw words *would, me, she* in the usual way by writing them on the board one at a time and pronouncing them. Have the children pronounce them and use them in oral sentences. Then write the sentences, underlining the outlaw words. If the children have trouble reading any of the outlaw words, simply tell them the words.

➤ Have the children open their Reading/Writing Connection books to pages 62–63, which provide additional practice with the /e/ sound spelled *e*. The children can complete page 62 by reading and copying the words and sentence. On page 63, help them label the pictures, read the pairs of words, and explain how the words in each pair are alike. Have the children complete the sentence at the bottom of the page by writing the sounds represented in the pictures and blending those sounds to make a word.

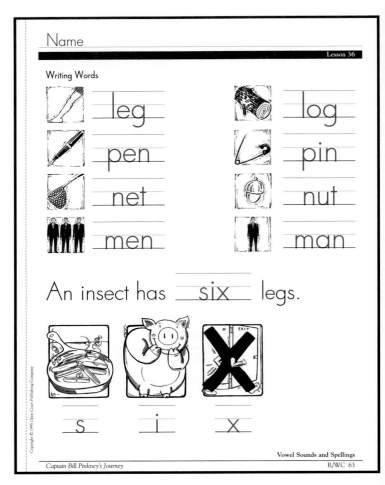

Reading/Writing Connection, page 62

Reading/Writing Connection, page 63

Captain Bill Pinkney's Journey
pages 8–9

Activating Prior Knowledge

Ask volunteers to sum up what they have learned about Captain Bill's commitment to his adventure and what the word *commitment* means.

Recommendations for Reading

- Display pages 8–9 of *Captain Bill Pinkney's Journey.* Read the captions and explain how both the globe and the flat map represent the earth. Point out that North America, South America, Africa, and other land areas are seen on the globe and the chart.
- Ask the children to talk about what they know about maps and what they are good for. Some children may have become familiar with maps while on a trip with their family. Let them share their experiences.

1 If no one questions the meaning of *continents,* wonder aloud about this word and help the children locate (on the flat map) the four that Captain Bill will touch: North America, South America, Africa, and Australia. The word appears in the Glossary.

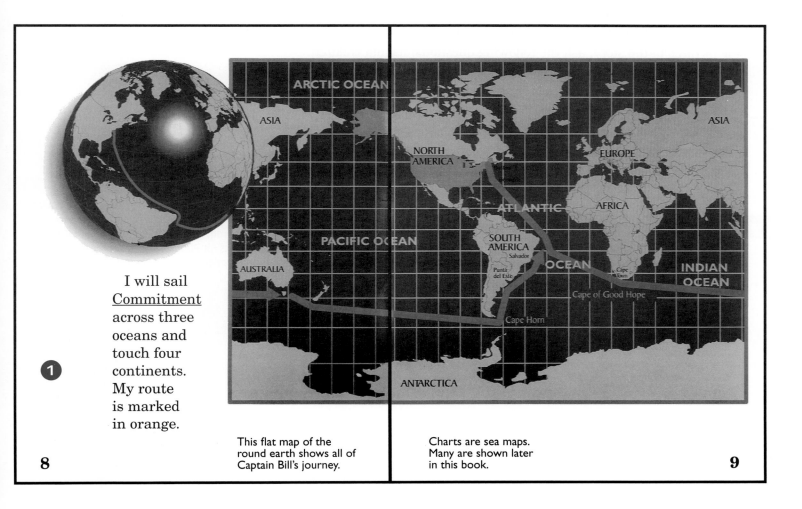

I will sail <u>Commitment</u> across three oceans and touch four continents. My route is marked in orange.

1

This flat map of the round earth shows all of Captain Bill's journey.

Charts are sea maps. Many are shown later in this book.

8

9

Responding

Display any maps you have available, including road maps, a world map, U.S. map, or a globe. Have the children compare these to the world map in *Captain Bill Pinkney's Journey.* Discuss how the different maps are used.

Call on volunteers to **sum up** what they have learned so far about geography, sailing, and commitment.

✳ READING A STEP-BY-STEP PRACTICE STORY

"Meg's Sled"
Story 17

Getting Ready to Read

Have the children put together Step-by-Step Practice Story 17. Call on a child to read the title. Ask what the children know about sleds.

Recommendations

Call on a different child to read each page of the story aloud. If a child has difficulty with a word, help blend it. Reread the story at least twice, calling on different children to read each time.

Responding

After reading, ask the children to tell in their own words what happened in the story and to discuss any difficulties they had in reading it. To check that the children are paying attention to the words as well as the pictures in the story, ask the following questions, having children point to the words in the story that answer each question:

What was the second animal Meg passed?

What was the first thing Meg did when she reached the top of the hill?

What did all of the animals cry as Meg sped past them on her sled?

Have the children read the story with a partner.

✳ READING ALOUD

Be sure to set aside time later in the day to read to the children. *Git Along, Old Scudder* by Stephen Gammel and *Maps and Globes* by Jack Knowlton are two of many books about using maps for travel that the children might enjoy. After reading, remember to ask the children what they have learned about maps from these or other books.

See **Learning Framework Card 5** for suggestions for reading aloud.

TEACHING TIP

Remind the children to read each book twice. When they finish today's book, they should get one from a previous lesson. Reading Assessment Sheets for Phonics Minibooks are available in *Assessment Masters, Grade 1.*

2 WRITING

✳ DICTATION AND SPELLING

Word-Building Game Have the children use Letter Cards *e, i, l, n, s, t* for this Word-Building game. Begin with the word *net*. Then have the children make the words that follow. This activity may be done with paper and pencil if you prefer.

net
let
set
sent
lent
lint
list

INDEPENDENT AND COLLABORATIVE WRITING

Start with Seminar. Have children share their pieces. Continue to encourage the children to elaborate on their ideas and extend their sentences by answering *where, how, why,* and *when* questions and adding that information to their stories. Discuss with the children whether the additions help make their pieces clearer or more interesting.

Before ending, select several pieces to use during a proofreading lesson on capitals and ending punctuation in the next lesson. Be sure to have the author's permission to use the piece.

Some children may want to explore making a map as a writing project. They might make a map of their room at home, of the classroom, or of their neighborhood. Encourage them to label the places on their maps.

TEACHING TIP

Make children feel that using their writing to help the whole class is special. Not only does it help the class but it means that the author gets special help proofreading. If possible, make transparencies of the pieces you will be proofreading.

3 GUIDED AND INDEPENDENT EXPLORATION

WORKSHOP

Remind the children that they may use this time to work on projects independently or in small groups. Make sure all the children know what their options are for this time and how to proceed with any projects they choose. Suggestions for teacher-guided, collaborative, and independent activities follow.

Work with the Teacher

- Working with small groups of children, use Outlaw Word Flash Cards to review the outlaw words that the children have learned thus far.
- Work with children to blend words with the /e/ sound.
- Reteach Sound/Spelling Card 5, Hen, and Step-by-Step Practice Story 17, "Meg's Sled," to those children who had difficulty earlier in the lesson.

Independent Work

- Activity Sheet 36 provides practice with following directions. Tell the children to cut out the pictures at the bottom of the sheet, then read each sentence and paste the pictures where the directions tell them to.
- Encourage children to read on their own. Provide a selection of books for them to choose.

Student Collaboration

- Pairs of children may review Alphabet Flash Cards with one another.

- With a partner, children may reread any Step-by-Step Practice Story. Remind them to follow the usual procedure.
- Invite the children to play Scrambled Sentences. Before Workshop begins, you might want to create some new sentences, using short *u,* short *e,* and the other sounds and spellings introduced in this unit. For a review of Scrambled Sentences, see **Games and Songs Teacher Tool Card 8.**
- Small groups of children may want to work together to make a map of the school. Have them discuss the places their maps should show.

Home/School Connection

- Distribute Home/School Connection 10, which explains to children's families what outlaw words are and how they can help their children to learn these words.
- Send home the take-home version of Phonics Minibook 5, *Panda Band,* for children to read to their families.

Name

Lesson 36

Put the pup in the box.
Put the duck on top of the box.
Put the dragon to the left of the box.
Put the egg next to the duck.
Put the pickle next to the dragon.

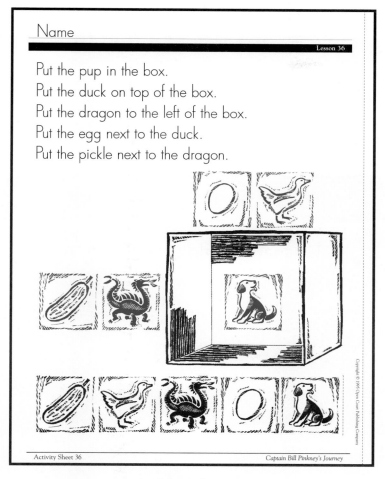

Activity Sheet 36

Captain Bill Pinkney's Journey

Activity Sheet 36

LESSON 37

Lesson Overview

New Learning

- /e/ spelled *ea*
- Capitals and end punctuation

Materials

- *Captain Bill Pinkney's Journey*, pages 10–15
- "Hen in a Pen," Step-by-Step Practice Story 18
- Sound/Spelling Card 5, Hen
- Learning Framework Cards 3, 4, 5
- Reading/Writing Connection, pages 64–65
- Activity Sheet 37

Prepare Ahead

- Fish for a Sound Cards (see page 75)
- Wonder Word Cards (see page 66)

GETTING STARTED

Choose one or more of the following activities to focus the children's attention and to review some of the concepts they have been learning.

Short-Vowel Song Have the children sing the /e/ verse for the "Short-Vowel Song" to the tune of "The Farmer in the Dell." Then have them sing all five verses with the other short vowels (see pages 22–23).

The short *e* is in hen
The short *e* is in hen
/e/ /e/ /e/-/e/ /e/-/e/
The short *e* is in hen.

Wonder Word Game Use cards with short vowel words. (You may have made a set of these for Workshop in Lesson 32.) Include cards with the following words printed on them: *left, less, smell, bend, tent.* Have the children sit in a circle and say this verse as you pass a card around the circle:

The wonder word goes round and round.
To pass it quickly you are bound.
If you're the one to have it last,
Then you must read it rather fast.

The child who has the card when the verse ends reads the word. This child picks the next card from the top of the deck and continues the game.

Listen for Vowel Sounds   Write the letter *e* on one end of the chalkboard and write letter *a* at the other end. Touch each letter and ask the children to say the sound. Then pronounce a series of words and have the children point to either the *e* or the *a* and say aloud the short vowel sound they hear in each word. You can use the following words:

pan	pen	leg	lag
tan	ten	mass	mess
bad	bed	pat	pet
send	sand	pest	past

1 READING

PHONICS

* **Blending**   Have the children blend the following words and sentences. For a complete discussion of the blending process, see **Learning Framework Card 3, Blending.**

Line 1:	head bread meant instead
Line 2:	big peg sag dug log
Line 3:	flip class block plant
Line 4:	apple pickle tumble
Sentence 1:	Ned should have bread instead of muffins.
Sentence 2:	She left the glass out on the deck.
Sentence 3:	Nell tickles the little pups.

Words   In line 1, the children are introduced to words that use the spelling *ea* for the /e/ sound. Although this spelling is not formally introduced on Sound/Spelling Card 5, Hen, tell the children that this is another way to spell the short *e* sound. Then, sound and blend the words in the usual fashion. Be sure to write the spelling *ea* as a unit and emphasize that the two letters together say /e/.

In line 2, point out that the words contain all five short vowel spellings. Invite the children to name the vowels and to pronounce the short sound of each.

As the children blend *apple* in line 4, have them blend each syllable individually, then put the syllables together. Point out that the *e* on the end of the word is silent. Repeat with the other words. After the

TEACHING TIP

You may want to write this spelling in red on Sound/Spelling Card 5, Hen. To differentiate the spelling from the *ea* for long *e*, which will be introduced later, you may want to write the spelling _ea_. This indicates that the spelling may fall in the middle of words or syllables only, not at the beginning or end of a word or syllable as the long *e* spelled *ea* may.

children have blended the words, have them clap the syllables to illustrate that each word has two syllables.

Review the words by pointing to a word, having a child read it, and asking children to use it in a sentence.

Sentences Introduce the outlaw words *should* and *out* before writing the sentences on the board. Write each word on the board, pronounce the word, and have the children use the word in oral sentences. Write the word *would* next to *should* and point out the spelling pattern *ould* to the children. (Note: *Would* was introduced in the previous lesson.)

Then write the sentences on the board. Help the children read *should* and *out* and any other outlaw words as necessary.

➤ Reading/Writing Connection, pages 64–65, reinforces /e/ spelled *ea*. Work with the children to complete page 64 and the top part of page 65.

Reading/Writing Connection, page 64

Name

Lesson 37

Completing Sentences

| instead | head | spread | fed | dead |

1. Ted _spread_ jam on his bread.

2. "The bug is _dead_," said Meg.

3. Greg _fed_ the red hen.

4. Peg will run _instead_ of Ben.

5. Can you fix the puppet's _head_?

Vowel Sounds and Spellings
64 R/WC   *Captain Bill Pinkney's Journey*

Reading/Writing Connection, page 65

Name

Lesson 37

Writing Words

| left | bed | instead | bread | nest |

nest   _bread_   _bed_

Dictation and Spelling

_____   _____
_____   _____
_____   _____
_____   _____

Captain Bill Pinkney's Journey

Decoding/Spelling
R/WC 65

Captain Bill Pinkney's Journey
pages 10–15

Activating Prior Knowledge

Invite volunteers to recall how Captain Bill spends his days and nights while *Commitment* is sailing.

Recommendations for Reading

- Display pages 10–11 and read the story segment. Then read the captions and have the children comment on anything of interest. Remind them that they have seen captions before in the Big Book *Animals.* Discuss how captions can add to the information given in a story. Help the children relate the pictures at the top of the pages with the representations of Captain Bill at work on his boat.
- Display pages 12–13 and read the story segment and the captions.
- Ask the children to comment on anything they find interesting and to ask any questions they may have.
- You might want to return to the globe or map to locate Bermuda and note on the bottom of pages 12 and 13 how many days Captain Bill has been sailing at this point in his journey.
- Display pages 14–15. Read page 14 and invite the children to wonder about how sailors might celebrate crossing the equator.
- Call attention to the picture on page 15. Tell the children that one of the men in the picture is Captain Bill Pinkney. Challenge the class to find his name on the page. Call on a volunteer to point to it and to his picture. Read the caption and ask how this might have helped him with his commitment to sail alone around the world.

STRATEGIC
R·E·A·D·I·N·G
PROMPTS
·
These prompts may be used
as guides when working with
reading strategies.

Captain Bill talks to students by radio.

He cooks his meals in the galley, the kitchen of the boat.

On Wednesday nights Captain Bill watches videos.

Captain Bill sleeps in his bunk.

Commitment is a snug home.
I do everything by myself.

Day and night it sails along,
even when I'm asleep.

10

11

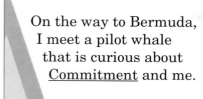

On the way to Bermuda,
I meet a pilot whale
that is curious about
<u>Commitment</u> and me.

Whales are not fish.
They are big mammals
that swim to the
surface to breathe air.

12

SAILING DAY 3

Houses on Bermuda
have special roofs
that collect rain for
drinking and washing.

After sailing for eight days, I see
land. It is the island of Bermuda,
far out in the Atlantic Ocean.

SAILING DAY 8

13

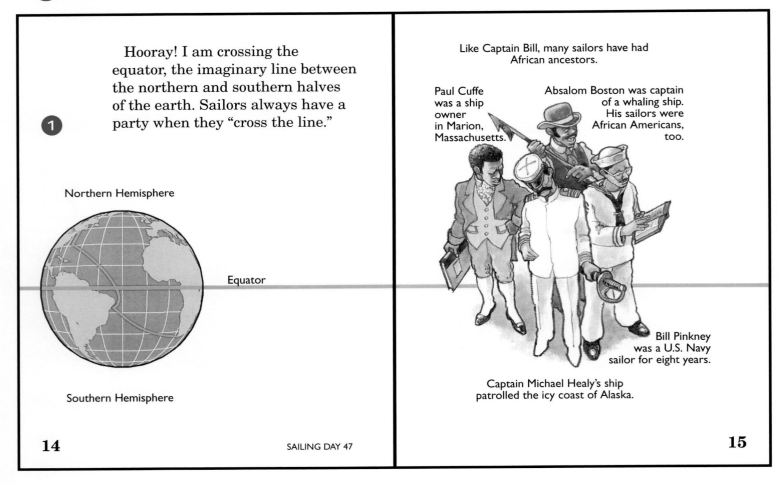

Hooray! I am crossing the equator, the imaginary line between the northern and southern halves of the earth. Sailors always have a party when they "cross the line."

1

Northern Hemisphere

Equator

Southern Hemisphere

14

SAILING DAY 47

Like Captain Bill, many sailors have had African ancestors.

Paul Cuffe was a ship owner in Marion, Massachusetts.

Absalom Boston was captain of a whaling ship. His sailors were African Americans, too.

Bill Pinkney was a U.S. Navy sailor for eight years.

Captain Michael Healy's ship patrolled the icy coast of Alaska.

15

1 If students wonder about the party that sailors have when they cross the line, share with them that this often includes practical joking.

Responding

Ask the children to comment on anything they found interesting on these pages.

✳ READING A STEP-BY-STEP PRACTICE STORY

"Hen in a Pen"
Story 18

Getting Ready to Read

Have the children put together Step-by-Step Practice Story 18. Call on a child to read the title of the selection. Make sure the children understand what a *pen* is in this context.

Recommendations

Call on a different child to read each page of the story aloud. If a child has difficulty with a word, have him or her refer to the Sound/Spelling Cards. If an outlaw word presents difficulty, tell children the word. Reread the story at least twice, calling on different children to read each time.

Responding

After reading, ask the children to tell in their own words what happened in the story and discuss any difficulties they had in reading it. To check that the children are paying attention to the words in the story, ask the following questions, having the children point to the words in the story that answer each question.

What was wrong with Henrietta's pen?

What did Ted keep saying about Henrietta's pen?

What did Ted feed Henrietta after he pulled her out of the bucket?

Have the children reread the story with a partner.

TEACHING TIP

Remind the children to read each book twice. When they finish today's book, they should get one from a previous lesson. Reading Assessment Sheets for Phonics Minibooks are available in *Assessment Masters, Grade 1.*

✳ READING ALOUD

You might want to share with the children some of the following books about undersea life and fantastic ocean adventures:

Come Away from the Water, Shirley by John Burningham

The Atlantic Ocean by Susan Heinrichs

John Tabor's Ride by Edward C. Day

The Magic School Bus: On the Ocean Floor by Joanna Cole

See **Learning Framework Card 5** for suggestions for reading aloud.

2 WRITING

✱ DICTATION AND SPELLING

Have the children turn to page 65 of their Reading/Writing Connection book and finish the bottom part of the page. Dictate the following words and sentence, using the suggestions for dictation that appear on **Learning Framework Card 4.**

Line 1:   let   left

Line 2:   list   lift

Sentence: The hen left the nest.

Help the children proofread their work.

Minilesson

Capitals and End Punctuation

Remind children that writers use capitals and end punctuation to make their writing easy for others to read. Take out *Captain Bill Pinkney's Journey* and the *Look Who's Reading!* Big Books. Have the children look for sentences that end with periods. Write examples of these on the board, noting the beginning capital and ending period.

Explain to the children that you use a special mark when you write a question. Make a question mark on the board. Turn to the story "What they Said" in *Look Who's Reading!* the first Big Book. Read several of the questions and note how the author begins with a capital but ends with a question mark.

Write the following sentences on the board or overhead projector. Read them or have the children read them and have children tell whether a period or question mark belongs at the end. Have them check for beginning capitals as well.

Can the man see the dog
the cat plays near Don
Is that hat big
where is the big rake

Next, write the student samples on the board or show them on an overhead projector. Read each sentence and check with the class to be sure that each sentence begins with a capital letter and ends with the appropriate punctuation. After this is done, have children work in pairs to proofread their own work.

Hold conferences with pairs of students focusing on proofreading.

If children need more time, encourage them to complete their pieces today during Workshop. If children would like to recopy their piece but already have their pictures in place, have them simply cut off the drawing or picture and attach it to a clean piece of paper. Remind children to put their names on their page and to use their best handwriting so others can read their work.

MONITORING DICTATION Collect children's dictation pages and scan them for accuracy in spelling and proofreading. Add notes to children's portfolios as appropriate.

TEACHING TIP

You may want to have children write their final copy on a piece of paper that has a suitcase on it. Draw a suitcase on a piece of paper, add writing lines, and leave space for a picture. Then duplicate it for all the children in the class.

3 GUIDED AND INDEPENDENT EXPLORATION

WORKSHOP

Remind the children that they may use this time to work on projects independently or in small groups. Make sure all the children know what their options are for this time and how to proceed with any projects they choose. Suggestions for teacher-guided, collaborative, and independent activities follow.

Work with the Teacher

- Have children read aloud Step-by-Step Practice Story 18.
- Revisit today's Blending lesson, emphasizing reading words as a whole rather than blending sound by sound.
- Have the children dictate words containing the /e/ sound for you to write on the chalkboard. Ask the children to help you spell the words.

Independent Work

- Activity Sheet 37 has the children use story context to complete a picture. Tell the children to read the sentences that tell about the picture, then draw in anything mentioned in the description that is missing from the picture.
- On the chalkboard, write the word *nest,* which appeared in today's Dictation lesson. Ask children to copy this word. Challenge them to make as many new words as they can by changing one letter at a time. They may use pencil and paper or letter cards for this activity.
- Children may want to continue working on their writing projects.

- Have the children prepare Letter Cards *e, f, i, l, s, t, y* for the Word-Building game in the next lesson.

Student Collaboration

- Encourage partners to reread Step-by-Step Practice Story 18, "Hen in a Pen." You might want to pair independent readers with those children who had difficulty during the initial reading of the story.
- Update the cards in the Fish for a Sound game and have the children play together in small groups.
- Have the children work in small groups to review the spelling of words with the /e/ sound. Each child can take a turn dictating a word for the group to spell. Once the group agrees on a spelling for a word, they should write it on their list. Tomorrow, each group can exchange lists with another group for proofreading.

Home/School Connection

Send home Step-by-Step Practice Story 17, "Meg's Sled," for the children to read to their families.

Name

At the Bus Stop

Amanda sits in the bus.
Max spills a bag of marbles.
Cliff has a ball in his hand
and a helmet on his head.

Captain Bill Pinkney's Journey

Activity Sheet 37

Activity Sheet 37

LESSON
38

• • • Lesson Overview

New Learning

- /y/ spelled *y*

Materials

- *Captain Bill Pinkney's Journey*, pages 16–19
- "The Stand," Step-by-Step Practice Story 19
- Sound/Spelling Card 25, Yaks
- Learning Framework Cards 2, 3, 5
- Reading/Writing Connection, pages 66–67
- Letter Cards *e, f, i, l, s, t, y*
- Activity Sheet 38

GETTING STARTED

Choose one or both of the following activities to focus the children's attention and to review some of the concepts they have been learning.

Short Vowel Spelling Review   Divide the class into two teams. On both ends of the chalkboard, write the following words: *fuss, bread, trick, brass, end, loss, band, head, mix, class, doll.* (If you have more than twenty-two students, you should include additional words with short vowel sound spellings.) Tell the children that you will say a sound and that one child from each team should go to the board, circle a word with that sound, and underline the letter or letters that spell that sound. For each sound that the children identify correctly, their team receives a point. At the end of the activity, point to each of the words one by one and have the children read them aloud together.

Sound Card Review Pronounce a sound and a word that contains the sound, for example, /e/ as in *bed.* Have children name the Sound/Spelling Card and the spelling of the sound. Use these examples

/a/ in *fat*	/e/ in *red*
/i/ in *sit*	/o/ in *hot*
/u/ in *fun*	/a/ in *cap*
/i/ in *tip*	/e/ in *step*

1 READING

PHONICS

25   Yaks

✱ **Introduce /y/ Spelled *y*** Turn Sound/Spelling Card 25, Yaks, and point out the line that follows the spelling *y* on the card. Explain that this means that the /y/ sound will only be found at the beginning of a word. Tell the children these animals are yaks and ask what the yaks seem to be doing. Tell the children that *yak* can also mean "to talk." Then read the Yak story that follows.

A discussion of the procedure for introducing a new sound can be found on **Learning Framework Card 2.**

Yolanda and Yoshiko are yaks.
They don't yell.
They don't yelp.
They don't yodel.
They don't yawn.
These young yaks just yak.
Yakety-yak, yakety-yak!
Can you hear the sound they make? /y/ /y/ /y/ /y/ /y/ /y/ /y/.

Yolanda and Yoshiko yak in the yard. /y/ /y/ /y/ /y/ /y/ /y/ /y/.
They yak on their yellow yacht. /y/ /y/ /y/ /y/ /y/ /y/ /y/.
They yak in the yam patch. /y/ /y/ /y/ /y/ /y/ /y/ /y/.
These yaks yak all year! /y/ /y/ /y/ /y/ /y/ /y/ /y/.

Do you think these yaks like to yak?
(Have the children answer) Yes!
(Ask the children to yak like Yolanda and Yoshiko.)

Have the children listen to some words and signal thumbs-up when they hear a word that begins with /y/. Use these words:

yellow	you	yarn
never	yodel	yawn
yak	young	yard

Ask the children to suggest other words that begin with /y/. Then have children tell how they can use the Yak card to help them remember this sound.

➤ Reading/Writing Connection, page 66, reinforces the sound /y/ spelled *y*. Have the children complete the top part of the page at this time.

✱ Blending Have the children blend the following words and sentences. For a complete discussion of the blending process, see **Learning Framework Card 3, Blending.**

Line 1:	**yell yet yarn yard**
Line 2:	**click stuck black speck clock**
Line 3:	**add dress address**
Line 4:	**problem rocket tremble**
Sentence 1:	**Greg wants to plant bulbs in the yard.**
Sentence 2:	**Lil wants the red yarn for art class.**
Sentence 3:	**Ben stepped in the black mud.**

Words In line 1, ask the children how many sounds are in *yell*. Remind them that although there are four letters, the spelling *ll* makes only one sound. Blend the word *yarn* as follows: /y/ /ar/ /n/, *yarn*. The spelling *ar* needs to be written as a unit. Emphasize that *ar* is one spelling. Repeat with the word *yard*.

The words in line 2 review the short vowel sounds. Have the children point to the Sound/Spelling Cards for each vowel as they sound and blend the words.

Ask the children what they notice about the words in line 3. They might comment on the final spelling of each word or on the fact that the first two words put together make the third.

Line 4 practices blending two-syllable words. Be sure to help the children blend them syllable by syllable.

Use clues such as the following to review the words:
• you use it to knit a sweater
• means the same as *to shake*
• tells where you live
• a color
• a small dot
• it tells time

Sentences Before writing the sentences, introduce the outlaw word *wants* in the usual manner. Then write the sentences. Have the children blend the words and read the sentences.

➤ Reading/Writing Connection, pages 66–67, provide additional practice with the sound /y/ spelled *y*. Have the children complete page 66 by reading and copying the words and sentence. Then for page 67, help the children match each sentence to its appropriate picture, then write the sentences in order on the spaces provided.

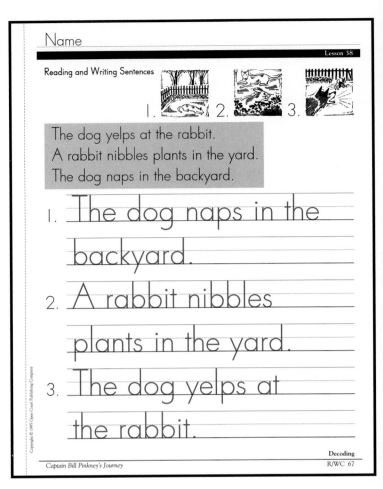

Name _____

Lesson 38

Sounds and Spellings _____

y—

_____

y _____

Y _____

Writing Words and Sentences _____

yam   yam   yes   yes

yell   yell   yet   yet

The cat has yards of yarn.

The cat has yards of yarn.

Consonant Sounds and Spellings

66 R/WC

Captain Bill Pinkney's Journey

Copyright © 1995 Open Court Publishing Company

Reading/Writing Connection, page 66

Name _____

Lesson 38

Reading and Writing Sentences

1.   2.   3.

The dog yelps at the rabbit.
A rabbit nibbles plants in the yard.
The dog naps in the backyard.

1. The dog naps in the backyard.

2. A rabbit nibbles plants in the yard.

3. The dog yelps at the rabbit.

Decoding

Captain Bill Pinkney's Journey

R/WC 67

Copyright © 1995 Open Court Publishing Company

Reading/Writing Connection, page 67

✱ READING THE BIG BOOK

Captain Bill Pinkney's Journey
pages 16–19

Activating Prior Knowledge

Call on volunteers to sum up what has happened so far in the story.

Recommendations for Reading

- Display pages 16–17 and call attention to the port of Boston on the map. Have a child point to it and then follow the course of Captain Bill's journey to Salvador, Brazil. Check the sailing calendar on page 3 to find out how long this portion of the journey took.
- Turn to pages 8–9 and point out this leg of the journey on the map.
- Read page 16, pointing out South America on the globe or world map. Invite the children to think of questions the children might have asked Captain Bill and what he might have said to them.
- Read the captions on page 17 and encourage comments and sharing of information about the rain forest.
- Display pages 18–19. Direct the children's attention to the pictures at the top of the pages. Read the paragraph on page 19. Invite the children to suggest questions they might have asked Captain Bill.
- Discuss and compare the information on the lower half of the pages.

STRATEGIC
R·E·A·D·I·N·G
PROMPTS
·
These prompts may be used
as guides when working with
reading strategies.

South America! In Salvador, Brazil, I meet children in a marching band, beating exciting rhythms on their drums.

BERMUDA
Boston
RAIN FOREST
Salvador
BRAZIL
PACIFIC OCEAN
ATLANTIC OCEAN
0°
10°S
20°S
30°S
40°S
50°S
16
60°W 50°W 40°W 30°W 20°W
SAILING DAY 61

Macaws live high in the trees of the rain forest.

Caimans live in swamps and rivers.

The world's biggest rain forest is in South America.

17

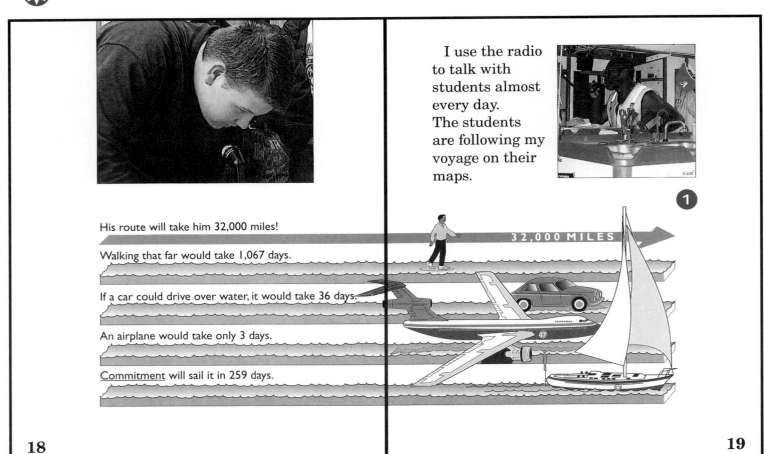

I use the radio to talk with students almost every day. The students are following my voyage on their maps.

His route will take him 32,000 miles!

Walking that far would take 1,067 days.

If a car could drive over water, it would take 36 days.

An airplane would take only 3 days.

<u>Commitment</u> will sail it in 259 days.

32,000 MILES

18

19

1 Model summing up by saying, *OK, what have we learned so far? Captain Bill Pinkney sailed his boat around the world and used many skills in order to accomplish his goal. He visited many interesting places.*

Responding

Ask for discussion of what the children found most interesting. Check the questions and wonderings list to see whether any questions have been answered and to add new ones.

Ask volunteers to **sum up** this part of the story.

✱ READING A STEP-BY-STEP PRACTICE STORY

"The Stand"
Story 19

Getting Ready to Read

Have the children put together Step-by-Step Practice Story 19. Call on a child to read the title of the selection. Ask children if any of them have ever seen the "Peanuts" cartoons in which Lucy has a booth where she helps people solve their problems in exchange for money. Or ask them if any of them have ever had a lemonade stand.

Recommendations

Call on a different child to read each page of the story aloud. If a child has difficulty with a word, follow the procedures shown on **Learning Framework Card 5.** Reread the story at least twice, calling on different children to read each time.

Responding

After reading, ask the children to tell in their own words what happened in the story and to discuss any difficulties they had in reading it. To check that the children are paying attention to the words in the story, ask the following questions, and have the children point to the words in the story that answer each question.

What does Tess say that T. Rex should have for a snack?
What does Tess say should fix Greg's stiff neck?
What is Deb's problem?

Have the children reread the story with a partner.

✱ READING ALOUD

Some books about South American culture, geography, and wildlife that you might want to share with the children are

A Family in Brazil by Olivia Bennett
Arroz con Leche: Popular Songs and Rhymes from Latin America
    by Lulu Delacre
South America by D.V. George
Explore the World of Exotic Rain Forests by Anita Ganeri

See **Learning Framework Card 5** for suggestions for reading aloud.

TEACHING TIP

Set aside ten minutes for partner reading every day. During this time, you should read with individuals, recording their progress. Reading Assessment Sheets for Phonics Minibooks are available in *Assessment Masters, Grade 1.*

2 WRITING

Word-Building Game   Have the children use Letter Cards *e, f, i, l, s, t, y* for this Word-Building game, or they may use paper and pencil. The list of words for the game follows:

yes

yet

let

left

lift

sift

Challenge the children to suggest other words than can be made with the letters.

Today the children will organize their class book. Talk about how the book should be organized. This may be easily done by listing the different places on the board and talking about places that seem to belong together and the title they would like to call this section. Suggestions might include Places I've Been, Trips near Home, Faraway Trips, Trips to Visit My Family, Summer Trips, Places I Want to Go. Have children read their pieces and talk about where they might fit in the book. Be sure children have put their name and a title on their pages, then put all the pages together. Talk about the need for numbering pages. If children want to create dividers for different sections, do so. At the end have the children talk about a title and what to put on the front page. This need not be elaborate. You may want to have a simple title, like Special Trips, and then have each child write his or her initials around the title. If children created individual books, have them make covers and staple the left sides to make a book.

If you do not make a class book, you may want to create a travel area in the classroom and post all the children's pages in one area.

3 GUIDED AND INDEPENDENT EXPLORATION

WORKSHOP

Remind the children that they may use this time to work on projects independently or in small groups. Make sure all the children know what their options are for this time and how to proceed with any projects they choose. Suggestions for teacher-guided, collaborative, and independent activities follow.

Work with the Teacher

- Play the Word-Building game with children who need to work on their spelling. Repeat today's word list or select a previous list, based on the children's needs.
- Reteach Sound/Spelling Card 25, Yaks, and Step-by-Step Practice Story 19, "The Stand," to those children who need extra help with new sounds and spellings.
- Invite some of the advanced readers to read aloud to you from the books of their choice. You might suggest that they select books that tell about ships or journeys. Invite some of the other children to listen in.

Independent Work

- Activity Sheet 38 reviews the /e/ sound and spellings. Tell the children to read each word, then choose a rhyming word from the box and write it on the line.
- Challenge the children to use at least three words from today's Blending exercise in two or three sentences. Suggest that they write something about a rocket trip. If time permits, they may illustrate their work.

Student Collaboration

- Allow pairs of children to read the books of their choice. Tell them to follow the usual procedure for reading with a partner.
- Have the children work in small groups to create a poster titled, *I Pack My Bag.* The poster should display the name and a picture of each item the children decide to take. They may draw the pictures themselves or cut them from magazines. They should write the name of each item next to or beneath its picture.
- Have children work in pairs to play the Scrambled Sentence game. Once they have unscrambled a sentence, the children should copy and illustrate it.

Home/School Connection

Send home Step-by-Step Practice Story 18, "Hen in a Pen," for students to read aloud to their families.

Name

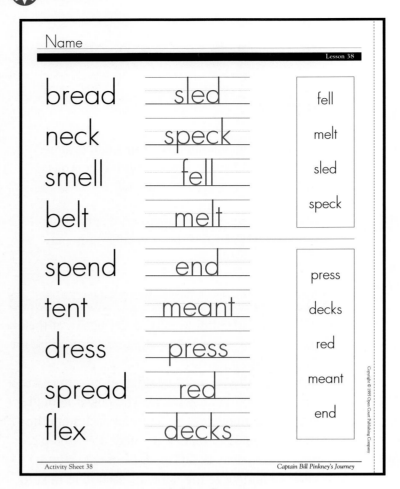

bread	sled
neck	speck
smell	fell
belt	melt

fell

melt

sled

speck

spend	end
tent	meant
dress	press
spread	red
flex	decks

press

decks

red

meant

end

Captain Bill Pinkney's Journey

Activity Sheet 38

LESSON

39

Lesson Overview

New Learning

- /w/ spelled *w_*
- /hw/ spelled *wh_*

Materials

- *Captain Bill Pinkney's Journey*, pages 20–23
- "Wendell Gets a Pet," Phonics Minibook 7, *Wendell's Pets*
- Sound/Spelling Card 23, Washer
- Sound/Spelling Card 28, Whales
- Learning Framework Cards 2, 3, 4, 5
- Reading/Writing Connection, pages 68–69
- Outlaw Word Flash Cards
- Activity Sheet 39

GETTING STARTED

Choose one or both of the following activities to focus the children's attention and to review some of the concepts they have been learning.

Consonant Riddle Game   Tell the children that you are thinking of a word that rhymes with *hat* and starts with *b*. Encourage the children to guess your word. Then, repeat with other words, such as a word that:

- rhymes with *sad* and starts with *d (dad)*
- rhymes with *land* and starts with *s (sand)*
- rhymes with *sit* and starts with *p (pit)*
- rhymes with *bat* and starts with *c (cat)*
- rhymes with *log* and starts with *d (dog)*
- rhymes with *dug* and starts with *b (bug)*

Keep the Card Game   Place in a paper bag Outlaw Word Flash Cards and/or index cards with words containing spellings you want to review. Divide the class into teams of five children each. Have one player on each team draw a card out of the paper bag and look at it. (The player's team members will also see the card.) If the player says the word correctly, he or she may put the card on the table in front of his or her team. If the player misses, the card will go back in the bag. The teams take turns. The team with the most cards at the end of five minutes wins the game.

1 READING

PHONICS

* **Introduce /w/ Spelled *w_*** Turn Sound/Spelling Card 23, Washer, and tell the children this is the Washer card. Point out the spelling and discuss why a blank line appears after the letter. (It indicates that the /w/ sound is always followed by another letter, a vowel.) Then read the Washer story.

   A discussion of the procedure for introducing a new sound can be found on **Learning Framework Card 2.**

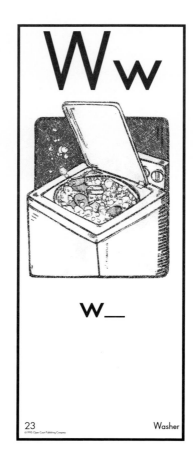

23   Washer

Willie the Washer washed white clothes all week.
When he washed, he went: /w/ /w/ /w/ /w/ /w/ /w/ /w/.

All winter, Willie worked well. /w/ /w/ /w/ /w/ /w/ /w/ /w/.
But last Wednesday, Willie was weak. **(softly)** /w/ /w/ /w// w// w/ /w/ /w/.
This week he got worse. **(slower and slower)** /w/. . ./w/. . ./w/. . .
Poor Willie was worn out. **(slowest)** /w/

Then a worker came and fixed Willie's wires.
Willie felt wonderful. **(more loudly)** /w/ /w/ /w/ /w/ /w/ /w/ /w/!
Now Willie can wash and wash wildly!
(quickly) /w/ /w/ /w/ /w/ /w/ /w/ /w/!

How does Willie the Washer sound now when he washes?
(Have the children join in) /w/ /w/ /w/ /w/ /w/ / w/ /w/.
Can you wash just like Willie?
(Have the children respond) /w/ /w/ /w/ /w/ /w/ /w/ /w/.

   Review the card by having children tell how they can use it to remember the /w/ sound.

* **Introduce /hw/ Spelled *wh_*** Turn Sound/Spelling Card 28, Whales. Tell the children that this is the Whale card and explain that this sound is very much like the /w/ sound. Explain that you are introducing the two cards at the same time because the two sounds are so similar. Then read the Whale story.

Look! It's Whitney the Whispering Whale!
Listen to her whisper: /hw/ /hw/ /hw/ /hw/ /hw/.

When Whitney meets with other whales,
She entertains them, telling tales.
She whispers: /hw/ /hw/ /hw/ /hw/ /hw/.
She's Whitney the Whispering Whale.

What ocean wonders does Whitney relate?
Does she whisper of whirlpools or whales that are great?
We're only people, so we'll never guess.
She's Whitney the Whispering Whale! /hw/ /hw/ /hw/.

Whatever Whitney whispers must be fun.
The other whales whistle when she's done.
They whoop and whack the white-capped waves.
They love Whitney the Whispering Whale! /hw/ /hw/ /hw/.

If you were Whitney, what sounds would you whisper
To your whale friends as they gathered to listen?
(Have the children whisper) /hw/ /hw/ /hw/ /hw/ /hw/.

28
Whales

Review the card by having the children tell about the picture, the sound, and the spelling. Ask what the blank means with the *wh_* spelling. Point out that this spelling is found at the beginning of words or syllables and is followed by a vowel sound.

The children should be able to suggest words that begin with /w/ or /hw/. You may want to write the words on the board as the children suggest them to call attention to the spellings. If the children have difficulty thinking of words that begin with these sounds, have them listen for the sounds at the beginning of the following words:

wagon	window	water
week	well	wish
Wednesday	work	winter

whistle	wheel	wheat
whisper	what	which
whale	whisker	white

TEACHING TIP
Do not try to make the children differentiate between these sounds if they do not do so naturally.

✱ Blending   Have the children blend the following words and sentences. For a complete discussion of the blending process, see **Learning Framework Card 3, Blending.**

Line 1:	wig wag win wet
Line 2:	swift swim swept
Line 3:	went west wind will
Line 4:	when whip
Sentence 1:	Where is Mack's black wig?
Sentence 2:	When will Dad fix the wall ?
Sentence 3:	Will grabbed a log as he swam in the pond.

Words   Have the children blend and read the words. Point out the *sw* cluster in the words in line 2.

Words that may be unfamiliar include *wig, wag, swift,* and *swept.* Have the children use these words in sentences.

Sentences   Introduce the outlaw word *where* before writing the sentences. Then write the sentences on the board. Point out that the question words *where* and *when* both begin with /hw/.

In sentence 2, you may need to review the special spelling pattern *all* before children read the word *wall.* Invite the children to suggest other words that have this spelling pattern. Ask why sentences 1 and 2 end with question marks. As the children read these sentences, notice whether their intonation reflects the fact that they are asking a question.

➤ Reading/Writing Connection, pages 68–69, reinforces the sound /w/ spelled *w,* and the /hw/ sound spelled *wh.* Have the children complete page 68 and the top of page 69.

Reading/Writing Connection, page 68

Name _____

Lesson 39

Sounds and Spellings

_____

W_

_____

W _____

W _____

Writing Words and Sentences

wet _wet_   wag _wag_

wiggle _wiggle_   well _well_

Will you get a wagon?

Will you get a wagon?

Consonant Sounds and Spellings

68 R/WC   *Captain Bill Pinkney's Journey*

Reading/Writing Connection, page 69

Name _____

Lesson 39

Sounds and Spellings

_____

wh_

_____

when _when_   whiz _whiz_

Dictation and Spelling

_____   _____

_____   _____

_____   _____

_____   _____

_____   _____

_____   _____

Decoding/Spelling

Captain Bill Pinkney's Journey   R/WC 69

✱ READING THE BIG BOOK

Captain Bill Pinkney's Journey
pages 20–23

Recommendations for Reading

- Display pages 20–21 and trace the journey from Brazil to Cape Town. Ask the children what they know about Africa, the continent to which Captain Bill is headed. Turn back to pages 8–9 and point out this leg of the trip on the world map.
- Read pages 20–21 with the captions and encourage children to comment and question freely.
- Have the children study pages 22–23 and tell what is happening. Ask them how they think Captain Bill is feeling as the storm gathers and whether they think he is afraid.
- Read pages 22–23 and allow for any comments or questions.

STRATEGIC R·E·A·D·I·N·G PROMPTS

These prompts may be used as guides when working with reading strategies.

1 Model responding to unfamiliar words by saying, Ancestor *is a hard word. The sentence gives you a clue that it means someone who lived in the past, in this case, a person from whom one is descended—parents, grandparents, all the way back into ancient times.*

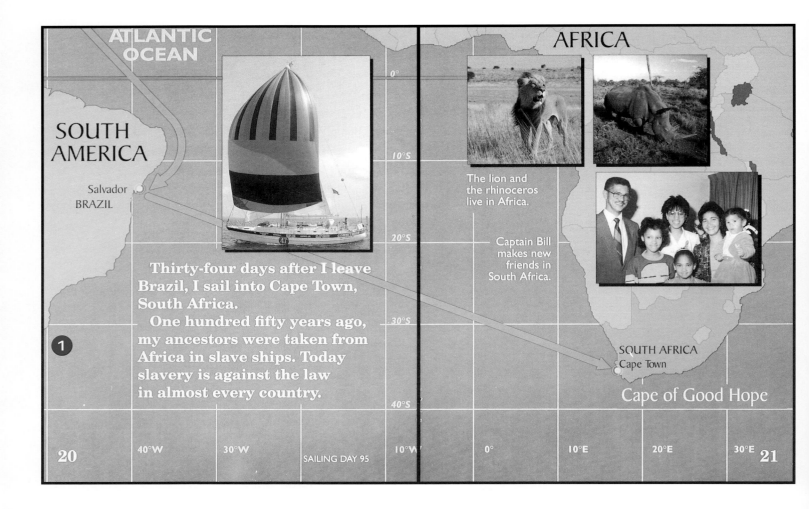

ATLANTIC OCEAN

SOUTH AMERICA

Salvador BRAZIL

Thirty-four days after I leave Brazil, I sail into Cape Town, South Africa.
One hundred fifty years ago, my ancestors were taken from Africa in slave ships. Today slavery is against the law in almost every country.

1

20

40°W 30°W SAILING DAY 95 10°W

AFRICA

The lion and the rhinoceros live in Africa.

Captain Bill makes new friends in South Africa.

SOUTH AFRICA Cape Town

Cape of Good Hope

0° 10°E 20°E 30°E 21

0° 10°S 20°S 30°S 40°S

Storm! Only eight days away from Cape Town, <u>Commitment</u> is rolling and pitching in strong winds and waves.

This is no fun! The waves are as tall as apartment buildings. I hold on tight and hope the storm ends soon.

22   SAILING DAY 103   23

Responding

Discuss what the children found interesting. Ask them what new things they learned. Call on volunteers to **sum up** what happened in this part of the story.

"Wendell Gets a Pet"
Phonics Minibook 7, Story 1

Getting Ready to Read

Reading the Title   Read the book title aloud and remind the children that the book contains two separate stories, the titles of which are also listed on the cover. Have the children turn to the first page of the first story and invite them to read the story's title, "Wendell Gets a Pet," silently. Then call on two or three children to read the title aloud.

Browsing the Story   Invite the children to page through the first story, commenting on the illustrations and telling what they think the story will be about.

Recommendations

• Call on a different child to read each page of the story aloud. If a child has difficulty with a word, help her or him blend the word. Reread the story at least twice, calling on different children to read each time.

OPEN COURT and ✱ are registered trademarks of Open Court Publishing Company.

Copyright © 1995 Open Court Publishing Company

All rights reserved for all countries. No part of this book may be reproduced by any means without the written permission of the publisher.

Printed in the United States of America

ISBN 0-8126-1277-9   10 9 8 7 6 5 4 3 2 1

2

Wendell Gets a Pet

Wendell wanted a pet.
He got his net and went to the pond.

3

Frogs swam in the pond.
One frog was on a pad.

4

Wendell grabbed his net.
He stepped on a log
to get next to the frog.

5

He dipped his net
into the pond.
The frogs swam away.

6

The log was wet,
and Wendell slipped.

7

Wendell fell off the log.
He landed in the pond.
His net fell to the bottom.

8

Wendell was wet,
but he got lots of pets!

9

Responding

Ask the children to tell in their own words what happened in the story and to discuss any difficulties they had in reading it. To check that the children are paying attention to the words in the story, ask the following questions, having the children point to the words in the story that answer each question.

Why did Wendell step on a log?
Why did Wendell slip on the log?
What happened to Wendell's net?
What did Wendell get?

Have the children reread the story with a partner.

✳ READING ALOUD

You might want to share one or more of the following books about children living in or near Cape Town, South Africa:
Somewhere in Africa by Ingrid Mennen and Niki Daly
Armien's Fishing Trip by Catherine Stock
Charlie's House by Reviva Schermbrucker

ASSESSMENT Listen to several individuals each read a story from one of the Phonics Minibooks read so far. Using a Reading Assessment Sheet, record your observations and add them to each student's folder.

After reading, remember to ask the children what new things they learned about this part of the world from these or other books. See **Learning Framework Card 5** for suggestions for reading aloud.

2 WRITING

✱ DICTATION AND SPELLING

Have the children turn to page 69 of the Reading/Writing Connection book so that they can finish the bottom of the page. Dictate the following words and sentence, using the suggestions for dictation that appear on **Learning Framework Card 4.**

Line 1:	yes yet
Line 2:	set sent
Sentence:	The pups yelp for help.

Help the children proofread each line.

EXPLORING THE WRITER'S CRAFT

During the next few lessons, the children will work on planning a trip. This planning can take many forms, depending upon the children in your class. Some children may be writing sentences while other children may just write lists. Encourage all children, however, to do some writing. This is their plan book, and they can approach it anyway they choose. Some children may wish to work in small groups.

Tell the children that before Captain Bill Pinkney set sail on his journey around the world, he had to do lots of planning. Have the children discuss some of the things that Captain Bill needed to think about before he set sail, for example, clothes, food, equipment, maps, and the like. You may want to revisit the Big Book and have children find some examples. Ask the children to think of the places they wrote about for the class book. What kind of plans did they make for their trips? If children wrote about imaginary trips, encourage them to think of what they might need.

Have the children generate a list of places to go to. These could be places they have never been before or the places they have written about previously. Encourage children to think not only of faraway or imaginary places but also interesting places close to home. Write the children's suggestions on a piece of paper with their names next to it. Tell them that tomorrow they will begin planning their trip to that place.

During Workshop children may want to look in books and magazines about possible places to visit. They can note these in their journals.

TEACHING TIP

If there is a field trip coming up, you may want to use these lessons to plan that trip with the whole class.

TEACHING TIP

Since children will use several pages for their Planning a Trip project, you may want to make booklets for them to work in.

3 GUIDED AND INDEPENDENT EXPLORATION

W O R K S H O P

Remind the children that they may use this time to work on projects on their own or in small groups. Be sure that each child knows what projects he or she may choose and how to complete any independent work. Suggestions for teacher-guided, collaborative, and independent activities follow.

Work with the Teacher

- Get out the cards from the Keep the Card game and add to them some new cards with words that contain the spellings *w* and *wh*. Use these cards to hold a Reading Relay between two small teams of children. Have the children on each team form a line. Start the game by inviting the first child on one team to select a card and read the word on that card. If the player reads the word correctly, he or she may take the card and go to the end of the line. If not, the first child on the other team has the opportunity to read the word. Continue the game, alternating turns between teams, until each child on one team has correctly read a word. That team then wins the relay. The Reading Relay game can be found on the **Games and Songs Teacher Tool Card 9.**
- To assess their progress, listen to individuals or pairs of children reread Phonics Minibook 7.
- Preteach Sound/Spelling Card 29, Bird, to those children who may need additional help with *er, ir,* and *ur.*

Independent Work

- Activity Sheet 39 reviews some of the outlaw words that the children have learned thus far. Tell the children that they can complete the sentences by writing the correct words in the blanks. They can then draw a picture of their favorite sentence in the box provided.
- Invite the children to answer, in writing, sentences 2 and 3 from the Blending exercise. Tell them that their answers should be complete sentences; such as, Mack's black wig is _____, Dad will fix the wall when _____. When they have finished writing, the children may illustrate their work.
- Encourage the children to revisit favorite selections in their small copies of *Look Who's Reading!* and *Animals*. Encourage them to make note of how many words they can now read on their own.

Student Collaboration

- Children may wish to reread Phonics Minibook 7 with a partner. Remind them to follow the usual procedure for partner reading.
- Reinforce the /w/ sound by inviting the children to look through magazines and cut out pictures of things that begin with the /w/ sound. Have them glue the pictures to a sheet of poster board or chart paper in such a manner that the pictures form a *W*. Beneath the *W,* they should try to print the names of all the items on the poster, using the Sound/Spelling Cards for help.
- Some of the children might enjoy forming read-aloud groups. One or two of the more independent readers can select a book to read to a small group of listeners. Provide a selection of interesting books that the children will be able to read fluently.

Home/School Connection

Have the children take home Step-by-Step Practice Story 19 to share with their families.

Name

Lesson 39

| away | does | out | should | four | where |

1. A ram has __four__ legs.

2. The cat ran __away__ when Meg let him __out__.

3. You __should__ sit and rest.

4. __Where__ is my handbag?

5. This dog __does__ lots of tricks.

(Student art appears here.)

Captain Bill Pinkney's Journey

Activity Sheet 39

Activity Sheet 39

LESSON

40

Lesson Overview

New Learning

- /er/ spelled *er, ir, ur*

Materials

- *Captain Bill Pinkney's Journey*, pages 24–27
- "Wendell's Pets," Phonics Minibook 7, *Wendell's Pets*
- Sound/Spelling Card 29, Bird
- Learning Framework Cards 2, 3, 5
- Reading/Writing Connection, pages 70–71
- Activity Sheet 40

Prepare Ahead

- /er/ word list (see page 110)
- Fish for a Sound Cards (see page 110)

GETTING STARTED

Choose one or both of the following activities to focus the children's attention and to review some of the concepts they have been learning.

What I Saw Game   Tell the children that today they can pretend to go on a journey and see many things that start with /w/. Ask the children to suggest an item beginning with /w/, such as *wagon, waterfalls, waffles*. Model how they should respond: "On my journey, I saw a . . . . It begins with /w/." Tell the children to listen carefully to avoid repeating each other's words.

Sound Card Review   Name a Sound/Spelling Card and call on the children to say the sound that card represents. Then call on a child to give a word that contains the sound and identify where the sound is heard in the word. Continue reviewing other cards in this fashion.

1 READING

✳ **Introduce /er/ Spelled *er, ir, ur*** Turn Sound/Spelling Card 29, Bird, and tell the children that this is the Bird card. Explain that this card represents the /er/ sound. Then direct their attention to the spellings on the card and ask how this sound can be spelled. Write *er, ir,* and *ur* on the chalkboard. Then read the Bird story.

A discussion of the procedure for introducing a new sound can be found on **Learning Framework Card 2.**

> Bertie the Bird is the oddest bird
> That anyone has ever heard.
> He doesn't caw like a crow or a gull,
> Or tweet like a robin or a wren.
> Instead, he makes a chirping sound—
> Over and over again! /er/ /er/ /er/, /er/ /er/ /er/
>
> Bertie can't fly, since his wings are too short.
> He arranges his feathers in curls.
> He admits, "I've short wings
> And I really don't sing,
> But I still am an interesting bird!"
> /er/ /er/ /er/, /er/ /er/ /er/!
>
> Can you chirp like Bertie the Bird?
> (**Have children say**) /er/ /er/ /er/, /er/ /er/ /er/!

Have the children listen to some words and signal thumbs-up when they hear a word with the /er/ sound. Use the words that follow:

bird	girl	beach
curl	dirt	stir
her	were	turn

✳ **Blending** Have the children blend the following words. For a complete discussion of the Blending process, see **Learning Framework Card 3, Blending.**

Line 1:	her sir fir fur
Line 2:	hurt hurl herd
Line 3:	bird stir curl fern
Line 4:	sister farmer winter summer
Sentence 1:	We helped Uncle Bert stir <u>the</u> batter.
Sentence 2:	The farmer picked <u>the</u> turnips.
Sentence 3:	<u>The</u> tart smells wonderful.

Words When you write the words, be sure to write the *er, ir, ur* spellings as a unit for the children to sound.

After the children blend *fir* and *fur* in line 1, point out that these words are *homophones,* that is, they sound the same, but have different meanings and spellings. Ask the children what meanings they know for the words *fir* and *fur.* If they are unable to give meanings, tell them that *fir* is a kind of tree, while *fur* is the name for an animal's coat.

In line 2, have the word *herd* used in a sentence so that the children understand the meaning. ("A herd of cattle," should bring instant recognition of the word.) If necessary, explain that *heard,* the past tense of *hear,* is spelled differently.

In line 4, blend the words syllable by syllable.

Ask the children if there are any unfamiliar words and have children who think they know what these words mean use them in sentences. Review the words by asking the children to find and erase:
- the name of an animal
- two words that rhyme
- a plant
- someone in a family
- a group of cows

TEACHING TIP

If the children enjoy working with homophones, you might read aloud *Eight Ate* by Marvin Terban, or *What's Mite Might?* by Giulio Maestro.

Reading/Writing Connection, page 70

Reading/Writing Connection, page 71

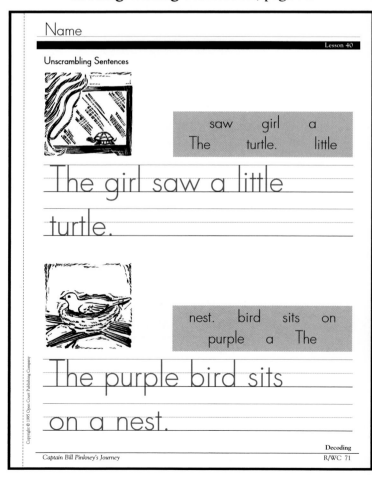

Sentences Introduce the outlaw word *we* by writing it on the board, pronouncing it, and having children use it in oral sentences before you write the sentences on the board. Then write the sentences and have the children blend them.

In sentences 1 and 2, point out the *-ed* endings and ask the children what this ending tells them. In sentence 3, the children may need help blending *wonderful.* Blend the first syllable with the /o/ sound. When the children recognize the word, they will adjust their pronunciation and say the word naturally.

❥ Reading/Writing Connection, pages 70–71, provide practice with the sound /er/ spelled *er, ir,* and *ur.* Have the children read and copy the words and sentences on page 70. Then, on page 71, help the children unscramble the groups of words, and write sentences that describe each picture on the lines provided.

✴ READING THE BIG BOOK

Captain Bill Pinkney's Journey
pages 24–27

Recommendations for Reading

- Display pages 24–25 of Big Book 3 and note the sailing day, the chart designations, and Tasmania (an island that is part of Australia), where Captain Bill stayed for a long time. Refer to the calendar on page 3 and note the date of his arrival in Hobart, Tasmania, Australia, and the reason for his long stay.
- Read the story segment and the captions.
- Encourage comments and questions on interesting things Captain Bill saw during his time there.
- Display pages 26–27 and invite comments and questions. The children should now be in the routine of noting the number of sailing days in the lower right corner of the page.
- Read the paragraph on page 26 and help the children relate to the passage of time—63 days. You might show the dates on the calendar on page 3, December 24, 1991, through February 25, 1992, and point them out again as you turn the pages of an actual wall calendar. Ask the children to recall holidays that fall on and between these dates, and ask them to talk about how the weather in their area changes during those dates.
- Read the captions and story segment on pages 26–27. Invite comments on how Captain Bill might have spent his time and how he may have felt during those days and nights with only sea animals and birds for company.

The storm is over! I sail on to Tasmania, a part of Australia.

The Tasmanian devil is small but fierce.

INDIAN OCEAN

AUSTRALIA

Tasmania Hobart

NEW ZEALAND

24 SAILING DAY 51

The kangaroo bounces on its strong hind legs.

The koala lives in eucalyptus trees and almost never touches the ground.

The kookaburra's voice sounds like silly laughing.

The platypus has a duck bill and a beaver tail. It lays eggs like a bird.

PACIFIC OCEAN

25

I leave Australia for the longest part of my trip—fifty-two days without seeing land!

A bird rests on Commitment.

A hawksbill turtle swims by.

26 SAILING DAY 185

I check my charts and listen to weather reports. Animals that live far from land are my only company.

White sharks live under the waves.

27

Responding

Invite volunteers to tell what they found most interesting or exciting about this part of the journey. Encourage children to comment on anything they know about the animals pictured on these pages.

Call on volunteers to **sum up** what happened during this part of Captain Bill's journey.

✱ READING A PHONICS MINIBOOK

"Wendell's Pets"
Phonics Minibook 7, Story 2

Getting Ready to Read

Reading the Title   Read the book's title aloud and remind the children that the book contains two separate stories. Have the children turn to page 1 and read the titles of the two stories. The children may notice that the book title and the title of the second story are the same. You might wish to ask for comments on the titles by having the children recall what happened in the first story and then asking them to tell what they think the second story might be about.

Browsing the Selection   Invite the children to page through the second story, commenting on any words or illustrations they find interesting.

Recommendations

Call on a different child to read each page of the story aloud. If children have difficulty with words, help them blend the words. Reread the story at least twice, calling on different children to read each time.

Wendell's Pets

Wendell had lots of pets.
He had a cat and a duck.

12

He had a rabbit and a lizard.
He had frogs and a tub of bugs.

13

When the pets went to class,
the class was glad.
But Mr. Allen was not.

14

"Where will you put all the pets, Wendell?"
said Mr. Allen.

15

"Here!" said Wendell.
"Next to me!"

16

Responding

After reading, ask the children to tell in their own words what happened in the story and discuss any difficulties they had in reading it. To check that the children are paying attention to the words in the story, ask the following questions, having the children point to the words in the story that answer each question.

What kinds of pets did Wendell have?

Where did the pets go with Wendell?

Who was not glad to see the pets?

Where did Wendell put his pets?

Have the children reread the story with a partner.

ASSESSMENT Listen to several individuals each read a story from one of the Phonics Minibooks read so far. Using a Reading Assessment Sheet, record your observations and add them to each student's folder.

✳ READING ALOUD

Many books, both nonfiction and fiction, have been written about or set in Australia. You may want to share one or more of the following with the children:

Koalas and Kangaroos: Strange Animals of Australia by Toni Eugene

Take a Trip to Australia by David Truby

Wombat Stew by Marcia K. Vaughan

Bossyboots by David Cox

Ask the children what new things they learned about Australia after reading these or other books. See **Learning Framework Card 5** for suggestions for reading aloud.

2 WRITING

✳ DICTATION AND SPELLING

Word-Building Game The children will need to use paper and pencil for today's Word-Building game. Write the letters *er* on the board and tell the children that they will use this spelling in the first two words that they will make. Tell them to write *her* on their papers. Then have them add a letter to make *herd*. Write *ir* on the board and tell the children to use this spelling to write the word *bird*. Have them change *bird* to make the new word *stir*. Then write *ur* on the board and have the children use this spelling to make *turn,* then *burn*. The children's word list should be

her

herd

bird

stir

turn

burn

INDEPENDENT AND COLLABORATIVE WRITING

Review the places that the children would like to visit. Invite volunteers to read or recall some of the suggestions. If you wrote the names of the children next to their destinations, have them find their names and help them read where they wanted to go. If any children want to change their minds, add their new destinations to the chart. In order to help children get started, tell them about somewhere you would like to go and add your destination to the board. Talk about how you will plan this trip, then list those things under your destination. For example, perhaps you want to visit a friend that lives in another city. In order to get there, you will drive. Since this is a new place, you will need a map. You'll be staying overnight so you'll need clothes, and so on. Unlike Captain Bill, you will not need food since you can easily stop at restaurants.

Then have the children work alone or with partners to plan their trip. They need to think about the place they are going and what they will need. Have them write their destination on the paper and make a list of things they will need for the trip. They may want to start this page with "What I will need to go to _____." Tell them not to worry about spelling. If they are unsure of how to spell something, they can use the Sound/Spelling Cards or ask their partner or a friend. They can also draw pictures.

Circulate among the children as they work. Help those having problems deciding what they will need. If children are having problems, ask questions that will help them think through their plan. For example, How long will you be gone? What is the weather like there? While pictures are an option, encourage children to do some writing. Tell them not to worry about spelling. If there are children who do not want to work on this, encourage them to write in their journals.

Have several children share their plans during Seminar. Choose children who are going different places. Remind children before class ends to put their names on their papers (or booklets if you are using them) and to put them in their writing folders. Tomorrow they will continue with their trip planning.

TEACHING TIP

Remind the children to date their work and to keep the pieces in their folders.

3 GUIDED AND INDEPENDENT EXPLORATION

WORKSHOP

Remind the children that they may use this time to work on projects on their own or with small groups. Be sure that each child knows what projects he or she may choose and how to complete any independent work. Go over worksheets, games, and projects before sending children off to work independently. You may want to work with small groups to reinforce the /e/ sound spelled *e*.

Work with the Teacher

- Repeat today's Blending exercise with a small group of children. Have them take out their copies of Step-by-Step Practice Story 20, "What Is It?" and locate as many words as they can from the exercise. Each time a child locates a word, invite him or her to read aloud first the word and then the entire sentence in which the word is located.
- Listen to individuals or pairs of children reread Step-by-Step Practice Story 20.
- Play an oral spelling game with a small group of children. Ask them to dictate several words containing the /er/ sound. Write each word on the chalkboard, asking the children to help you spell it. Make sure your word list includes words with all three of the /er/ spellings *(er, ir, ur)*. For word ideas, the children may refer to today's Blending exercise and Step-by-Step Practice Story 20, "What Is It?"

Independent Work

- Activity Sheet 40 provides practice with the /er/ sound and spellings. Tell the children to read each sentence and write *yes* or *no* in the blanks depending on whether the sentence could be true or not. Finally, they should illustrate one of the silly sentences in the box at the bottom of the page.

- Invite the children to write and illustrate sentences using the homophones *fir* and *fur* from today's Blending exercise.
- Encourage the children to read or browse books on their own. Provide a selection of tradebooks for them to choose from. You may want to make available some of the read-aloud selections from recent lessons.

> **TEACHING TIP**
> Encourage the children to read to each other. You, too, should choose children to read with. As you read with each child, note his or her progress.

Student Collaboration

- Encourage the children to read Step-by-Step Practice Story 20, "What Is It?" with a partner.
- Suggest that children work in small groups to make up hints for words that contain the /w/ sound with either of its spellings. When each group has made up at least two hints, they may pose them to members of another group. For example, "What begins with *w* and names a season?" *(winter)*
- Update the cards for the Fish for a Sound game and invite small groups of children to play.

Name _____

1. A zipper can get stuck.   <u>yes</u>

2. A turtle has antlers.   <u>no</u>

3. A helicopter can land on a nest.   <u>no</u>

4. You can have hamburgers for
   dinner.   <u>yes</u>

5. A bird has fur.   <u>no</u>

6. A lobster can send a letter.   <u>no</u>

7. A carpenter has a hammer and a
   ladder.   <u>yes</u>

(Student art appears here.)

Activity Sheet 40   Captain Bill Pinkney's Journey

Activity Sheet 40

LESSON

41

Lesson Overview

Materials

- *Captain Bill Pinkney's Journey*, pages 28–29
- "What Is It?," Step-by-Step Practice Story 20
- Learning Framework Cards 4, 5
- Reading/Writing Connection, pages 72–73
- Outlaw Word Flash Cards
- Activity Sheet 41

Prepare Ahead

- Bingo (see page 119, and Games and Songs Teacher Tool Card 5)

GETTING STARTED

Choose one or both of the following activities to focus the children's attention and to review some of the concepts they have been learning.

Middle Consonants   Use this activity to develop the children's awareness of sounds in the middle of words. Say a word and ask the children to repeat it and then identify the middle sound. Have a child identify the Sound/Spelling Card that represents the middle sound in the word. Confirm the children's responses by saying the sound as you point to the Sound/Spelling Card. For example, "That's right. You heard /g/ in *rugged.*" Use these words:

rugged	cabin
fuzzy	sailing
chorus	runner
lesson	

Dictate to the Teacher   Write *well* on the chalkboard, point to it, and ask, "If this is the word *well*, then how would you spell *yell?*" Have a volunteer dictate the spelling to you and add the new word to the board. Continue with this procedure, moving through the following sequence of words:

well	yell
yell	yet
yet	wet

Then have children take out scratch paper and allow about a minute for them to list as many *ell* or *et* words as they can. Have children dictate words from their lists for you to write on the board. Have the group read the lists from the board.

1 READING

Review Short Vowel Sounds Have the children take the vowel cards from their Letter Cards and place all five vowels in front of them in order: *a, e, i, o, u.* Tell the children that you will say some words and that they should listen for the vowel sounds. They should wait until you nod your head to hold up the card that stands for the sound they hear in each word. Say the following words.

sat	bed	hid	mop	bug
pet	tap	stop	lips	zap
fish	box	tub	nest	skip
patch	bus	spot	step	sit

For additional practice, have the children join in singing all five verses of the "Short-Vowel Song."

✳ Blending

Have the children blend the following words and sentences. For a complete discussion of the blending process, see **Learning Framework Card 3, Blending.**

Line 1:	big bigger biggest
Line 2:	curb nurse purse turtle
Line 3:	hammer ladder zipper dinner
Line 4:	unzip unpack unlock
Sentence 1:	The biggest insects are in the dirt in my garden.
Sentence 2:	The rabbit ran under the deck in my back yard.
Sentence 3:	When will you get a better pen?

Words After blending the words in line 1, ask children to give a sentence for each one. Remind them that sometimes a final consonant in a base word is doubled when an ending is added.

Before blending the words *nurse, purse,* and *turtle* in line 2, tell the children that the final *e* is silent. Then proceed as usual.

Ask what the children notice about the words in line 3. Some children may point out the *-er* ending for each word, while others might notice the double letters.

In line 4, point out the prefix *un-* and discuss what it means in each word. Encourage the children to suggest other words that use this prefix.

Review the words by having the children choose a word to fill in the
blank in sentences such as:
- An ant is small. A bear is _____.
- A bear is _____ than a dog.
- A whale is the _____ animal in the ocean.
- I like to have dessert with my _____.
- When I get home from vacation I _____ my suitcase.

Sentences   Write the sentences on the board and have the children
read them. Tell the children any outlaw words they are having difficulty
reading.

Talk with the children about the final punctuation in each sentence.
Why do some sentences end with a period while others end with a
question mark? Which word in sentence 3 is the question word?

➤ Pages 72–73 of the Reading/Writing Connection book review short
vowel sounds and spellings. On page 72, help the children make three
words in each box by filling in each blank with one of the vowels provided. Each vowel should only be used once. In some cases, more than
one vowel may fit in a word; the other words in the box will help determine which letter should be used. There is only one right combination
of letters in the words.

Reading/Writing Connection, page 72

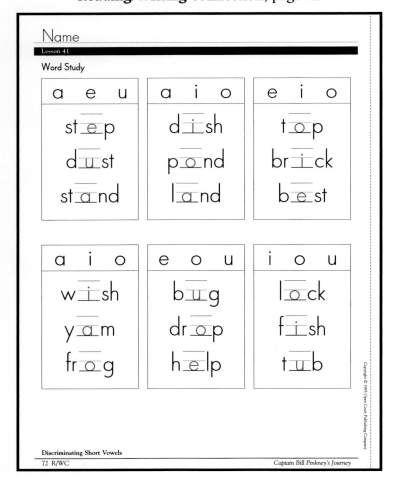

Reading/Writing Connection, page 73

Name

Lesson 41

Completing Sentences

1. Sam had bread and butter. | better / butter

2. Mom stopped the car. | stepped / stopped

3. Herb packed his bag. | packed / pecked

4. The girls dig in the dirt. | dig / dog

Dictation and Spelling

Decoding/Spelling

Captain Bill Pinkney's Journey   R/WC 73

The children can complete the top half of page 73 by choosing the appropriate word for each sentence and writing it in the blank.

✱ READING THE BIG BOOK

Captain Bill Pinkney's Journey
pages 28–29

Activating Prior Knowledge

Ask the children to tell what they remember about Captain Bill's journey since he left Australia. The children may want to return to the globe or world map to show the longest part of the journey.

Recommendations for Reading

- Help the children find where the map inset fits in the square marked on the map on page 28.
- Read the paragraphs on page 28 and then have volunteers trace the final days of the journey and the ports visited by Captain Bill.
- Read the caption on page 29 and invite discussion about the instruments and books shown in the pictures. Ask the children why they think reading was Captain Bill's most important skill.

STRATEGIC
R·E·A·D·I·N·G
PROMPTS
•

These prompts may be used as guides when working with reading strategies.

1 Wonder aloud about the skills Captain Bill needed to survive and encourage the children to wonder and offer suggestions. You might also wonder aloud how Captain Bill might be feeling as he gets closer to home and let the children who have been on trips share their feelings as they started for home.

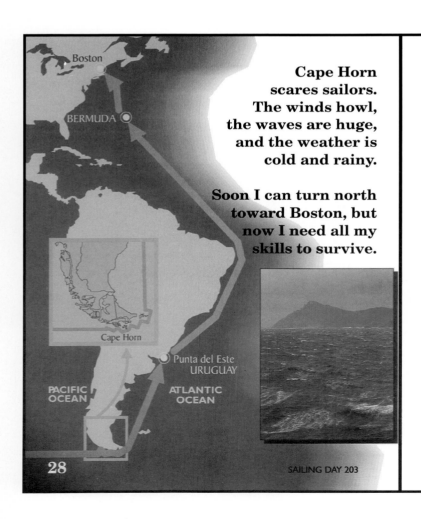

Cape Horn scares sailors. The winds howl, the waves are huge, and the weather is cold and rainy.

Soon I can turn north toward Boston, but now I need all my skills to survive.

28

SAILING DAY 203

To make this trip, Captain Bill had to study math, geography, and science. Reading, however, was his most important skill.

29

Responding

Call on volunteers to tell what they found most interesting on pages 28–29. Invite questions and wonderings and check the list to see how many questions and wonderings have already been answered.

✳ READING A STEP-BY-STEP PRACTICE STORY

"What Is It?"
Story 20

Getting Ready to Read

Have the children put together Step-by-Step Practice Story 20. Call on a child to read the title of the selection. Tell the children that today's story has something to do with baking. Ask them if they have ever had the chance to cook something at home. If so, have them share the experience and the steps they went through to make something edible.

Recommendations

Call on a different child to read aloud each page of the story, or divide each page into two parts and call on two readers. Reread the story until all children have read. Finally, go over each page by calling on a single reader to read slowly. The other children should raise their hands when they hear the sound /er/. The child who points out the word with that sound may write it on the board.

Responding

After reading, ask the children to tell in their own words what happened in the story and discuss any difficulties they had in reading it. To check that the children are paying attention to the words in the story, ask the following questions, having the children point to the words in the story that answer the questions:

What did Uncle Art put into the mixer first?

What were the last ingredients to go into the mixer?

What did Uncle Art suggest that Bert should drink with his carrot bread?

Have the children reread the story with a partner.

✳ READING ALOUD

You may want to read one or more of the following books about ships and ocean voyages to the children:

Ships and Seaports by Katherine Carter

Oars, Sails and Steam: A Picture Book of Ships by Edwin Tunis

Dear Daddy . . . by Phillippe Dupasquier

If I Sailed a Boat by Miriam Burt Young

See **Learning Framework Card 5** for suggestions for reading aloud.

TEACHING TIP

Set aside ten minutes for partner reading every day. During this time, you should read with individuals, recording their progress. Reading Assessment Sheets for Phonics Minibooks are available in *Assessment Masters, Grade 1.*

2 WRITING

✳ DICTATION AND SPELLING

Have the children turn to page 73 of the Reading/Writing Connection book. Dictate the following words and sentence following the regular procedure. See **Learning Framework Card 4** for a review of dictation.

Encourage the children to check the Sound/Spelling Cards and to ask if they are unsure of which spelling for the /er/ sound to use.

✎ **Line 1:** wet   went

Line 2: girl   turn

Sentence: Her dog had wet fur.

Help the children proofread each line.

INDEPENDENT AND COLLABORATIVE WRITING

Children usually think of planning for a trip as thinking about what they need to take with them, but planning should also include how to get where one is going. Initiate a discussion of various ways to travel. List the children's suggestions on the board. Point out that different ways of travel require different plans. For example, if they are going by car, they might need to get a map and plan a route. If they are going by train, they need to think about tickets, when the trains leave and arrive, and how they will get from the train station to their final destination.

Have the children choose a way they might like to travel. If they are going to an imaginary place, they may want to come up with an imaginary form of transportation. On a sheet of paper or on the next page in their planning booklet, have them write how they would travel and what plans they would need to make. Their response may be as simple as "I am planning to go to _____. I will get there by _____. I will need to _____."

Circulate among the children and help them to decide on a mode of transportation. If several children are using the same form of transportation, you may want to hold small group conferences to have them share ideas and support each other.

Another option is for children to create a map of where they are going or have been. Remind children that the map in *Captain Bill Pinkney's Journey* showed the route he followed and the names of the places that he visited. Children should include the names or pictures of important places they would pass along their way. These maps may be as simple as a picture of the children's houses, a street or highway with a sign on it, and then a picture of the final destination. Good examples of easy maps can be found in a number of children's publications. These include *As the Crow Flies: A First Book of Maps* by Gail Hartman and the September, 1993 issue of *Ladybug* magazine.

Hold a Seminar to allow children to share their travel plans. Continue to have children keep their work in their folders. Tomorrow, they will write about what they plan to do when they get to their destination.

TEACHING TIP

You may designate part of a bulletin board as a place where children can display their writing about trips so they can see all the places the class has written about.

3 GUIDED AND INDEPENDENT EXPLORATION

W O R K S H O P

Remind the children that they may use this time to work on projects on their own or in small groups. Be sure that each child knows what projects he or she may choose and how to complete any independent work. Suggestions for teacher-guided, collaborative, and independent activities follow.

Work with the Teacher

- Play Bingo with the children to review recently introduced sounds and spellings. Before Workshop begins, prepare Bingo cards containing the spellings *e, u, er, ir, ur, w, wh, y, l,* and *z;* then write a list of words that contain these spellings. (You may be able to use word cards from recent Wonder Word, Keep the Card, and Reading Relay games.) For complete Bingo instructions, see **Games and Songs Teacher Tool Card 5.**
- Use Outlaw Word Flash Cards to review outlaw words.
- Invite the children to practice reading words with /e/ by reading their choice of Step-by-Step Practice Stories 17, 18, or 19.

Independent Work

- Activity Sheet 41 reviews number words. Tell the children to read each sentence and fill in the missing number, using the pictures to help them. They should then draw a line from each sentence to its matching picture.
- Children who enjoyed reading *Wendell's Pets* might like to draw pictures of pets that they would like to bring, or would like to see a classmate bring, to school. Under each picture, they should write a sentence telling about the pet.
- Have the children prepare Letter Cards *a, h, i, l, m, p, s, w* for the Word-Building game in the next lesson.

Student Collaboration

- Encourage pairs of children to reread Phonics Minibook 7, *Wendell's Pets,* or a recent Step-by-Step Practice Story. You might want to assign each pair a target sound (/e/, /o/, /l/, /ir/, /y/, or /w/) and have the children list the words in the story that contain that sound. As one child reads, the other can write, changing places after each page.
- Pairs or small groups of children can review outlaw words. Give each pair or group a few Outlaw Word Flash Cards. Tell the children to work together to read each word and to write sentences using the words.
- Another form of map is one used in a treasure hunt. Several children may want to draw a map that others could follow to find something special in the classroom.

Home/School Connection

Send home the take-home version of Phonics Minibook 6, *In the Pond,* for children to share with their families.

ASSESSMENT TIP Listen to several students as they each read a story from one of the Phonics Minibooks to you. Using a Reading Assessment sheet, record your observations and add them to each student's folder.

Name

| One | Two | Three | Four | Five |

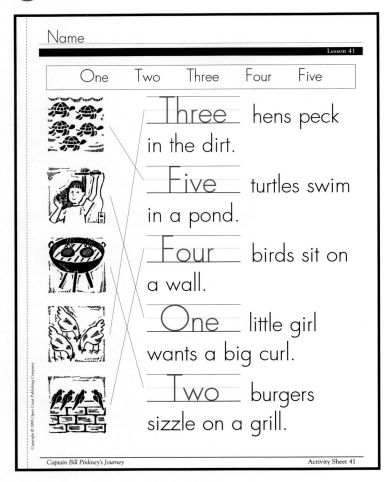

Three hens peck in the dirt.

Five turtles swim in a pond.

Four birds sit on a wall.

One little girl wants a big curl.

Two burgers sizzle on a grill.

Captain Bill Pinkney's Journey   Activity Sheet 41

Activity Sheet 41

LESSON 42

Lesson Overview

New Learning

- /sh/ spelled *sh*

Materials

- *Captain Bill Pinkney's Journey*, pages 30–31
- "Jen's Web," Step-by-Step Practice Story 21
- Sound/Spelling Card 30, Shark
- Learning Framework Cards 2, 3, 5, 6
- Reading/Writing Connection, pages 74–75
- Letter Cards *a, h, i, l, m, p, s, w*
- Activity Sheet 42

GETTING STARTED

Choose one or both of the following activities to focus the children's attention and to review some of the concepts they have been learning.

Word Sort   Print the spellings *er*, *ir*, and *ur* on the chalkboard. Write words with the /er/ sound on cards and place them in a container. Have children select a card, read the word, and place the card under the correct spelling for the /er/ sound. At the end of the activity, have the children chorally read all the words under each spelling. Some suggested words:

girl	curl	her
skirt	burn	winter
dirt	turn	sister
bird	fur	herd
shirt		

Quick Change Teams   Have the children work in teams of four or five and make sure that each team has a sheet of paper. Write the word *tip* on the chalkboard. Then give the following directions and have the first team member write the new word on the paper and pass the paper to the next team member. Give the next set of directions for that child to write a new word and to pass the paper on. Keep giving directions and having the paper passed until each team member has had a turn to write a word. List the words on the chalkboard and have the teams compare their lists with yours. Call on children to use the words in sentences.

The directions you should give follow:

- Change the vowel to *o*. *(top)*
- Change the vowel to *a*. *(tap)*
- Change the last letter to *g*. *(tag)*
- Change the vowel to *u*. *(tug)*
- Change the first letter to *b*. *(bug)*
- Change the vowel to *i*. *(big)*
- Change the vowel to *e*. *(beg)*

1 READING

PHONICS

* **Introduce /sh/ Spelled *sh*** Turn Sound/Spelling Card 30, Shark, and tell the children that this is the Shark card. Point out the Shark's fin and tell the children that the shark is holding its fin in front of its mouth. Hold your finger in front of your mouth in a shushing position and ask what this gesture means. Have the children make the /sh/ sound with you. Point out the spelling and have the children name the letters. Explain that when the letters *s* and *h* come together, they make a new sound. They don't have the sound of the *s* or the sound of the *h*. Then read the Shark story. A discussion of the procedure for introducing a new sound can be found on **Learning Framework Card** 2.

Sharon the Shark rushes to shush the other fish.
Her baby sister needs a nap.
Sharon knows that when Baby Shark is tired,
She's likely to snip and snap!

Sharon hears Shirley the Shrimp shouting.
"Hush, Shirley!" Sharon whispers. /sh/ /sh/ /sh/ /sh/ /sh/!
"Don't wake up Baby!"

Sheila the Shellfish is splashing in shallow water.
"Hush, Sheila!" Sharon whispers. /sh/ /sh/ /sh/ /sh/ /sh/!
"Don't wake up Baby!"

What would happen if Shirley or Sheila woke up Baby Shark?
She'd flash her tiny shark teeth!

Help Sharon make it quiet so Baby Shark can sleep.
(Have the children join in:) /sh/ /sh/ /sh/ /sh/ /sh/!

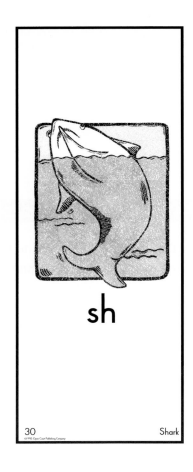

sh

30   Shark

Have the children signal with a thumbs-up when they hear the /sh/ sound at the beginning of a word. Pronounce these words:

shell	shelf	feather
shoe	chipmunk	shower
shadow	shingle	sheet

Ask the children to suggest other words that begin with /sh/. Then have them signal when they hear /sh/ at the end of words. Use these words:

push	rush	smash
bath	fish	wish
crash	flag	crush

* **Blending** Have the children blend the following words and sentences. For a complete discussion of the blending process, see **Learning Framework Card 3, Blending.**

Line 1:	ship shop shut shell
Line 2:	shack shark shirt shrimp
Line 3:	rash smash flash crash
Line 4:	dish dishes wish wishes
Sentence 1:	The dog hid under the bushes.
Sentence 2:	The men unpacked the shipment of plums.
Sentence 3:	Sam rushed to the market to get fresh fish.

Words Be sure to write the spelling *sh* as a unit before having the children say the sound. Remind the children that the *sh* spelling makes one sound, /sh/. Blend the words sound by sound. For example, in line 1, blend the word *ship* as follows: /sh/ /i/ /p/, *ship*. The children can use this same procedure to blend the other words.

In line 4 point out that the *-es* ending added to *dish* and to *wish* makes the words plural. Have the children clap the syllables and make the point that adding *-es* adds a second syllable to each word. Ask the children in what other way they can make a word tell about more than one. If necessary, explain they sometimes just add *s.*

Review the words by asking questions such as the following:

- Which word means a big boat?
- Which word means more than one plate?
- Which word means something that you hope for?
- Which word names an animal?
- Which word names something to wear?
- Which word is the opposite of open?

Sentences To encourage fluency, have the sentences reread several times.

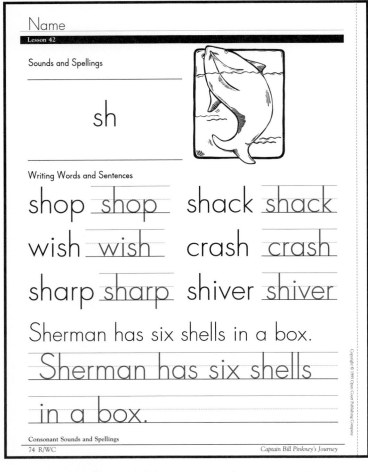

Reading/Writing Connection, page 74

Reading/Writing Connection, page 75

➤ Reading/Writing Connection, pages 74–75, reinforces the /sh/ sound spelled *sh*. Have the children read and copy the words and sentence on page 74. For the top of page 75, the children should label each picture with the correct word. At the bottom of the page, have them identify and write the sounds represented by the pictures and blend those sounds to make a word.

✳ READING THE BIG BOOK

Captain Bill Pinkney's Journey
pages 30–31

Recommendations for Reading

- Let the children talk about what they think is happening in the pictures on pages 30–31.
- Ask whether anyone can read any of the words on the banner the children are holding. Let the children point to the words as they read them.
- Let volunteers suggest what Captain Bill and the children might be feeling as they meet on the dock in Boston.

STRATEGIC
R·E·A·D·I·N·G
PROMPTS
•
These prompts may be used as guides when working with reading strategies.

1 It might be helpful to have the children sum up what they have learned about Captain Bill Pinkney's difficult journey.

I made it! I have kept my promise. I have made my dream come true.

On the dock in Boston, some of the students who were my radio friends are waiting. I am so happy to be back. I have so many stories to share with them.

30

SAILING DAY 259

31

Responding

Ask the children to tell what they liked best about the story. Encourage them to tell about something they learned that they had not known before.

"Jen's Web"
Story 21

Getting Ready to Read

Have the children assemble Step-by-Step Practice Story 21, "Jen's Web," in the usual manner. Then ask a child to read the title of the story. Discuss where this story is taking place and what the the title might mean.

Recommendations

Call on a different child to read aloud each page of the story. If children have difficulty with words, help them blend or remind them of the outlaw word. Also, follow the suggestions on **Learning Framework Card 6.** Reread the story at least twice, calling on different children to read. You might have the entire class do a responsive reading of the story while you or a child read the part of Jen.

Responding

- After reading, have a few children tell in their own words what happened in the story.
- Ask whether children have questions about anything they read. Ask them to point out words that were difficult to blend, outlaw words they did not know or did not remember, and sentences that were difficult to understand.
- To determine whether the children are focusing on the words in the story, ask the following questions, having children point to the word in the story that answers each question.

     What is the spider's name?
     What is the web for and what is it not for?
     What animals are in this story?

Have the children reread the story with a partner.

You may want to share one or more of the following books about boats with your class:

Busy Boats by Peter Lippman
Harbor by Donald Crews
Boat Book by Gail Gibbons
Boats by Anne Rockwell

TEACHING TIP

Remind the children to read each book twice. When they finish today's book, they should get one from a previous lesson. Reading Assessment Sheets for Phonics Minibooks are available in *Assessment Masters, Grade 1.*

See **Learning Framework Card** 5 for additional suggestions for reading aloud.

2 WRITING

✱ DICTATION AND SPELLING

Word-Building Game   For the Word-Building game, have the children use Letter Cards *a, h, i, l, m, p, s, w* or use paper and pencil. Begin by having them place the letters *s* and *h* together and pronounce the sound. Then have them make the word *ship.* Remember to write the word on the board or the overhead for the children to check their work. Have them continue building the words that follow:

slip
slim
slam
lamp
lash
wash
wish

As you have the children change *lash* to *wash*, point out that the sound of the letter *a* changes when it comes after *w.*

INDEPENDENT AND COLLABORATIVE WRITING

Review with the children some of the places they are going, what they plan to bring, and how they plan to travel. Tell them that today they should think about what they will do once they get there. For example, if some are planning to go to the beach, they might go swimming, build sandcastles, and look for shells. Visiting a cousin or a friend might involve playing with favorite toys. Have some children share their ideas, then have children continue working alone or with their partners. They may work in their plan book or on a new sheet of paper to tell about what they will do once they arrive at their destinations. If children would prefer, they can continue writing their daily entries into their journals.

Circulate among the children and hold conferences with individuals or with small groups.

During Seminar have children share what they will be doing on their trip. Encourage children to ask each other questions and to help each other expand their ideas. You may want to model some questions and comments, such as, "That's an interesting thing to do. Can you tell us more?" "Who will be there to play with you?" "Have you ever built sandcastles before? Will you need to put pails and shovels on your list of things to take?" "When you go to the museum, what special things do you hope to see?"

3 GUIDED AND INDEPENDENT EXPLORATION

WORKSHOP

Remind the children that they may use this time to work on projects on their own or in small groups. Be sure that each child knows what projects he or she may choose and how to complete any independent work. Suggestions for teacher-guided, collaborative, and independent activities follow.

Work with the Teacher

- Listen to children reread "Jen's Web," Step-by-Step Practice Story 21.
- Preteach Sound/Spelling Card 31, Thongs, and tomorrow's Blending exercise to children who may need additional support with new sounds.
- Using a new list of words, repeat the Fill in the Blank game from Getting Started with those children who are having trouble with *er, ir,* and *ur.*

Independent Work

- Activity Sheet 42 provides practice with antonyms. For each word given, tell the children to choose from the word list the word with the opposite meaning. They should write that word in the blank, then again in the corresponding puzzle boxes. Remind the children that they can use the arrows to help them write their answers correctly in the puzzle.
- Challenge children to extend and illustrate a sentence from today's Blending exercise.
- Encourage children to work on a writing project of their choice. If you have a writing center, remind the children of its use.

Student Collaboration

- Encourage partners to reread "Jen's Web," Step-by-Step Practice Story 21.
- Pairs or groups of children can make up alliterative sentences containing the /sh/ sound. The sentences need not make sense. Encourage groups to choose one sentence and illustrate it, or exchange a sentence with another group for that group to read and illustrate.
- Children may want to write sentences using the antonyms in Activity Sheet 42, or they may want to come up with different sets of antonyms and use them in sentences.
- Have children write the antonyms from Activity Sheet 42 on cards and play Go Fish! matching the opposites.

TEACHING TIP

Encourage the children to read to each other. You, too, should choose children to read with. As you read with each child, note his or her progress.

Home/School Connection

- Send home "What Is It?" Step-by-Step Practice Story 20, and encourage the children to share the story with their families.

Name

Lesson 42

| subtract | whisper | winter | first | finish | sharp |

↓ 1. last

first

↓ 2. yell

whisper

↓ 3. summer

winter

→ 4. start

finish

→ 5. add

subtract

→ 6. dull

sharp

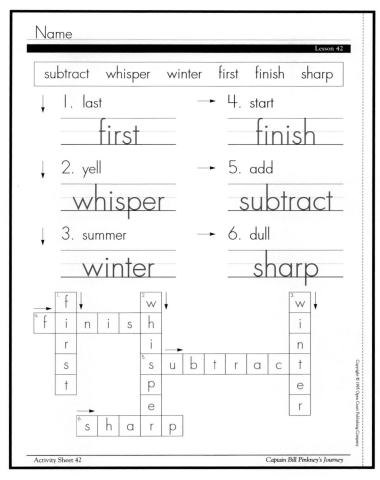

Activity Sheet 42   *Captain Bill Pinkney's Journey*

Activity Sheet 42

LESSON 43

Lesson Overview

New Learning

- /th/ spelled *th*

Materials

- *Captain Bill Pinkney's Journey*, page 32
- "Seth's Bath," Step-by-Step Practice Story 22
- Sound/Spelling Card 31, Thongs
- Learning Framework Cards 2, 3, 4, 5, 6
- Reading/Writing Connection, pages 76–77
- Activity Sheet 43

Prepare Ahead

- Flash Cards with words containing the /sh/ sound (see page 131)

GETTING STARTED

Choose one or both of the following activities to focus the children's attention and to review some of the concepts they have been learning.

Substituting the /sh/ Sound   Say the word *dip* and ask the children what sound they hear at the end. Tell them that you are going to make a new word by changing the /p/ sound to /sh/, and then say the word *dish*. Then tell the children that you will have them make new words by changing either the beginning or ending sound of a word to /sh/. Give the words that follow and tell the children either to change the beginning or end sound. Alternate calling on individuals and asking for whole-group responses.

hop (beginning)	tell (beginning)	Fred (end)
mutt (beginning)	keep (beginning)	flat (end)
dirt (beginning)	splat (end)	put (end)

A Tisket, a Tasket Game   To practice reading words with /sh/, have the children sit in a circle and invite a volunteer to be the traveler. Give the traveler a basket that contains cards printed with words containing the /sh/ sound. The traveler should move around the circle and say

> A tisket, a tasket
> a green and yellow basket,
> I took a word to my friend
> and on the way I dropped it.

On the last line, the traveler should stop in front of another child and drop one of the cards. That child should pick up the card and read the word. She or he then becomes the new traveler. Use the following words: *ship, shell, wish, fisherman, push, shot, ashes, shop, shed, dash, rush, shin, shirt.*

1 READING

PHONICS

✴ **Introduce /th/ Spelled *th***   Turn Sound/Spelling Card 31, Thongs, and tell the children that this is the Thongs card. If necessary, explain that thongs are shoes that people usually wear at the beach or swimming pool. Then read aloud the Thongs story.

A discussion of the procedure for introducing a new sound can be found on **Learning Framework Card 2.**

> In summer Thelma likes bare feet,
> But sometimes it's too hot.
> She puts on thongs to beat the heat,
> And when she walks they say (**softly**) /th/ /th/ /th/ /th/ /th/.
>
> On Thursdays, Thelma plays with Theo.
> They run and throw a ball.
> Running makes her thongs so loud,
> This time the thongs say (**in normal voice**) /th/ /th/ /th/ /th/ /th/.
>
> Now if you were walking here or there
> What sounds might your thongs make?
> (**Have the children answer softly**) /th/ /th/ /th/ /th/ /th/.
> If you were running as Thelma does,
> What sounds might your thongs make?
> (**Have the children answer in normal voice**) /th/ /th/ /th/ /th/ /th/.

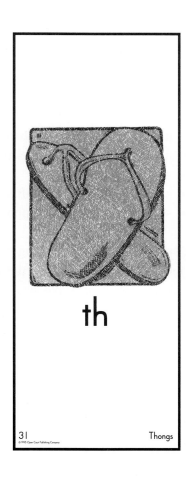

31   Thongs

Have the children signal thumbs-up when they hear a word that begins with /th/. Read these words:

thumb	**thump**	**think**	**thin**
fan	**thimble**	motor	**thistle**
this	tap	**thanks**	**there**

Ask children to suggest other words that begin with /th/. Then have them listen for /th/ at the end of words and signal when they hear it. Use these words:

with	path	teeth	wreath
push	math	both	feet
beneath	ask	bath	moth

✱ **Blending**   Have the children blend the following words and sentences. For a complete discussion of the blending process, see **Learning Framework Card 3, Blending.**

Line 1:	thin thud that this
Line 2:	math bath path
Line 3:	third birth with
Line 4:	thunder bother finish monster
Sentence 1:	That monster splashes <u>water</u> in <u>the</u> bathtub.
Sentence 2:	Did Seth finish dinner?
Sentence 3:	This mattress is <u>too</u> thin.

Words   When you write the words be sure to write the *th* spelling as a unit before having the children say the sound. Emphasize that the spelling for /th/ is *th* and that the two letters together make the /th/ sound.

Review the words by asking the children to find and erase one of the following:

- a word that rhymes with *cat*
- a word that names something you learn at school
- a word that means *end*
- something that comes after *second*
- something that is the opposite of *fat*

Sentences   Before writing the sentences on the board, introduce the outlaw word *water.* Write the word on the board, read it, and have the children repeat it. Have several children use the word in oral sentences. Then write the sentences on the board.

After the children blend each sentence, have them read the sentence several times until they can read it fluently. Vary the reading by asking individual children to read the sentence and then having the class read it together.

❯ Reading/Writing Connection, pages 76–77, reinforce the /th/ sound and spelling. Help the children complete these pages at this time. On the top of page 77, they should unscramble the words and write a sentence that describes the picture.

TEACHING TIP

The fact that *th* has two sounds, voiced and unvoiced as in *thin* and *then,* should not be a problem for the children. When they blend and recognize the word, they will naturally pronounce it correctly.

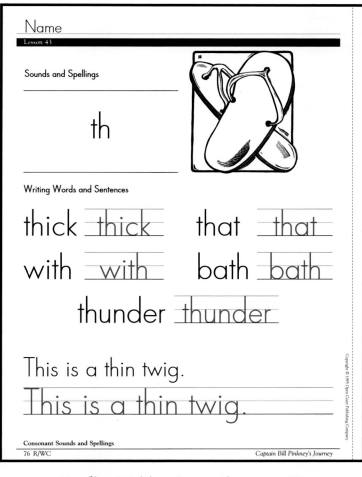

Name _____

Lesson 43

Sounds and Spellings _____

th

Writing Words and Sentences

thick [thick]   that [that]

with [with]   bath [bath]

thunder [thunder]

This is a thin twig.

This is a thin twig.

Consonant Sounds and Spellings
76 R/WC   Captain Bill Pinkney's Journey

Reading/Writing Connection, page 76

Name _____

Lesson 43

Unscrambling Sentences

bird   feathers.   This   red   has

This bird has red

feathers.

Dictation and Spelling

_____   _____
_____   _____
_____   _____
_____   _____
_____   _____

Decoding/Spelling
Captain Bill Pinkney's Journey   R/WC 77

Reading/Writing Connection, page 77

✳ **READING THE BIG BOOK**

Captain Bill Pinkney's Journey
page 32

Activating Prior Knowledge

Call on volunteers to recall any unusual or interesting words they
might remember from the book. Write their suggestions on the board.

Recommendations for Reading

- Turn to the Glossary on page 32. Invite observations and comments
  about anything of interest to the children. Read the first entry, *bunk,*
  and its definition. The children may notice that the glossary gives the
  meaning of words. Some may observe this is something like a diction-
  ary. Call attention to the alphabetical listing of the words.
- Explain that a glossary gives meanings of words as they are used in
  a particular book. Tell the children that all the words in this glossary
  appear in this book and are words that have to do with sailing, geography, boats, or other things of importance in this book.

- Refer to the interesting words that you and the children listed on the chalkboard. Read each word and point out its beginning letter. Help a child look for the word in the glossary. Read the definition of any word that is found.
- Turn to page 8 and read the first sentence. Point to the word *oceans* and read it. Then turn to page 32 and call on a volunteer to point to the word *ocean*. Read the word and its definition. Ask the children whether the glossary definition gave any information about *ocean* that was new to them.
- Repeat the procedure with the word *continents* in the same sentence on page 8.

GLOSSARY

BUNK: A bed on a boat.
CAPE: A piece of land sticking out
  into the water.
CONTINENT: One of seven very large bodies
  of land on the earth.
CHART: An ocean map used by sailors.
HARBOR: A shelter along a coast that
  protects ships.
HEMISPHERE: Half of the earth.
ISLAND: A piece of land entirely surrounded
  by water.
OCEAN: A very large body of salt water.
RADAR (RAdio Detecting And Ranging): A radio
  device that helps ships and planes find their
  way at night or in bad weather.
ROUTE: The path from one place to another.
ROLL: To rock from side to side.
PITCH: To rock from front to back.
VOYAGE: A long trip.

32

Responding

Ask the children how a glossary is useful.

"Seth's Bath"
Story 22

Getting Ready to Read

Have the children assemble Step-by-Step Practice Story 22 in the usual manner. Then ask a child to read the title of the story. Discuss where this story is taking place and ask the children what they think the title means.

Recommendations

Call on a different child to read aloud each page of the story. If children have difficulty with words, help them blend or remind them of the outlaw word. Follow the suggestions on **Learning Framework Card 6.** Reread the story at least twice, calling on different children to read. Perhaps have the entire class read the story aloud as a choral reading.

The children may need help with the word *rafts.*

Work with consonant clusters in this lesson: *st-* in *stepped, sh-* in *ship,* and *-sh* in *fish* and *finished; -st* in *cast; -nd* in *hands;* and *-ck* in *deck.* In *monster* they must split the word into *mon* and *ster* and then blend. The same is true with *under* and *abandon,* which must be split into syllables and blended.

Responding

- After reading, have a few children tell in their own words what happened in the story.
- Encourage the children to ask any questions they may have about the story. Ask them to point out difficult points in the story, words that were difficult to blend, outlaw words they did not know or remember, and sentences that were difficult to understand. Call on volunteers to answer these questions.
- To help children focus on the words in the story, ask them to find and read words that have the /sh/ sound. Then ask them to find and read words with two syllables. Ask them to find and read any words with more than two syllables.

Have the children reread the story with a partner.

Continuing with the many books written about travel, you might want to share one or more of the following books with the children.
How to Travel with Grownups by Elizabeth Bridgman
Grandfather's Journey by Allen Say
Follow the Dream: The Story of Christopher Columbus by Peter Sis

TEACHING TIP

Set aside ten minutes for partner reading every day. During this time, you should read with individuals, recording their progress. Reading Assessment Sheets for Phonics Minibooks are available in *Assessment Masters, Grade 1.*

See **Learning Framework Card 5** for additional suggestions for reading aloud.

2 WRITING

✳ DICTATION AND SPELLING

Have the children turn to page 77 of their Reading/Writing Connection book and finish the bottom of the page. Dictate the following words and sentence, using the suggestions for dictation that appear on **Learning Framework Card 4.**

Line 1: shop   shelf

Line 2: dish   flash

Sentence: I wish I had a ship.

Have the children proofread their work as usual.

INDEPENDENT AND COLLABORATIVE WRITING

Review with the children some of the ideas they were writing about in the previous lesson. Discuss any ideas the children may have gotten from Seminar that they might like to include in their work.

Encourage the children to continue working on writing about their plans for their trip. They may want to look over all their previous pages to see if they want to add or change anything. Those children who are writing sentences should look for capitals and end punctuation. Encourage them to extend their sentences. They may add any illustrations they would like.

Circulate among the children holding individual conferences, or you may want to hold small group conferences with children who may be writing about similar trips.

Take time for small group Seminars. Have children tell their group where they are going, something they plan to take, and something they plan to do when they arrive.

3 GUIDED AND INDEPENDENT EXPLORATION

WORKSHOP

Remind the children that they may use this time to work on projects on their own or with small groups. Be sure that each child knows what projects he or she may choose and how to complete any independent work. Suggestions for teacher-guided, collaborative, and independent activities follow.

Work with the Teacher

- Review all of the sounds and spellings that the children have learned so far. Have a small group of children take out pencil and paper. Point to a Sound/Spelling Card at random and call on a child to pronounce the sound, to write down its spelling or spellings, and to say a word containing the sound. Repeat until each child has had at least one turn.
- Repeat today's Blending with children who need additional practice. Encourage them to read each word as a whole word, rather than blending it sound by sound.
- To assess their progress, listen to children reread Step-by-Step Practice Story 21, "Jen's Web."

Independent Work

- Activity Sheet 43 reviews the /sh/ and /th/ sounds and spellings. Have the children cut out the boxes and rearrange the tops and bottoms of the pictures so that they match. The children can then work in pairs to write the names of the pictures.
- Have children fold a sheet of paper into thirds. In each of the front thirds, they should write a word that contains /sh/ spelled *sh.* They should then turn over the paper and write in each of the remaining thirds, a word that contains /th/ spelled *th.* When they are finished writing, they should draw a picture to go with each word.
- Have the children prepare Letter Cards *a, c, h, i, m, n, p, u* for a Word-Building game in the next lesson.

Student Collaboration

- Encourage partners to reread Step-by-Step Practice Stories 20 and 21, "What Is It?" and "Jen's Web." Make sure each partner reads alternate pages of each story, rather than reading one story in its entirety.
- Small groups of children may want to make *th* and *sh* posters. Instruct them to make block letters *th* or *sh* on a sheet of poster board, then fill in the letters with drawings and magazine cut outs of items that contain the /th/ or /sh/ sound. Encourage them to label each item.
- The children may work with a partner to compose and illustrate sentences. Have them use the cards from the A Tisket, a Tasket game and try to make sentences with the words.

TEACHING TIP

Encourage the children to read to each other. You, too, should choose children to read with. As you read with each child, note his or her progress.

Home/School Connection

Send home Step-by-Step Practice Story 21 and encourage the children to read it to their families. The book of Step-by-Step Practice Stories contains a letter that can be sent home with this story.

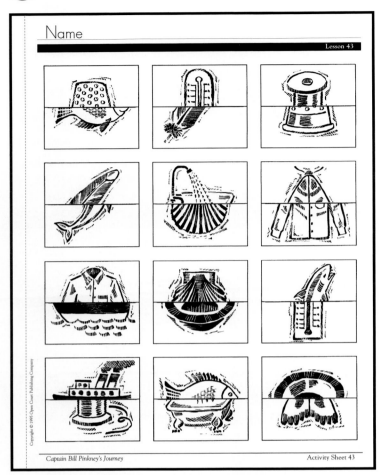

Name

Lesson 43

Captain Bill Pinkney's Journey

Activity Sheet 43

Activity Sheet 43

LESSON
44

Lesson Overview

New Learning

- /ch/ spelled *ch*

Materials

- *Captain Bill Pinkney's Journey,* pages 4–17
- Sound/Spelling Card 32, Chipmunk
- Learning Framework Cards 2, 3, 5
- Reading/Writing Connection, pages 78–79
- Letter Cards *a, c, h, i, m, n, p, u*
- Activity Sheet 44

Prepare Ahead

- Go Fish! Cards (see page 144 and Games and Songs Teacher Tool Card 7)

GETTING STARTED

Choose one or more of the following activities to focus the children's attention and to review some of the concepts they have been learning.

Listen for Vowel Sounds   On the chalkboard write the vowels *a, e, i, o,* and *u,* leaving as much space between letters as possible. Point to one letter at a time and ask what sound the vowel makes. Say the following words and ask the children to point to and name the vowel that they hear in each word. Example words are:

hog	flash	duck	mix
ant	up	egg	step
pet	stick	ox	man

Vowel Card Review   Ask how children can tell which Sound/Spelling Cards show short vowel sounds. Ask a child to name any card with green at the bottom. That child may call on three other children to say words with the sound of the card. Continue until each short vowel card has been named.

> **TEACHING TIP**
>
> As an alternative, have the children suggest words for each vowel sound. As an extra challenge, specify whether the sound should be at the beginning or in the middle of the words.

1 READING

PHONICS

✱ **Introduce /ch/ spelled *ch*** Before you display Sound/Spelling Card 32, Chipmunk, you may want to cover the *_tch* spelling that will be discussed in the next lesson. Display Sound/Spelling Card 32 and tell the children this is the Chipmunk card. Ask what they know about chipmunks. Then read aloud the Chipmunk story.

A discussion of the procedure for introducing a new sound can be found on **Learning Framework Card 2.**

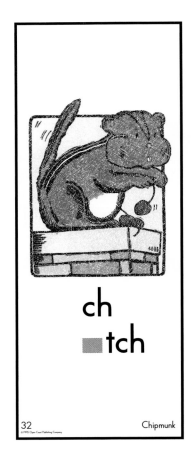

32
Chipmunk

> Chipper the chipmunk is cheerful and chubby.
> He chats and he chatters all day. /ch/ /ch/ /ch/ /ch/ /ch/ /ch/
> He sits on a chimney.
> Can you hear him chat?
> He chats and he chatters this way: /ch/ /ch/ /ch/ /ch/ /ch/ /ch/.
>
> Chipper stuffs cherries into his cheek.
> Then he chatters: /ch/ /ch/ /ch/ /ch/ /ch/ /ch/
> Chipper likes chestnuts and acorns to eat.
> Then he chatters: /ch/ /ch/ /ch/ /ch/ /ch/ /ch/
>
> Can you children chatter like Chipper?
> **(Have the children answer)** /ch/ /ch/ /ch/ /ch/ /ch/ /ch/
>
> Now chat with the chipmunk child beside you.
> **(Ask partners to have chipmunk conversations)**
> /ch/ /ch/ /ch/ /ch/ /ch/ /ch/

Have the children listen to some words and signal thumbs-up when they hear a word that begins with /ch/. Use these words:

cheese	cherry	cheek
chocolate	theater	chimpanzee
button	chicken	chop

Ask the children to suggest other words that begin with /ch/. Then have them review the card and tell how it will help them remember the /ch/ sound. Remind them that the letters *ch* stand for a single sound.

Have the children look at Sound/Spelling Cards Shark, Thongs, and Chipmunk, and compare the spellings. Ask what the second letter is in each spelling. Point out to the children that when they blend words, they should remember that the letter *h* after a consonant is often a clue that the consonant and the *h* will have a new sound.

✱ **Blending** Have the children blend the following words and sentences. For a complete discussion of the blending process, see **Learning Framework Card 3, Blending.**

Line 1:	chin chill chat chop
Line 2:	chest check chimp champ
Line 3:	church lunch bench branch
Line 4:	children chicken
Sentence 1:	Beth hurt her chin on the branches.
Sentence 2:	The chimp has two bunches of bananas.
Sentence 3:	Chuck sat on a bench at church.

Words   Before you have the children blend the words, remind them that *c* and *h* together make the /ch/ sound. You may want to point out the *ll* in *chill*, the *ck* in *check* and *chicken*, and the *mp* in *chimp* and *champ*.

Review the words by asking questions such as the following:
- Which one-syllable word names part of a tree?
- Which two-syllable word names something you can eat?
- Which one-syllable word means to cut?
- Which word names a meal?
- Which word names an ape?
- Which word means to talk?

Sentences   In sentences 1 and 2, point out the plural words *branches* and *bunches*. Ask the children to give the singular form of each word. In sentence 2, you may need to help the children blend *bananas*. Have the children sound out each syllable before blending the parts.

➤ Reading/Writing Connection, pages 78–79, reinforces the /ch/ sound and spelling. On page 79, help the children label each picture with the correct word, then have them write a sentence using as many of the words from the box at the top of the page as they wish.

Name
Lesson 44

Sounds and Spellings

ch

Writing Words and Sentences

chin chin   church church

chick chick   inch inch

chill chill   bunch bunch

The children munch on chips.

The children munch on

chips.

Consonant Sounds and Spellings
78 R/WC   *Captain Bill Pinkney's Journey*

Reading/Writing Connection, page 78

Name
Lesson 44

Writing Words

| check | chop | chimp | chicken |
| ranch | bench | much | lunchbox |

chicken   bench   chop

chimp   lunchbox   check
(Student sentences will vary.)

Captain Bill Pinkney's Journey   Decoding
                                                R/WC 79

Reading/Writing Connection, page 79

❋ **READING THE BIG BOOK**

Captain Bill Pinkney's Journey
pages 4–17

Activating Prior Knowledge
   Display Big Book 3 and ask a volunteer to read the title. Invite the children to tell what part of Captain Bill's book they found the most important or most interesting.

Recommendations
• Read through the first part of the text, pointing to each word and pausing to have the children read with you any words that they can.
• Discuss the different kinds of information on the pages and the ways it is presented (photographs, drawings, maps, diagrams, captions). Discuss times when children might use different forms of illustration in their own writing. You might mention that the children could use pictures cut from magazines as well as drawings to illustrate their work.
• With the children, browse pages 4–17 for favorite parts that they might like you to reread.
• Discuss why a certain part is a favorite.

Responding

Ask the children whether they are still wondering about anything in this section of the story.

TEACHING TIP

Have the children do partner reading daily. Using previously read Phonics Minibooks and Step-by-Step Practice Stories for this purpose will help the children review and solidify their knowledge of the sounds and spellings they have learned. Read with children individually and record their progress.

✳ READING ALOUD

Many books have been written about faraway places. You may want to share one or more of the following books with your class:

A Country Far Away by Nigel Gray, illustrated by Phillippe Du Pasquier

Sleep Rhymes Around the World, edited by Jane Yolen

Street Rhymes Around the World, edited by Jane Yolen

See **Learning Framework Card 5** for additional suggestions for reading aloud.

2 WRITING

✳ DICTATION AND SPELLING

Word-Building Game   Have the children use Letter Cards *a, c, h, i, m, n, p,* and *u* or paper and pencils for this activity. Have them put the letters *c* and *h* together; then have them add letters to make the word *chip.* Continue with the words that follow:

chimp
champ
chump
chum
much
munch
inch
chin

EXPLORING THE WRITER'S CRAFT

Discuss different ways people might write to each other, such as invitations, letters, Valentines, seasonal cards. During his trip, Captain Bill talked with students regularly by radio to tell them about his journey. When some people travel they send postcards to tell others about their trip. Discuss times children may have sent or received postcards. Note that postcards are also used for other purposes, such as reminding patients of medical or dental appointments. Have children tell about how they feel when they receive mail.

To introduce the children to letter writing, you may want to share one or more of these books or put them in a reading center for children to read on their own.

The Jolly Postman or Other People's Letters by Janet and Allen Ahlberg

Willaby by Rachel Isadora

Your Best Friend Kate by Pat Brisson

3 GUIDED AND INDEPENDENT EXPLORATION

WORKSHOP

Remind the children that they may use this time to work on projects on their own or in small groups. Be sure that each child knows what projects he or she may choose and how to complete any independent work. Suggestions for teacher-guided, collaborative, and independent activities follow.

Work with the Teacher

- Review Sound/Spelling Card 32, Chipmunk, and today's Blending exercise with those children who would benefit from additional practice. You might introduce tomorrow's spelling, _tch, to some children.
- Play the Word-Building game with children who need help with their spelling. Repeat a previous word list or create your own word list, depending on the children's needs.
- Have some of the more independent readers select books to read aloud to you. Invite other children to listen.

Student Collaboration

- Children may wish to draw chipmunks and make up chipmunk sentences for them, using words that contain the /ch/ sound.
- Small groups of children can play Go Fish! Before Workshop begins, prepare some new cards for the Go Fish! decks, using recently introduced sounds and spellings. For further information, see **Games and Songs Teacher Tool Card 7.**

- Some children might want to form read-aloud groups. One or two independent readers might select a book to read to a small group of listeners. You may want to provide a selection of fiction and nonfiction books about other countries.

Independent Work

- Distribute Activity Sheet 44. Tell the children to choose the word that completes each sentence and to write it in the blank. They should be sure to write the first letter of each word in the box at the beginning of the blank. When they have finished, the children should copy the letters from these boxes into the corresponding boxes at the bottom of the page. The letters will spell out a message for the children to read.
- Challenge children to write a sentence containing two or more words from today's blending and to illustrate it.
- Encourage children to write friendly notes to classmates.

Name

Lesson 44

| napkin | rattle | illness | after |
| antlers | children | dash | end |

1. His **illness** kept him in bed.

2. She has gifts for the **children**.

3. The elk's **antler's** are big.

4. Do you have a soft **napkin** ?

5. Can you fix the car's **rattle** ?

6. Let's skip to the **end** of the block.

7. The dog ran **after** the chipmunk.

8. I will add a **dash** of pepper.

I c a n r e a d
1 2 3 4 5 6 7 8

Captain Bill Pinkney's Journey

Activity Sheet 44

LESSON 45

••• Lesson Overview

New Learning

- /ch/ spelled _tch_

Materials

- *Captain Bill Pinkney's Journey*, pages 18–31
- "Patch Gets the Ball," Step-by-Step Practice Story 23
- Sound/Spelling Card 32, Chipmunk
- Learning Framework Cards 3, 4, 5, 6
- Reading/Writing Connection, pages 80–81
- Activity Sheet 45

GETTING STARTED

Choose one or both of the following activities to focus the children's attention and to review some of the concepts they have been learning.

Quick Change Teams Have the children work in teams and make sure each team has a sheet of paper. Have the first team member write the word *ship* at the top of the page and then pass the paper to the next team member. Give directions for making a new word. Each team member should write the new word beneath the old word and pass the paper on. Keep the game moving quickly. At the end of the game write the list of words on the chalkboard and have the teams check their lists. Call on children to use the words in sentences. Use the directions that follow:

Change the vowel to *o*. (shop)
Change /sh/ to /ch/. (chop)
Change the vowel to *i*. (chip)
Change the last letter to *n*. (chin)
Change the /ch/ to /th/. (thin)
Change the /n/ to /s/. (this)

Consonant Discrimination Game Write the spellings *th, sh,* and *ch* on the chalkboard, with as much space as possible between them. Touch each spelling and ask the children to say the sound it makes. Explain that you will say some words. Each word has either the /th/, the /sh/, or the /ch/ sound in it. After you say each word, the children should point to the sound they hear and say the spelling. You may wish to alternate whole-group responses with individual responses. Use the words:

chocolate	think	then
should	sandwich	pinched
finish	peach	bush
arithmetic	patient	pitcher

1 READING

PHONICS

Plurals with -es   Write the following words on the chalkboard:

dish   fox   ranch   inch

Point to the word *dish* and ask the children to read it aloud. Touch the word and say, "This word means one dish. If I had more, I would say 'many _____.'" Have the children suggest the word to complete the sentence. When they give the word *dishes*, write the word under *dish*. Ask what letters are added to *dish* to show more than one. Point out that the letters *es* added a new syllable to the word.

Have the children read the word *fox*. Then ask what word you would use to tell about more than one fox. Call on a child to write the new word *foxes* under *fox*. Continue in the same manner with the other two words. When complete, have the group read all eight words with you.

✱ **Introduce /ch/ Spelled _tch**   Point to Sound/Spelling Card 32, Chipmunk, and ask the children what sound the spelling *ch* makes. Tell them that there is another way to spell /ch/, then uncover the *_tch* spelling on the card. Ask the children if they can tell you anything special about this spelling. Help them explain that the green box before the *tch* means that the spelling always comes after a short vowel. Have the children point out other green box spellings they have learned *(ck, x)*. Have the children summarize how this card can help them remember the /ch/ sound.

✱ **Blending**   Have the children blend the following words and sentences. For a complete discussion of the blending process, see **Learning Framework Card 3, Blending.**

Line 1:   itch switch witch which

Line 2:   latch catch patch match

Line 3:   ditch ditches inch inches

Line 4:   butcher pitcher

Sentence 1:   Mitch stitches patches on his pants.

Sentence 2:   The pitcher tosses the ball to the catcher.

Sentence 3:   Chester went to the butcher for hamburger.

Words In writing these words it is important that the children see the *tch* spelling as a unit whose sound is /ch/.

The words *witch* and *which*, in line 1, will be homophones for many children. To help the children see the difference in their meanings, have each word used in a sentence. You may want to point out that many question words begin with *wh*, so they can remember the word that asks a question begins with *wh*.

Line 3 reviews the *-es* ending for plurals.

In line 4, the *u* in *butcher* is not quite a short *u*, but the children will adjust their pronunciation as they blend and recognize the word.

Review the words. Tell the children that you are going to say a sentence using a word in line 4. Then say a sentence and ask the children to erase the word you used. For example say, "I buy meat at the butcher shop." The children should erase *butcher*. Repeat with other words in other lines.

(line 2) I have a latch on my door.

(line 3) The table is ten inches wide.

(line 1) Poison ivy will make you itch.

Sentences The children may need some help blending *hamburger* in sentence 3. Write the word syllable by syllable. Have the children blend each syllable and then blend the syllables together.

▶ Reading/Writing Connection, pages 80–81, reinforces the /ch/ sound spelled *_tch*. Help the children complete page 80 and the top of page 81.

✳ READING THE BIG BOOK

Captain Bill Pinkney's Journey
pages 18–31

Recommendations for Reading

- Read through the second part of the text, pages 18–31, pausing to have the children read any words that they can along with you.
- Discuss the kinds of information on the pages and the ways it is presented (photographs, drawings, maps, diagrams). Discuss what kind of text can be illustrated with photographs (text about real places, people, or things). Encourage children to think about using different forms of illustration in their writing.
- Pause to allow the children to tell why a certain part is a favorite. Give each child who wishes an opportunity to point to a word or group of words and read aloud.

Responding

Ask the children if there is anything in the story that they still wonder about.

Name _____

Lesson 45

Sounds and Spellings

ch

▇tch

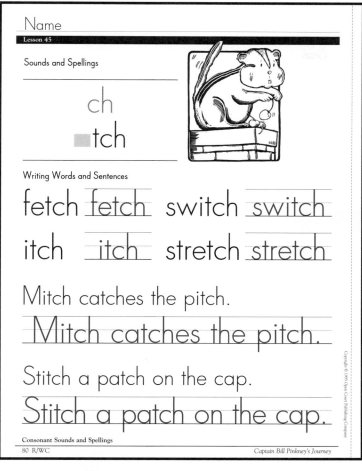

Writing Words and Sentences

fetch _fetch_   switch _switch_

itch _itch_   stretch _stretch_

Mitch catches the pitch.

Mitch catches the pitch.

Stitch a patch on the cap.

Stitch a patch on the cap.

Consonant Sounds and Spellings

80 R/WC   *Captain Bill Pinkney's Journey*

Name _____

Lesson 45

Writing Words

| fetch | patches | crutches | catch | ditch | scratch |

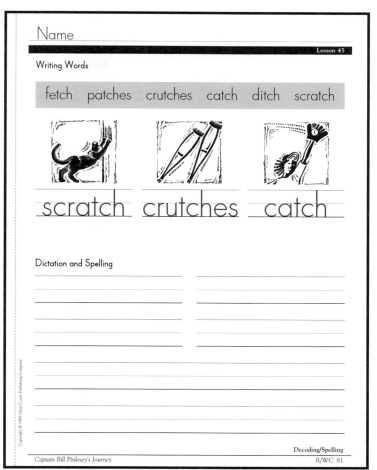

scratch   _crutches_   _catch_

Dictation and Spelling

_____   _____
_____   _____
_____   _____
_____   _____
_____   _____

Captain Bill Pinkney's Journey

Decoding/Spelling

R/WC 81

Reading/Writing Connection, page 80   Reading/Writing Connection, page 81

✳ READING A STEP-BY-STEP PRACTICE STORY

"Patch Gets the Ball"
Story 23

Getting Ready to Read

Have the children assemble Step-by-Step Practice Story 23 in the usual manner. Then ask a child to read the title of the story. Discuss where this story takes place and what the children think the title means.

Recommendations

Have the children read each page of the story to themselves, then call on a different child to read the page aloud. If children have difficulty with words, help them blend them or remind them of the outlaw word. Follow the suggestions on **Learning Framework Card 6.** Reread the story at least twice, calling on different children to read. Perhaps have the entire class read the story aloud as a choral reading.

Responding

After reading, have the children tell in their own words what happened in the story. To determine whether children are focusing on the words in the story, ask the following questions, having children point to the words in the story that answer each question.

Where did Lil, Elena, and Chuck meet?

What kind of player did Lil say she would be?

What kind of player did she say Chuck would be?

Who ran past the grass?

Where did he run?

What did Elena tell her dog to do?

Have the children reread the story with a partner.

✳ READING ALOUD

Many books have been written for children about the concepts of place and time. You may want to share one or more of the following books with your class:

Where in the World is Henry? by Lorna Balian

Where Does the Sky End Grandpa? by Martha Alexander

Time of Wonder by Robert McCloskey

See **Learning Framework Card 5** for additional suggestions for reading aloud.

TEACHING TIP

Remind the children to read each book twice. When they finish today's book, they should get one from a previous lesson. Reading Assessment Sheets for Phonics Minibooks are available in *Assessment Masters, Grade 1.*

2 WRITING

✳ DICTATION AND SPELLING

Have the children turn to page 81 of their Reading/Writing Connection book. Dictate the following words and sentence, using the suggestions for dictation that appear on **Learning Framework Card 4.**

Line 1: bath   math

Line 2: chip   chimp

Sentence: Tim chats with Chuck.

Have the children proofread their work as usual.

✳ INDEPENDENT AND COLLABORATIVE WRITING

You may want to bring to class postcards of the city or town where you live or have children bring some in. Display and discuss the postcards, pointing out that there is limited space for the message and a space for the name and address of the person they are sending the card to. Many postcards have interesting pictures. As you discuss postcards, suggest that the children write to someone at home or to a classmate, or someone else in the school. Their postcards can tell something special about school, where they live, or anything else they would like to share.

You may want to make postcards for the children to use. Simply cut out rectangles from poster board and draw a line down the middle on one side of each card. One advantage of making your own cards is that you can make the cards larger than a standard postcard, leaving more room for children to write. Children can draw on the front and then do their writing on the back.

Remind children to write as neatly as possible so the person receiving the card can read it.

Circulate among the children as they write. Encourage children to sound out words they are having trouble spelling and to use the Sound/Spelling Cards. They can also ask a friend to help them spell a word. If a number of children ask how to spell the same words, write the words on the board; this will make them accessible to everyone and save you time.

Have the children save their cards in their writing folder. They will work on addressing the cards in the next lesson.

TEACHING TIP

Create a class mailbox and encourage children to send friendly notes to each other.

3 GUIDED AND INDEPENDENT EXPLORATION

WORKSHOP

Remind the children that they may use this time to work on projects on their own or in small groups. Be sure that each child knows what projects he or she may choose and how to complete any independent work. Suggestions for teacher-guided, collaborative, and independent activities follow.

Work with the Teacher

- Review the *ch* and *_tch* spellings of the /ch/ sound, stressing where each may appear in a word. You may wish to review today's or an earlier Blending exercise.
- Listen to children reread Step-by-Step Practice Story 23. Encourage them to point out words that contain the /ch/ sound and to note how the sound is spelled in each word.
- Use flash cards to review outlaw words with small groups of children who need additional practice.

Independent Work

- Activity Sheet 45 has the children use story context to complete a picture. Tell the children to read the sentences and draw in anything mentioned in the description that is missing from the picture.
- Encourage children to read a book on their own. Provide a selection of books for them to choose from.
- Children may want to continue writing friendly notes to classmates.

Student Collaboration

- Encourage children to read Step-by-Step Practice Story 23 with a partner. When they finish reading, they should return to the story, copy each word that contains the /ch/ sound, and write it in a sentence.
- Children may want to make cards for a Go Fish! or Concentration game. Have them use words from the Blending exercise or Step-by-Step Practice Story 23. Have them make two cards for each word and then play a game.
- Have children work together to write an alliterative sentence using words that begin with /th/, /sh/, or /ch/. Have them illustrate their sentences.

TEACHING TIP

Encourage the children to read to each other. You, too, should choose children to read with. As you read with each child, note his or her progress.

Home/School Connection

Send home Step-by-Step Practice Story 22 and ask the children to read it to their families.

Name

Under the Sun

A ship is on the water.
Big and little fish swim
under the ship. The girl next
to the cliff picks up a shell.

Captain Bill Pinkney's Journey   Activity Sheet 45

Activity Sheet 45

LESSON
46

●●● Lesson Overview

New Learning

- Addressing cards or letters

Materials

- "The Trash Stash," Step-by-Step Practice Story 24
- Learning Framework Card 3, 5
- Reading/Writing Connection, pages 82–83
- Activity Sheet 46

Prepare Ahead

- Index cards printed with words containing /ch/ and /th/ sound spellings (see page 154)
- Bingo materials (see page 159 and Games and Songs Teacher Tool Card 5)
- Scrambled Sentences Game (see page 159 and Games and Songs Teacher Tool Card 8)

GETTING STARTED

Choose one or more of the following activities to focus the children's attention and to review some of the concepts they have been learning.

Sound Card Review   Say the word *shoe.* Then ask which Sound/Spelling Card represents the beginning sound in *shoe* and have children name the spelling. Then say *car* and ask which card represents the vowel sound. Have children name the spelling. Continue saying words and asking children to name the card and spelling that represents the beginning or the vowel sound in the word. You might ask children to say words of their own to challenge classmates.

Wonder Word Game   Use the cards from the A Tisket, a Tasket game in Lesson 43 and add words containing the /ch/ and /th/ sounds, such as *chant, pinch, death, thin, third, panther,* and *chicken.* Have the children sit in a circle and say this verse as you pass a card around the circle:

The wonder word goes round and round.
To pass it quickly you are bound.
If you're the one to have it last,
Then you must read it rather fast.

The child who has the card when the verse ends reads the word. This child picks the next card from the top of the deck and continues the game.

Before and After Game Have the children sit in a circle. Give each child a letter card for one of the alphabet letters from *b* to *y*. Walk around the outside of the circle and tap a child on the shoulder. Ask, "What letter do you have? What letter comes after yours in the alphabet?" After the child answers, he or she can walk around the circle, tap someone else, and repeat the game. The child takes the new traveler's place in the circle.

Vary the game by having the children name the letter that comes before theirs.

TEACHING TIP

Start the game by having the children name the letter that comes after, as it is much easier than naming the letter that comes before.

1 READING

PHONICS

Review /ch/ Spelled _tch Ask the children what a baseball mitt helps a player do. Elicit that you can use the mitt to *catch* a ball. Write the word *catch* on the chalkboard and point to the *_tch* spelling. Point to Sound/Spelling Card 32, Chipmunk, and remind the children that *_tch* is one way to spell this sound. Say *catch* again and have the children repeat the word.

Write several other words that contain the *_tch* spelling for /ch/. Blend each word with the children. Words include

patch
stitch
match
ditch

Extend the activity by asking the children to tell the plural of each word and explain how it is formed.

✱ **Blending** Have the children blend the following words and sentences. For a complete discussion of the blending process, see **Learning Framework Card 3, Blending.**

Line 1:	strip stretch scrap scratch
Line 2:	splash splatter splinter
Line 3:	march crunch fetch switch
Line 4:	lead read thread instead
Sentence 1:	Ellen hit <u>the</u> ball with her tennis racket.
Sentence 2:	The timid ducks <u>would</u> not cross <u>the</u> path.
Sentence 3:	Chad scratched <u>the</u> red spot on his neck.

Words Lines 1 and 2 give the children practice reading words with clusters of three consonants. Provide help as needed. You might circle each cluster and review the sounds before reading the word.

Line 4 reviews the *ea* spelling for the short *e* sound. Before writing the first word, remind the children that in some words, short *e* is spelled *ea*. Then point out the word *lead*. Below it, write *led*. Tell the children that these words are homophones, that is, they sound the same but are spelled differently and have different meanings. Point to each word as you use it in a sentence and invite the children to explain what it means. Repeat with *read* and *red*. Blend the last two words.

Ask the children whether they have heard all of the words. Invite volunteers who are familiar with the words to use them in sentences. Then review the words by asking questions such as:

- Which word tells what a dog does with a ball?
- Which word is something that you sew with?
- Which word is a little piece of wood that gets stuck in your hands or feet?
- Which word is the noise you make when you jump in the water.
- Which word means a little bit of paper?
- Which word is what you do when you have an itch?

Reading/Writing Connection, page 82

Reading/Writing Connection, page 83

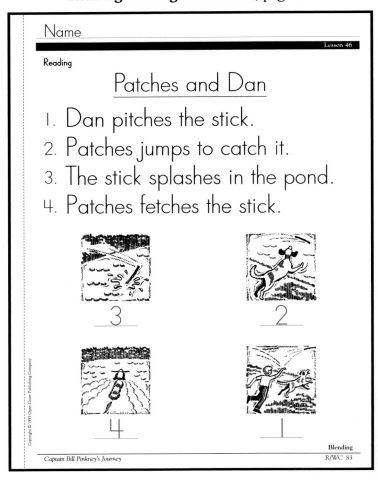

Sentences   The children may need support with their blending of the words *racket*, *timid*, and *scratched*. You may want to blend these in syllables.

❯ Reading/Writing Connection, pages 82–83, focuses on three-letter clusters. Have the children complete the sentences on page 82 by writing the correct word in each blank. On page 83, the children should number the pictures to match the sentences and show the order of the story.

✱ **READING A STEP-BY-STEP PRACTICE STORY**

"The Trash Stash"
Story 24

Getting Ready to Read
Browsing the Story   Have the children assemble Step-by-Step Practice Story 24, "The Trash Stash." Ask a child to read aloud the title of the story. Encourage the children to discuss anything they noticed about the story as they put it together.

Recommendations
Follow the standard procedure for reading a Step-by-Step Practice Story:
- Have the children read each page to themselves before you call on a different child to read each page of the story aloud. Clarify any difficulties and discuss anything of interest on each page before going on.
- Reread the story at least twice, calling on different children to read. Have the entire class read the story aloud as a choral reading.

Responding
- Invite the children to discuss any questions they had about the story.
- Have the children discuss what the story was about and what they liked about it.
- To make sure the children are focusing on the words in the story, rather than simply on the pictures, have them answer the following questions by pointing to and reading aloud the words:
    Who had a stash of trash?
    What kind of bench was in the stash?
    How many dishes were in the stash?
    How many lunch boxes were in the stash?
    Where did Mitch put his stash of trash?
    What did Mitch say to the children?
- Call on volunteers to read entire sentences.

Have the children reread the story with a partner.

TEACHING TIP

Set aside ten minutes for partner reading every day. During this time, you should read with individuals, recording their progress. Reading Assessment Sheets for Phonics Minibooks are available in *Assessment Masters, Grade 1*.

Additional books about world travel that you might like to share with the children include

The Armadillo from Amarillo by Lynne Cherry
My Grandmother's Journey by John Cech
Where Is Papa Now? by Celeste Conway

See **Learning Framework Card 5** for suggestions for reading aloud.

2 WRITING

✳ **DICTATION AND SPELLING**

Word-Building Game   Have the children use paper and pencil for today's activity. Write the consonant clusters *scr, spl, str* on the chalkboard. Have the children copy *scr* on their paper, then have them make the word *scrap*. Write the word under the cluster for the children to check their work. Point to *spl* and have the children copy it on their paper. Then tell them to make the word *split*. Write the word for them to check. Continue with *str* and the word *stretch.* Repeat with the words *scram, splotch,* and *strum.*

Challenge the children to suggest another word for each cluster.

Minilesson

Addressing Cards and Letters

Take a few minutes to discuss the cards the children wrote in the previous lesson. Hold Seminar and have volunteers share their cards.

Tell the children that now that the cards have been written, they need to address them. Writing addresses correctly is very important. If the address is not correctly written or clearly written, the post office will not be able to deliver it. Ask for a volunteer to give his or her full name. As you write the name on the board, remind the children that every name begins with a capital letter. For the second line, ask the volunteer to give his or her street address. Note that the name of the street or road is also capitalized because it is a name. The words *Street, Road, Avenue* and the like are also capitalized because they are part of the name. Then complete the address with the name of the city or town and state. Note that these too are names, so ask what to do when you write them. If the child knows his or her zip code, add this to the last line. Summarize the address by reminding the children:

• All the words in an address are capitalized.
• The first line has the full name of the person to whom the letter or card is being sent.
• The second line has the house number and street.
• The third line has the city, state, and zip code.

TEACHING TIP

Children may want to write the address on a piece of paper and then glue or tape it on their cards so if they make a mistake it won't ruin the card.

Circulate through the class. Have children write the name and address of the person the postcard is going to. If children need to know the address of the school, write it on the board for them. The important points children need to remember from this lesson are to include the name and address of the person and to write it legibly.

Have the children deliver their cards to classmates or take them home to family members.

3 GUIDED AND INDEPENDENT EXPLORATION

WORKSHOP

Remind the children that they may use this time to work on projects on their own or in small groups. Be sure that each child knows what projects he or she may choose and how to complete any independent work. Suggestions for teacher-guided, collaborative, and independent activities follow.

Work with the Teacher

- Review today's Blending lesson with small groups of children who would benefit from additional practice. Encourage them to read words as whole units rather than blending them sound by sound.
- Listen to children reread Step-by-Step Practice Story 24.
- Play Bingo with the children to review the sounds and spellings that they have recently learned. Prepare cards that include the spellings *sh, th, ch,* and *_tch.* If you feel that the children are ready, you might also include some of the three-letter clusters from today's lesson. Look to recent Blending exercises for word ideas. Detailed information about Bingo is provided on **Games and Songs Teacher Tool Card 5.**

Independent Work

- Activity Sheet 46 reviews reading words with the /ch/ sound. Have the children use the story context to complete the picture. Tell them to read the sentences and draw in anything mentioned in the description that is missing from the picture.
- Have children copy a word from today's blending exercise, then challenge them to form as many new words as they can by changing or adding one letter at a time. Encourage them to write and illustrate sentences using one of their new words.
- Encourage children to read on their own. Provide a selection of books for them to choose from.

Student Collaboration

- Encourage pairs of children to reread "The Trash Stash" or any of the previous Step-by-Step Practice Stories. Remind them to follow the usual procedure for partner reading.
- Small groups of children may enjoy playing Scrambled Sentences. Provide each group with an envelope of game materials, and review with the children the procedure for playing the game. If time permits, the groups may exchange envelopes for a second round of play. Detailed information can be found on **Games and Songs Teacher Tool Card 8.**
- Have children use the words from A Tisket, a Tasket cards in sentences. Challenge them to use more than one word in a sentence.

Home/School Connection

Send home Step-by-Step Practice Story 23, "Patch Gets the Ball." Encourage the children to read the story to their families.

Name _____

At Camp

Dad chops logs with a hatchet.
Trish and Mom pitch the tent.
Mitch gets sandwiches from the
picnic basket.

Activity Sheet 46   *Captain Bill Pinkney's Journey*

Activity Sheet 46

LESSON
47

Lesson Overview

New Learning

- /k/ spelled *k*

Materials

- Phonics Minibook 8, *The Market*
- Sound/Spelling Card 11, Camera
- Learning Framework Cards 2, 3, 4, 5
- Reading Writing Connection, pages 84–85
- Activity Sheet 47

Prepare Ahead

- /ch/ and /k/ Flash Cards (see page 170)

GETTING STARTED

Choose one or both of the following activities to focus the children's attention and to review some of the concepts they have been learning.

Reading Relay Game Form two teams of children and have the players on each team sit one behind the other. Use the index cards from the Wonder Word game in the previous lesson. To play the game, the first child on one team picks a word card, reads the word, then takes the card and goes to the end of the line. If a child reads the word incorrectly, the opposite team has an opportunity to say the word. The teams take turns choosing a card and reading the word.

Find a Word Game Write words on the chalkboard that contain some of the sound spellings that the children have recently learned. Name a Sound/Spelling Card and have a child find and read a word on the board that contains that sound. The child should identify the spelling used in the word and then erase the word. Continue with other children. You might want to use some of the following words:

munch	patch	shirt	snack
theft	flash	broth	stick
watch	shop	bath	such

1 READING

PHONICS

✱ **Introduce /k/ Spelled *k*** Turn Sound/Spelling Card 11, Camera, and ask the children which other Sound/Spelling Card has a camera pictured on it. Ask what two ways the children know to spell the /k/ sound. Explain that the letter *k* alone also spells this sound. Point out that the spellings *c, _ck,* and *k* appear on both cards. To remind the children of the /k/ sound, read aloud the Camera story.

A complete review of the procedure for introducing sounds and spellings can be found on **Learning Framework Card 2.**

Carlos has a new camera. When he takes pictures, his camera makes a clicking sound like this: /k/ /k/ /k/ /k/ /k/.

In the garden, Carlos takes pictures of caterpillars crawling on cabbage:
/k/ /k/ /k/ /k/ /k/.
At the zoo, Carlos takes pictures of a camel, a duck, and a kangaroo:
/k/ /k/ /k/ /k/ /k/.
In the park, Carlos takes pictures of his cousin flying a kite:
/k/ /k/ /k/ /k/ /k/.
In his room, Carlos takes pictures of his cute kitten, Cozy:
/k/ /k/ /k/ /k/ /k/.

Can you help Carlos take pictures with his camera?
(Have the children join in) /k/ /k/ /k/ /k/ /k/ /k/ /k/.

Ask the children to name words they remember from the story that begin with the /k/ sound. Write the words on the board as the children name them. Have children erase the words that begin with *c,* then read with them the words that begin with *k.*

✱ **Blending** Have the children blend the following words and sentences. For a complete discussion of the blending process, see **Learning Framework Card 3, Blending.**

Line 1:	**kill skill skillet**
Line 2:	**kit skit skirt skin**
Line 3:	**park milk ask mask**
Line 4:	**kitchen kitten kettle**
Sentence 1:	**The children put on masks for the skit today.**
Sentence 2:	**Ken went to the market with Mark.**
Sentence 3:	**The kittens slept in the dark kitchen.**

Words Some of the words, such as *skill, skillet,* and *skit,* may be
unfamiliar to the children. Invite children who are familiar with the
words to use them in sentences, or give sentences of your own.
　　Review the words by asking questions such as the following:
• Which word has the sound /ar/ in the middle?
• Which word has the sound /ir/ in the middle?
• Which words start with the sound /sk/?
• Which words have two syllables?

Sentences Before writing the sentences on the board, introduce the
outlaw word *today* in the usual manner. Then write the sentences for
the the children to read. Have the sentences read several times to
encourage fluent reading.

▶ Reading/Writing Connection, pages 84–85, provide additional practice with the /k/ sound spelled *k*. Help the children complete page 84
and the top of page 85.

Reading/Writing Connection, page 84

Name
Lesson 47
Sounds and Spellings

c
■ck
k

k
K

Writing Words and Sentences

kick　kick　bark　bark

kitchen　kitchen　silk　silk

The kitten laps milk.
The kitten laps milk.

Consonant Sounds and Spellings
84 R/WC　　　　　*Captain Bill Pinkney's Journey*

Reading/Writing Connection, page 85

Name
Lesson 47
Writing Words

park　kept　breakfast　mask　kick　kettle

kettle　　mask　　park

Dictation and Spelling

Captain Bill Pinkney's Journey　　Decoding/Spelling　R/WC 85

The Market
Phonics Minibook 8

Getting Ready to Read

Reading the Title Read the title of the book and point out that it contains two stories whose titles are also listed on the cover. Have the children turn to page 3 and read the title of the first story, "Can I Help You?"

Browsing the Story Allow the children to page through the book, commenting on the illustrations and discussing what they think the stories will tell them.

Recommendations

Follow the standard procedure for reading a Phonics Minibook:

- Call on a different child to read each page of the story aloud. Clarify any difficulties encountered on a page, then have a different child reread the page before going on.
- Reread the story at least twice, calling on different children to read.
- Repeat these steps when reading the second story.

2

Can I Help You?

"Have a ham,"
said the man to the clam.

"I do not want a ham!
I'm a clam!" said the clam.

3

"Grab a hat,"
said the man to the bat.

"I cannot grab a hat! I'm a bat,"
said the bat.

4

"Do you want a dish?"
said the man to the fish.

"What for?" said the fish.
"I'm a fish."

5

"Here's a rug,"
said the man to the bug.

"No, I do not want a rug,"
said the bug.

6

"Want a tub?"
said the man to the sub.

"I'm too big for a tub,"
said the sub.

7

"Have a wig,"
said the man to the pig.

"Not a wig!" said the pig.
"I'm a pig!"

8

"I can't sell a thing today."

9

The Lamp

10

"Have a lamp,"
said the man to the lad.

"What does it cost?" asked the lad.

11

"It costs a nickel,"
said the man to the lad.

"A nickel!" said the lad.
"What can I do with it?"

12

"First rub the lamp,"
said the man.
"Then stand back
and wish."

13

"I wish!" said the lad.

14

"This lamp is scratched.
It's full of dirt.
I do not want it," said the lad.

15

"We can't sell a thing today."

16

Responding

- Ask the children to discuss any difficult words they encountered in their reading and how they figured out these words.
- To make sure the children are focusing on the words in the story, rather than simply on the pictures, ask questions such as the following and have the children answer by pointing to and reading aloud the words:

Story 1: "Can I Help You?"
What does the man offer to the clam?
What does the clam say about the ham?
What does the man tell the bat to do?
What does the man ask the fish?
What does the fish ask the man?
What does the sub say about the tub?

Story 2: "The Lamp"
Who wants to sell the lamp?
How much does the lamp cost?
What does the man say the lad should do first?
What does he say the lad should do next?
What does the lad say about the lamp?

- Invite children to tell what they like best about the story.

Have the children reread the story with a partner.

* READING ALOUD

A number of children's books tell about children who live in other countries. You may want to share some of these:

A Family in Japan by Judith Elkin
At the Crossroads by Rachel Isadora
Fiesta! Cinco de Mayo by June Behrens

For additional suggestions for reading aloud, see **Learning Framework Card 5.**

2 WRITING

* DICTATION AND SPELLING

Have the children turn to page 85 of their Reading/Writing Connection book. Dictate the following words and sentence, using the procedure for dictation on **Learning Framework Card 4.**

Line 1:	catch pitch
Line 2:	itch stitch
Sentence:	Mitch can patch the rip.

Encourage children to ask for help if they are unsure of which spelling to use for the /ch/ sound. Help the children proofread each line.

INDEPENDENT AND COLLABORATIVE WRITING

Postcards are a good writing activity for children because they require short messages. Another way to communicate with friends is to write notes. Discuss informal letters or notes you might send to friends and have children tell why they might like to write a letter to someone.

If you have read *The Jolly Postman and Other People's Letters*, *Willaby*, or *Your Best Friend Kate*, discuss the kinds of letters that the characters sent and received. Another good book to read is *The Southpaw* by Judith Viorst. In both *The Southpaw* and *The Jolly Postman and Other People's Letters* you can point out the places where the letter writer made a mistake and simply crossed it out and continued writing.

Suggest that the children think about someone they might like to write a note to. Have them take a few minutes to brainstorm what they might like to write about: something that happened at school, something new they have learned, something that happened over the weekend, or something special that has happened at home. Make a list of children's suggestions and write next to each suggestion the name of the child who made it. Have children begin writing a letter to someone about anything they wish.

TEACHING TIP

Remind the children to read each book twice. When they finish today's book, they should get one from a previous lesson. Reading Assessment Sheets for Phonics Minibooks are available in *Assessment Masters, Grade 1.*

MONITORING DICTATION Collect students' Reading/Writing Connection books and scan the dictation pages to make sure children are proofreading and to see whether they are having difficulty spelling any sounds. Add your observations to students' portfolios, if appropriate.

TEACHING TIP

At this point, the children are writing casual or informal notes. They should probably remember that letters start with a greeting, Dear _____, and end with the letter writer signing his or her name.

3 GUIDED AND INDEPENDENT EXPLORATION

W O R K S H O P

Remind the children that they may use this time to work on projects on their own or in small groups. Be sure that each child knows what projects he or she may choose and how to complete any independent work. Suggestions for teacher-guided, collaborative, and independent activities follow.

Work with the Teacher

- Play a spelling game to review three-letter clusters. Dictate a word such as *rap* and ask the children how to spell it. Write it on the chalkboard as they spell it out. Then have them build the words *trap* and *strap*. Other word lists you might use include

rip	sand	fit	run	red	pin
trip	stand	fist	ran	shed	pinch
strip	strand	first	ranch	shred	punch

- Listen to individuals or pairs of children reread Phonics Minibook 8. Encourage them to point out the /k/ words and to comment on how /k/ is spelled in each word.
- Take out flash cards on which you have written words containing /ch/ spelled *ch* and *_tch,* and /k/ spelled *c, k,* and *_ck*. (You may be able to use cards from previous Wonder Word and Reading Relay games.) Have children read each word and identify the spelling of /ch/ or /k/.

Independent Work

- Activity Sheet 47 provides practice with rhyming words. Tell the children to choose a word from the box that rhymes with each given word, and write it on the appropriate blank. You might remind the children that often there are different spellings for the same sound.

- Children may use this time to work on unfinished writing projects. They may want to write notes to classmates.
- Encourage children to read on their own. Provide a number of books for them to choose.

Student Collaboration

- Invite pairs of children to reread Phonics Minibook 8. You might ask the pairs to locate and copy each word that contains the /k/ sound and underline the letter or letters that make the sound.
- Pairs of children may want to make a list of things the characters in *The Market* might buy, such as a new shell for a clam, or nice mud for the pig.

> **TEACHING TIP**
> Encourage the children to read to each other. You, too, should choose children to read with. As you read with each child, note his or her progress.

Home/School Connection

Send home Step-by-Step Practice Story 24 and encourage the children to read it to their families.

Name

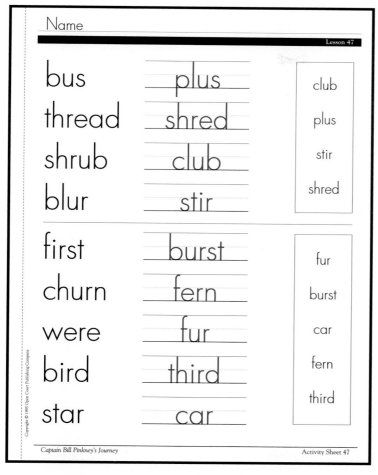

bus	plus
thread	shred
shrub	club
blur	stir

club
plus
stir
shred

first	burst
churn	fern
were	fur
bird	third
star	car

fur
burst
car
fern
third

Captain Bill Pinkney's Journey

Activity Sheet 47

Activity Sheet 47

LESSON 48

Lesson Overview

New Learning

- /ā/ spelled *a* and *a_e*

Materials

- *Captain Bill Pinkney's Journey*, pages 3–32
- "Gull and Crane," Step-by-Step Practice Story 25
- Sound/Spelling Card 33, Long A
- Learning Framework Cards 3, 5
- Reading/Writing Connection, pages 86–87
- Outlaw Word Flash Cards
- Activity Sheet 48
- Home/School Connection 11

Prepare Ahead

- Go Fish! Cards (see page 179 and Games and Songs Teacher Tool Card 7)

GETTING STARTED

Choose one or both of the following activities to focus the children's attention and to review some of the concepts they have been learning.

Fill in the Blank Print the spellings *sh, th,* and *ch* on the chalkboard. Point to the spellings one at a time and have the children make the sound. Then tell the children that you are going to print some words on the chalkboard with some of the spellings missing. The children have to decide which spelling belongs in the blanks: *sh, th,* or *ch.* Encourage them to experiment with all the possibilities before deciding which is the word. Some spellings may make more than one word. Write in the missing spellings the children suggest. Have the group read all the words.

__ip (*ship, chip*)
__is (*this*)

__ark (*shark*)

bun__ (*bunch*)

__under (*thunder*)

cra__ (*crash*)

di__ (*dish*)

ba__ (*bath, bash*)

__icken (*chicken*)

__ick (*thick, chick*)

__imp (*chimp*)

bran__ (*branch*)

Keep the Card Game   Place in a paper bag Outlaw Word Flash Cards and/or index cards with words containing spellings you want to review. Divide the class into teams of five students each. Have one player on each team draw a card out of the paper bag and look at it. (The player's team members will also see the card.) If the player says the word correctly, he or she may put the card on the table in front of his or her team. If the player misses, the card will go back in the bag. The teams take turns. The team with the most cards at the end of about five to ten minutes wins the game.

TEACHING TIP

This would be a good time to recycle some of the words from previous Wonder Word; A Tisket, a Tasket; and Reading Relay games.

1 READING

PHONICS

This lesson introduces the first long vowel sound and spellings. Unlike the other Sound/Spelling Cards, no story accompanies the introduction of long vowels. The picture on each long vowel Sound/Spelling Card is an elongated (or long) version of the letter. The picture of the letter is to remind the children that the long vowel sound is the name of the pictured vowel. All the long vowel spellings are presented on a yellow background.

Some children may initially have difficulty blending words that have long vowel spellings. This is normal. It is very important that you not wait for mastery of each spelling before going on to the next. Proficiency will come through repetition and practice.

✱ **Introduce /ā/ Spelled *a***   Tell the children that they will learn about a new vowel sound and discuss what they know about vowels. Remind them, if necessary, that all words and syllables contain a vowel and that vowels have more than one sound. They have learned the short vowel sound and spelling for each vowel, and today they will learn the first long vowel sound and spellings. Tell the children that the long vowel sound says the name of the vowel and that there are several spellings for each long vowel sound. Explain briefly that a vowel often needs help from other letters to say its name. Then follow the procedure outlined below to introduce long *a*.

Display Sound/Spelling Card 33, Long A. Tell the children that this is the Long A card. Remind the children that the long sound of a vowel is the same as the vowel's name, then ask what would be the long sound of *a.* Point out the spellings on the card and tell the children that all of these spellings will make the /ā/ sound in words.

Encourage the children to discuss the card. Point out that the letter *a* is long and thin. Ask them to tell how this card can help them remember the sound /ā/. Have the children repeat the sound.

Sing "Apples and Bananas," substituting the /ā/ sound in the second verse.

I like to eat eat eat
Apples and bananas.

I like to ate ate ate
ay-ples and bay-nay-nays.

Contrast the short and long sounds by pointing to the Lamb card and having the children say the sound /a/, then pointing to the Long A card and having the children say /ā/. Then teach the children the following rhyme:

A's my name,
Two sounds I make:
Short *a* in *lamb,*
Long *a* in *cake.*

Have the children repeat the rhyme several times with you.

Point to the spellings *a* and *a_e* on the card and tell the children that today they will read words with these two spellings for the long *a* sound. Have the children say the sound /ā/ as you point to each spelling. Explain that the blank in *a_e* means that a consonant goes in between the two letters in words and that the *e* helps the *a* to say its name. As an example, write *ate* on the chalkboard and read the word. Point out the consonant between *a* and *e.* Other example words are *cake, date, same.*

Say some words with long *a* at the beginning and have the children signal (thumbs-up, for example) if the word has the /ā/ sound. Use the following words:

ape	ice	eat
acorn	**apron**	under
use	**April**	**Amy**

Next say some words with long *a* in the middle and have the children signal if they hear the long *a* sound. Use the following words.

bake	sell	tickle
cave	hop	**grape**
book	duck	**sale**
hat	**lake**	pin

plate	stop	brick
ant	paper	state

Encourage the children to think of other words with the long *a* sound. Finally, review the Long A card and the spellings that have been introduced.

* **Blending**　Have the children blend the following words and sentences. For additional suggestions for blending, see **Learning Framework Card 3.**

Line 1:　**April　able　paper　staple**

Line 2:　**late　skate　sale　whale**

Line 3:　**came　trade　shake　chase**

Line 4:　**mad　made　plan　plane**

Sentence 1:　**The table is made of maple.**

Sentence 2:　**Kate ate pancakes and bacon for supper.**

Sentence 3:　**Dale got skates and games at the yard sale.**

Words　Blend the words in line 1, syllable by syllable with the /ā/ sound at the end of the first syllable. (For example, A—pril, April) After the children blend the words in line 1, ask what they notice about the words. Point out that the words all have two syllables and that the *a* spelling for /ā/ occurs at the end of a syllable.

In line 2, build *late* as follows: Write *l* and ask the children what sound it makes. Then write *a_e* and blend through the vowel: /l/—/ā/, *lā.* Then write *t* in the blank and have the children say /t/. Blend the whole word. Repeat with the other words in the line. It is important to write the spelling *a_e* as a unit to signal the children to give the sound /ā/.

In line 4, contrast the short *a* and long *a* spelling patterns. Again, write *a_e* as a unit before having the children give the sound. Point out that *e* makes the vowel say its long sound. You may want to give other examples, such as *can* and *cane, cap* and *cape, at* and *ate.*

To review the words, play a game with a sponge die marked with numbers 1–4 and two stars. Tell children to choose a word line and to roll the die. The number on the die tells which word in the line to read. If a star is rolled, the child may read any word in the line.

Sentences　In sentence 2, help the children blend *pan* and *cakes* separately and then put the words together to make *pancakes.*

▶ Reading/Writing Connection, pages 86–87, reinforces the /ā/ sound spelled *a* and *a_e*. Have the children read and copy the words and the sentence on page 86. They can complete the sentences on page 87 by writing the correct word in each blank.

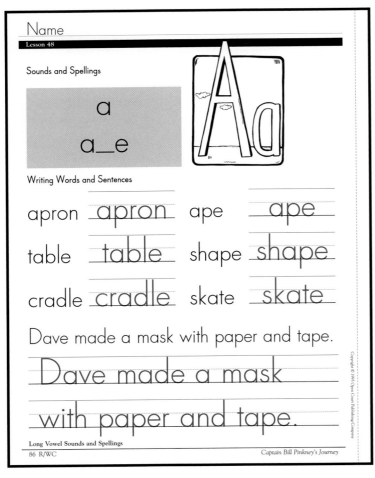

Reading/Writing Connection, page 86

Name _____

Lesson 48

Completing Sentences

1. Ted has a _cap_ on his head.

   cap
   cape

2. Pat fixed his model _plane_.

   plan
   plane

3. A whale _can_ swim.

   can
   cane

4. Mark _made_ muffins.

   mad
   made

5. Kate has a _fat_ kitten.

   fat
   fate

Decoding

Captain Bill Pinkney's Journey

R/WC 87

Reading/Writing Connection, page 87

✱ READING THE BIG BOOK

Captain Bill Pinkney's Journey
pages 3–32

Activating Prior Knowledge

Ask the children to recall some of the questions they had as they went through Big Book 3. Remind them of the list they made as they studied the many kinds of information contained in the book.

Recommendations for Reading

- Begin reading from the list of questions and wonderings you have kept throughout the reading, pausing after each one to give the children time to think about whether and how it has been answered.
- Call on volunteers to answer or comment. Whenever possible, have the children turn to a place in the book that gave the answer, point to it, and read whatever words they can.

Responding

Discuss how the children would celebrate the arrival of someone special. You might want to plan a class celebration. The children might want to pretend to welcome Captain Bill home, or to celebrate the completion of the Big Book. Discuss how they want to celebrate.

"Gull and Crane"
Story 25

Getting Ready to Read

Browsing the Story   Have the children assemble Step-by-Step Practice Story 25, "Gull and Crane." Select a child to read aloud the title of the story. Encourage the children to discuss anything they noticed about the story while putting it together.

Recommendations

Follow the standard procedure for reading a Step-by-Step Practice Story:

- Call on a different child to read each page of the story aloud. Pause after each page to discuss with the class anything interesting they noticed and to clarify any difficulties they encountered. Have a different child reread the page before going on.
- Reread the story at least twice, calling on different childen to read; then have the entire class read the story aloud chorally.

Responding

- Invite the children to discuss any questions they had about "Gull and Crane."
- To make sure the children are focusing on the words in the story, rather than simply on the pictures, have them answer the following questions by pointing to and reading aloud the words:

    Where did Gull and Crane wade?
    What did Gull and Crane eat?
    What did Crane's shape do when he waded into the lake?
    Where was Snake's nest?
    Why did Snake hate Gull and Crane?

- Invite volunteers to point out any words they can read.
- Call on volunteers to read entire sentences.
- Finally, have the children discuss what the story was about and what they liked about it.

Have the children pair up and read the story to each other.

TEACHING TIP

Set aside ten minutes for partner reading every day. During this time, you should read with individuals, recording their progress. Reading Assessment Sheets for Phonics Minibooks are available in *Assessment Masters, Grade 1.*

The following books tell about similarities among people from different countries. You may want to share one or more of these with your class.

Everybody Cooks Rice by Norah Dooley
We Celebrate Family Days by Bobbie Kalman, Susan Hughes, and
    Karen Harrison
*This Is the Way We Go to School: A Book About Children Around the
    World* by Edithe Baer

After reading, ask the children questions such as, "What did you find most interesting in this book? Why?" and "What did this book make you wonder about?"

For additional suggestions for reading aloud, see **Learning Framework Card 5.**

2 WRITING

✳ DICTATION AND SPELLING

Word-Building Game   Beginning with this lesson, the children are being introduced to long vowel spellings. Since these often require more than one letter, it is recommended that from this point on the children should use paper and pencil for the Word-Building game. Have the children write the words in a list as you write at the board. Allow time for the children to proofread and to correct their words before writing the next word in the list. Encourage the children to ask which vowel spelling to use to write a word if they are unsure. Use the following words for today's Word-Building game:

at
ate
late
plate
plane
plan
pan
pane

INDEPENDENT AND COLLABORATIVE WRITING

Review the list the children generated yesterday. Children may want to write letters, postcards, or even stories about something that happened on a trip. They might want to use Step-by-Step Practice Story 13, "My Trip," for a model. If children are writing letters, they may want to fold and address them. If the letters are for other children in the class, have the writer put the child's name on it. You may want to provide the address of the school for those children who want to write a full address. Remind the children that they may also choose to write in their journals.

If your class is planning a celebration, encourage the children to work on posters, flags, or banners.

As the children write, you may want to write a note of your own.

Hold Seminar and have several students share their writing. In preparation for the minilesson on spelling in the next lesson, find examples of consonant-vowel-consonant words that children have spelled incorrectly. Ask the children if you may use their sentences, then copy the sentences in their entirety.

TEACHING TIP

If you are setting up a mailbox in your class, you may want to designate a postal carrier for the day. It is this child's responsibility to check the mailbox that day and deliver any mail to others in the class.

3 GUIDED AND INDEPENDENT EXPLORATION

WORKSHOP

Remind the children that they may use this time to work on projects independently or in small groups. Be sure that each child knows what projects he or she may choose and how to complete any independent work. Suggestions for teacher-guided, collaborative, and independent activities follow.

Work with the Teacher

- Repeat today's Blending exercise with children who would benefit from additional practice distinguishing among the spellings of long and short *a*.
- Use flash cards to review outlaw words with small groups of children who are having trouble remembering them.
- Introduce Sound/Spelling Card 10, Jump Rope, and Step-by-Step Practice Story 26, "Jane and Jake," to those children who may benefit from extra practice with the new sound and spellings.

Independent Work

- Activity Sheet 48 provides practice with the /ā/ sound spelled *a* and *a_e*. Have the children read each sentence and write *yes* or *no* in the blank depending on whether the sentence describes what is shown in the picture. When they have finished labeling the sentences, the children can work together in pairs to change one of the "no" sentences into one that correctly describes the picture, or to write a sentence of their own. They can write their sentence on the back of this sheet.
- Challenge children to write and illustrate a sentence containing at least one long *a* and one short *a* word. Have them use words from the Blending exercise.
- Children may want to continue writing postcards and notes.

Student Collaboration

- Encourage pairs of children to reread Step-by-Step Practice Story 25. You may want to encourage peer tutoring by pairing independent readers with less fluent readers.
- Small groups of children may enjoy playing Go Fish! or a memory game using the Go Fish! rhyming-word cards. Prior to the start of Workshop, you might prepare some new cards containing recently taught sounds and spellings. For further information about these games, see **Games and Songs Teacher Tool Card 7.**
- Some children may want to form read-aloud groups. Each group can select a book and the group to read it aloud.

TEACHING TIP

Encourage the children to read to each other. You, too, should choose children to read with. As you read with each child, note his or her progress.

Home/School Connection

- Send home the take-home version of Phonics Minibook 7 and encourage the children to read it with their families.
- Home/School Connection 11 tells of the completion of *Captain Bill Pinkney's Journey.* You may want to send the letter home at this time.

Name

SACK RACE

Finish

	yes / no
1. A dog sits in the shade.	yes
2. A plane lands in the grass.	no
3. Nate swims in the lake.	yes
4. A cat tastes the cake.	no
5. A dog wins the race.	no
6. Grapes are on the table.	yes

Captain Bill Pinkney's Journey

Activity Sheet 48

LESSON 49

Lesson Overview

New Learning

- /j/ spelled **j** and **_dge**
- Proofreading for spelling

Materials

- "Jane and Jake," Step-by-Step Practice Story 26
- Sound/Spelling Card 10, Jump rope
- Learning Framework Cards 2, 3, 4, 5
- Reading/Writing Connection, pages 88–89
- Activity Sheet 49

Prepare Ahead

- Reading Relay Flash Cards (see page 187)
- Spider Game Webs (see page 187 and Games and Songs Teacher Tool Card 6)

GETTING STARTED

Choose one or both of the following activities to focus the children's attention and to review some of the concepts they have been learning.

Long Sound/Short Sound Spellings   Use this activity to help the children distinguish between the spellings for the long *a* and short *a* sounds. Have the students stand up, at least an arm's length from each other. On the chalkboard write one word at a time. Have the children read the word quietly to themselves. Tell them that if the word contains a long *a* sound, they should hold their arms out to their sides. If the word contains a short *a* sound, they should hold their hands close together in front of them. After the children have done this, ask them to read the word aloud together. You might want to use some of the following words:

add	shake	ask
fake	name	act
ape		

> **TEACHING TIP**
>
> Having the children wait until you give a signal before making their response will increase the effectiveness of this activity.

Riddle Me This Point to the Sound/Spelling Cards Gopher, Robot, Long A, and Popcorn, saying the name of each picture as you point, and ask the children to guess your word: *grape*. Have a volunteer point to the correct spelling of the long *a* sound in the word (*grape*) as you write the word on the chalkboard. Repeat the process for other words. After one or two examples, ask the riddle by naming the Sound/Spelling Cards without pointing to them. Use words such as the following:

- Ball, Long A, Camera *(bake)*
- Lion, Long A, Ball, Hen, Lion *(label)*
- Nose, Long A, Monkey *(name)*
- Gopher, Long A, Timer *(gate)*

1 READING

PHONICS

* **Introduce /j/ Spelled *j* and *_dge*** You may want to cover the spellings *ge* and *gi_* until they are introduced in a later lesson. Turn Sound/Spelling Card 10, Jump rope, and tell the children this is the Jump rope card. Read aloud the Jump rope story that follows. You can find the procedure for introducing a new sound and spelling on **Learning Framework Card 2.**

> When Jenny jumps her jump rope, it sounds like this:
> /j/ /j/ /j/ /j/ /j/.
> When Jackson jumps his jump rope, it sounds like this:
> /j/ /j/ /j/ /j/ /j/.
>
> The judges generally agree
> That Jenny jumps most rapidly: **(quickly)** /j/ /j/ /j/ /j/ /j/.
> When Jenny jumps, she jumps to this jingle:
> "Jump, jump, jump so quick.
> Whenever I jump, I like to kick." /j/ /j/ /j/ /j/ /j/.
>
> The judges generally agree
> That Jackson jumps most quietly: **(quietly)** /j/ /j/ /j/ /j/ /j/.
> When Jackson jumps, he jumps to this jingle:
> "Jump, jump, nice and quiet.
> See what happens when you try it." /j/ /j/ /j/ /j/ /j/.
>
> (To the children) Jump rope like Jenny. **(quickly)** /j/ /j/ /j/ /j/ /j/
> (To the children) Jump rope like Jackson. **(quietly)** /j/ /j/ /j/ /j/ /j/

Point to the *j* spelling on the card. Ask the children whether any of their names contain this letter. Write these names on the chalkboard and read them. Ask what other words they can think of that begin with this sound, and write these words on the board. Point out that the spelling *j* usually occurs at the beginning of a word.

Point to the _dge spelling and explain that this is another spelling for /j/. Ask the children what they notice about this spelling. If necessary, remind them that the green box means that a short vowel comes before this spelling and that this spelling is found at the end of a word or syllable.

Have the children tell how they can use this card to help with their reading and writing.

* **Blending**   Have the children blend the following words and sentences. For additional suggestions for blending, see **Learning Framework Card 3.**

Line 1:	Jan Jane Jack Jake
Line 2:	jam jar job jump
Line 3:	edge ledge hedge
Line 4:	fudge judge ridge bridge
Sentence 1:	Jim will make fudge for Jennifer.
Sentence 2:	The snake would not budge from under the hedge.
Sentence 3:	Jane wants a milkshake for a snack.

Ask the children why the words in line 1 all begin with capital letters. Have the children read all four names aloud. Ask which names have the short *a* sound and which have the long *a* sound. Draw attention to the *a_e* spelling pattern in the long *a* names.

In lines 2, 3, and 4, have the children circle the letters that spell the /j/ sound.

Words such as *hedge* and *ridge* may be unfamiliar to the children. Invite volunteers to use these words in sentences.

Review the words by asking the children to find and erase

- a name with a short *a* sound
- a word with the /ar/ sound
- words for two sweet things
- a word for something that goes across a river
- a word that rhymes with *Bob*

Encourage the children to give one another clues to review other words.

▶ Reading/Writing Connection, pages 88–89, provides additional practice with the /j/ sound spelled *j* and *_dge.* Help the children complete page 88 and the top of page 89.

Name

Sounds and Spellings

j
■dge

j
j

Writing Words and Sentences

job   job   juggle   juggle

judge   judge   badge   badge

Jake cut the tall hedge.

Jake cut the tall hedge.

Consonant Sounds and Spellings
88 R/WC   Captain Bill Pinkney's Journey

Reading/Writing Connection, page 88

Name

Reading and Writing Sentences

Jack's dad jogs across the bridge.

Jan jumps across the ditch.

Jack's dad jogs across the bridge.

Dictation and Spelling

Captain Bill Pinkney's Journey   Decoding/Spelling
                                                          R/WC 89

Reading/Writing Connection, page 89

✳ **READING A STEP-BY-STEP PRACTICE STORY**

"Jane and Jake"
Story 26

Getting Ready to Read
Browsing the Story   Have the children assemble Step-by-Step Practice Story 26, "Jane and Jake." Ask a child to read the title of the story. Encourage the children to discuss anything they noticed about the story. Tell the children that Jane and Jake are trolls and ask if they know any stories that have trolls.

Recommendations
Follow the procedure for reading a Step-by-Step Practice Story:
• Call on a different child to read each page of the story aloud. Pause after each page to discuss with the class anything interesting they have noticed and to clarify any difficulties they have encountered. Have a different child reread the page before going on.
• Reread the story at least twice, calling on different childen to read, and then have the entire class read the story aloud chorally.

Responding

- Invite the children to discuss any questions they had about "Jane and Jake."
- To make sure that the children are focusing on the words in the story rather than simply on the pictures, have the children point to and read aloud the words that answer these questions:

  What did Jane bake for Jake?

  Where did Jane put the fudge?

  Where was Jake sitting?

  What did Jane do to Jake with the jar?

  What did Jake say he should not do?

  What did Jane say she wished?

- Call on children to read entire sentences.
- Finally, have the children discuss what the story is about and what they like about it.

Have the children pair up and reread the story to each other.

✳ READING ALOUD

TEACHING TIP

Set aside ten minutes for partner reading every day. During this time, you should read with individuals, recording their progress. Reading Assessment Sheets for Phonics Minibooks are available in *Assessment Masters, Grade 1.*

Be sure to set aside time to read aloud to the children. All of the following books focus on difficult journeys. You may want to share one or more of these books with your class:

Amos and Boris by William Steig

Benji on His Own by Joan M. Lexau

Journey Cake, Ho by Ruth Sawyer

After reading, be sure to ask the children questions such as, "What did you find most interesting about this book? Why?"

See **Learning Framework Card 5** for additional suggestions for reading aloud.

2 WRITING

As the long vowel spellings are introduced and used in Dictation, be sure to have the children check the Sound/Spelling Cards for spellings. Remind the children that they may ask you which spelling to use in a given word if they are unsure. For example, with the word *bake,* the children could ask, "Which spelling of long *a* do we use?" Tell them, *"a blank e."* This would also be a good time to remind the children that the spelling *a* for long *a* usually occurs at the end of a syllable in a two syllable word.

✳ DICTATION AND SPELLING

Have the children turn to page 89 of their Reading/Writing Connection book. Dictate the following words and sentence, using the suggestions for dictation that appear on **Learning Framework Card 4.**

✎ **Line 1:**	ate gate
Line 2:	rake brake
Sentence:	Jake made a cake.

Minilesson

Proofreading: Spelling It Right

The children have been introduced to all of the short vowels and to most of the consonants. They have been doing proofreading during Dictation and Spelling. Today they will begin applying the concept of proofreading to their own writing. Explain that it will be easier for others to read their writing if words are spelled correctly, or close to correctly. Today they will start to check the spellings of words that contain the vowels and consonants they have learned so far. (The focus will be on consonant-vowel-consonant words with short vowel sounds.)

On the chalkboard or the overhead, write sample sentences from the children's work, including misspellings. If you would prefer not to use examples from the children's writing, make up sentences of your own. For example,

Dan is nt ht. (Dan is not hot.)

It is bd to jmp on the bad. (It is bad to jump on the bed.)

Explain to the children that they can use their knowledge about letters and sounds to proofread their own writing. Read the first sentence as it was intended (Dan is not hot.) Ask the children if they can tell whether any of the words are spelled incorrectly. Then ask them to examine each word with you to see if all its sounds have been spelled. By having the children blend *Dan* and *is,* confirm that they are spelled correctly. When the children try to blend *not,* ask them if every syllable must have a vowel and have them figure out what sound is missing. Remind them to check the Sound/Spelling Cards and have them try each vowel alternative if they are unsure which to choose. Continue through the sentence in this way, correcting each word as necessary. Read the corrected sentence aloud to confirm the spellings. Repeat with the second sentence.

At the end of the lesson, the children can proofread their own writing in the same way. They should check each word to make sure none of the sounds are missing.

TEACHING TIP

Omissions of vowels and suffixes are among the most frequent errors in early spellings.

3 GUIDED AND INDEPENDENT EXPLORATION

WORKSHOP

Remind the children that they may use this time to work on projects on their own or in small groups. Be sure that each child knows what projects he or she may choose and how to complete any independent work. Suggestions for teacher-guided, collaborative, and independent activites follow.

Work with the Teacher

- Repeat today's Blending exercise with individuals or small groups of children. Encourage them to read whole words rather than blending the words sound by sound. Use this opportunity to assess the children's progress.
- Prepare flash cards to review /j/ spelled *j* and *_dge*. To these cards add some of the /ch/ and /k/ flash cards used in Lesson 17. Use the cards to have a Reading Relay with two teams of children.
- Have independent readers select books to read to you. Invite other children to listen in.

Independent Work

- Activity Sheet 49 has the children use pictures to help them put sentences in correct story order.
- Invite children to copy, extend, and illustrate a sentence from today's Blending lesson. Get them started by suggesting that they answer a question such as *how, where,* or *why*. Remind them that the Sound/Spelling Cards can help them spell unfamiliar words.
- Remind the children that they may always use this time to read on their own. Encourage them to revisit favorite Big Book selections or to select books from the classroom library.

Student Collaboration

- Encourage pairs of children to reread Step-by-Step Practice Story 26. When they have finished reading, they should return to the story and copy down all of the long *a* words and the /j/ words, then underline the letter or letters in each word that spell the target sound.
- Pairs or groups of children might enjoy playing the Spider game. Prior to Workshop, you should prepare some new webs, using sounds and spellings the children have learned recently. For further information, see **Games and Songs Teacher Tool Card 6**.
- Pairs or groups may want to continue working on their posters, banners, flags, or other projects for their celebration.

TEACHING TIP

Encourage the children to read to each other. You, too, should choose children to read with. As you read with each child, note his or her progress.

Home/School Connection

Send home Step-by-Step Practice Story 25 and encourage the children to read it to their families. In the book of Step-by-Step Practice Stories, you will find a letter to accompany this story.

Name

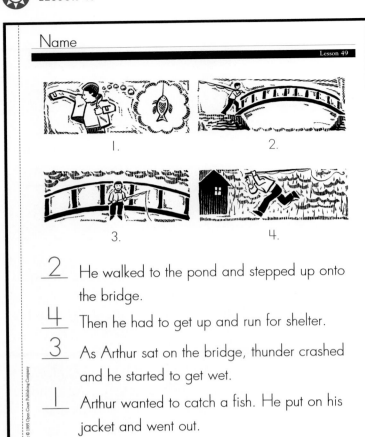

1.   2.

3.   4.

__2__ He walked to the pond and stepped up onto the bridge.

__4__ Then he had to get up and run for shelter.

__3__ As Arthur sat on the bridge, thunder crashed and he started to get wet.

__1__ Arthur wanted to catch a fish. He put on his jacket and went out.

Activity Sheet 49

LESSON
50

Lesson Overview

New Learning

- /j/ spelled *ge* and *gi_*

Materials

- "Magic Pages," Step-by-Step Practice Story 27
- Sound/Spelling Card 10, Jump Rope
- Learning Framework Cards 3, 5
- Reading/Writing Connection, pages 90–91
- Activity Sheet 50

Prepare Ahead

- Reading Relay Flash Cards (see page 194 and Games and Songs Teacher Tool Card 9)
- Scrambled Sentences Game (see page 194 and Games and Songs Teacher Tool Card 8)

GETTING STARTED

Choose one or both of the following activities to focus the children's attention and to review some of the concepts they have been learning.

Sound Review   Name a Sound/Spelling Card and have the children say the sound the card represents. Call on a child to say a word that contains the sound and to tell where the sound is heard in the word. Repeat with other cards.

Dictate to the Teacher   Writer the word *at* on the chalkboard and have the children read it. Then ask them how to change this word to *ate.* Continue having the children write the following words. Have them read each word.

gate	mad
game	made
same	mane
Sam	man
sad	

1 READING

✱ **Introduce /j/ Spelled *ge* and *gi*_**   Use the Sound/Spelling Card 10, Jump Rope, and briefly review the sound and the *j* and _*dge* spellings. Uncover or indicate the *ge* and *gi*_ spellings and tell the children that these are two other spellings for the /j/ sound. Ask the children what sound *g* usually makes. Explain that when the letter *g* is followed by *e* or *i* it often says /j/. Discuss that the blank after *gi* indicates that this spelling is not found at the end of a word. Write the words *geranium, giant,* and *geography* on the chalkboard and pronounce each one. Ask what sound the children hear at the beginning of each word. Then point out that each of these words begins with *ge* or *gi.*

✱ **Blending**   Have the children blend the following words and sentences. For additional suggestions for blending, see **Learning Framework Card 3.**

Line 1:	gem gentle gingerbread magic
Line 2:	age page cage rage
Line 3:	badge badger gadget
Line 4:	gift gill giggle get
Sentence 1:	Giraffes are large and gentle.
Sentence 2:	The gems glitter in the sun.
Sentence 3:	The man on the stage did a magic trick.

Words   In order to help the children identify that the *g* stands for the /j/ sound in the words in line 1, write the whole word for the children to blend, rather than building each word spelling by spelling.

In line 2, you may want to point out that the *e* has two jobs—it makes the *a* say its name and it makes the *g* say /j/.

In line 4, the children will see that not all words with *ge* or *gi* say /j/. Tell the children that they may have to try both sounds for *g* when they are blending a new word. Then they will have to decide which sound makes sense. Demonstrate by blending the first word as *jift* and then as *gift*. Ask which is a real word.

Some children may be unfamiliar with the words *badger, gadget, ginger, gem,* and *gill.* Ask volunteers who think they know what these words mean to use them in sentences.

Review the words by asking the children to find

- a word in which the *ge* makes a /g/ sound
- a word in which *gi* makes a /g/ sound
- a word in which *ge* makes a /j/ sound
- a word in which *gi* makes a /j/ sound
- an animal
- a part of a fish

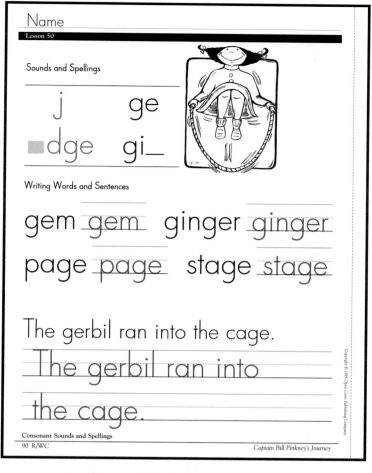

Reading/Writing Connection, page 90

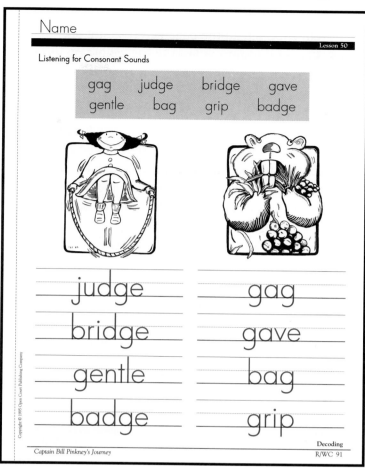

Reading/Writing Connection, page 91

▶ Reading/Writing Connection, pages 90–91, reinforces the /j/ sound spelled *ge* and *gi_*. Have the children blend and copy the words and sentence on page 90. Then, on page 91, help them write the listed words in the correct column, depending on whether they hear the /j/ or /g/ sound in each word.

✳ READING A STEP-BY-STEP PRACTICE STORY

"Magic Pages"
Story 27

Getting Ready to Read
Browsing the Story   Have the children assemble Step-by-Step Practice Story 27, "Magic Pages." Ask a child to read the title of the story. Encourage the children to discuss anything they noticed about the story while putting it together.

Recommendations
Follow the standard procedure for reading a Step-by-Step Practice Story:
• Call on a different child to read each page of the story aloud. Pause after each page to discuss with the class anything interesting they

TEACHING TIP

If the children have trouble deciding which pronunciation of *g* to use to blend a word, have them try both sounds and then decide which way makes sense.

noticed and to clarify any difficulties they encountered. Have a different child reread the page before going on.

- Reread the story at least twice, calling on different children to read, then have the entire class read the story aloud chorally.

Responding

- Invite the children to discuss any questions they had about this story.
- To make sure the children are focusing on the words in the story, rather than simply on the pictures, have them point to and read aloud the words that answer the following questions:

  What can the child in the story do when she turns her magic pages?

  What can she do with a whale?

  What can she do with large snakes?

  Where is the child at the end of the story?

- Invite volunteers to point out any words they can read.
- Call on children to read entire sentences.
- Finally, have the children discuss what the story was about and what they liked about it.

Have the children pair up and reread the story with a partner.

✳ READING ALOUD

Be sure to set aside time later in the day to read to the children. The following books tell about fantasy voyages. You might want to share one or more of these books with the children.

Boatride with Lillian Two Blossom by Patricia Polacco

Commander Toad in Space by Jane Yolen

Where the Wild Things Are by Maurice Sendak

After reading, be sure to ask the children such questions as "What did you like best about this book? Why?" and "What did you find most surprising in this book?"

For additional suggestions for reading aloud, see **Learning Framework Card 5.**

TEACHING TIP

Remind the children to read each book twice. When they finish today's book, they should get one from a previous lesson. Reading Assessment Sheets for Phonics Minibooks are available in *Assessment Masters, Grade 1.*

2 WRITING

✱ DICTATION AND SPELLING

Word-Building Game   Have the children use their own paper for the Word-Building game. Say each word, then write it on the chalkboard or an overhead transparency. Before writing each word, allow time for the children to write it on their own. Encourage the children to ask for help with spellings if they need it. Use the following words for today's lesson:

tape

ape

age

page

cage

wage

wake

Jake

Proofread the words as usual. Ask the children why *Jake* begins with a capital letter.

INDEPENDENT AND COLLABORATIVE WRITING

If your class is planning a celebration, have the children continue working on their projects. Plan to set aside time for the celebration during the next lesson, or children may continue writing postcards, writing a note to a friend, writing in their journals, or they may start a new piece.

Another idea that children may want to explore for writing is making a map. Discuss with the class how Captain Bill Pinkney used a map on his trip and how they were able to follow his trip around the world with a map. Discuss the possibility of making maps of the school, of the children's routes home, of the children's homes, or a room in the house. Ask the children about other kinds of maps, for example, maps for a treasure hunt that help you find some thing rather than some place. Talk with the children about what kinds of things they would include on these maps.

Meet with children and provide support as needed. If any children are still drawing rather than writing, encourage them to label their pictures. You may want to meet with groups of children to help them proofread their work by checking for the correct spelling of simple three-letter words.

> **TEACHING TIP**
> The children may enjoy seeing how many words they can form starting with *ake* or *age* and adding or deleting one spelling at a time.

3 GUIDED AND INDEPENDENT EXPLORATION

WORKSHOP

Remind the children that they may use this time to work on projects on their own or in small groups. Make sure each child knows what projects he or she may choose and how to complete any independent work. Suggestions for teacher-guided, collaborative, and independent activities follow.

Work with the Teacher

- Review the words and sentences from today's Blending exercise with those children who seemed confused during the initial teaching. Encourage them to extend the sentences or to make up their own sentences using some of the words.
- Make flash cards for words containing the sounds /j/ spelled *ge* and *gi_* and /g/ spelled *g*. Add them to yesterday's *j* and *_dge* cards and use them to hold a Reading Relay between two teams of children or simply to work with children who might benefit from the practice.
- Listen to children reread Step-by-Step Practice Story 27.

Independent Work

- For Activity Sheet 50, the children can complete the sentences by writing the correct spelling of each word in the blank provided.
- Invite the children to create nonsense sentences containing words from today's Blending lesson. Have the children illustrate their silly sentences and label the items in their pictures with the appropriate words, particularly those words with the /j/ and /ā/ sounds.

Student Collaboration

- Encourage the children to pair up and reread Step-by-Step Practice Story 27. Remind the pairs to follow the usual turn-taking procedure. When they finish reading, the partners can select a trade book to read or browse together.
- Have groups or pairs play Scrambled Sentences. You might want to prepare new sentences for them, using recently introduced sounds and spellings. When they finish playing, the children can prepare their own scrambled sentences for others to unscramble. Give them some index cards and an envelope. Tell them to think up a sentence, print each word on a separate index card, and place the cards inside the envelope. On the inside flap of the envelope, they should print an answer key. (To ensure that they are able to prepare a scrambled sentence on their own, have them use the game they just unscrambled as a model.) They may finish their work during tomorrow's Workshop if time runs out today.

TEACHING TIP
Encourage the children to read to each other. You, too, should choose children to read with. As you read with each child, note his or her progress.

Home/School Connection

Send home Step-by-Step Practice Story 26 for the children to share with their families.

Name

1. Germs can make you

   __sick__ .

   | sic |
   | sick |

2. Does the duck watch her

   __eggs__ ?

   | eggs |
   | eggz |

3. You can bake a

   __cake__ in the kitchen.

   | cak |
   | cake |

4. The __little__ girl

   runs fast.

   | littl |
   | little |

5. Can I snack on

   __fudge__ ?

   | fuge |
   | fudge |

Activity Sheet 50   *Captain Bill Pinkney's Journey*

Activity Sheet 50

LESSON 51

Lesson Overview

New Learning

- /ī/ spelled *i* and *i_e*

Materials

- "A Fine Parade," Step-by-Step Practice Story 28
- Sound/Spelling Card 34, Long I
- Learning Framework Cards 3, 4, 5
- Reading/Writing Connection, pages 92–93
- Activity Sheet 51
- Index cards from Lesson 47

Prepare Ahead

- Bingo materials (see page 201 and Games and Songs Teacher Tool Card 5)
- "Eye" poster boards (see page 201)

GETTING STARTED

Choose one or both of the following activities to focus the children's attention and to review some of the concepts they have been learning.

Tic-Tac-Toe   Make two different Tic-Tac-Toe grids on the chalkboard. Place the spellings *th, ch,* and *sh* on the grid. You might use the following patterns:

th	sh	sh		ch	sh	ch
sh	th	ch		th	th	ch
ch	th	ch		sh	sh	th

Have the children say each sound as you point to it. Then divide the children into two teams. Call out words containing these sounds. One person from each team goes to the chalkboard, locates the spelling, and crosses it out. The first team to fill a horizontal line completes the game.

Words to call out are

think	church	tenth
month	show	chalk
munch	thousand	rich
show	watch	shell
with	splash	chin

A Tisket, a Tasket Game   Give the traveler a basket with the index cards used during Workshop in Lesson 47. Follow the same procedure for playing A Tisket, a Tasket as in previous lessons.

1 READING

PHONICS

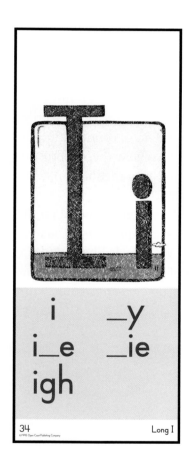

✱ **Introduce /ī/ Spelled _i_ and _i_e_**   Turn Sound/Spelling Card 34, Long I, and ask the children what they remember about cards like this one. If necessary, remind them that the picture of the long thin _i_ means that this card is the Long I card and that the spellings all say /ī/. Have the children repeat the sound. The procedure for introducing long vowels follows.

- To reinforce the long _i_ sound, have the children sing "Apples and Bananas" using the /ī/ sound in the verse.
- Contrast short _i_ and long _i_ by pointing to the Pig card and having the children say the sound. Have the children say the following ryhme with you:

I's my name,
Two sounds have I:
Short _i_ in **pig**,
Long _i_ in **pie**.

- Point to the spellings _i_ and _i_e_ on the Long I card. Have the children say /ī/ as you point to each spelling. Ask the children what the blank in the _i_e_ spelling means. If necessary explain that a consonant goes in the blank in words. Explain that the _e_ helps _i_ say its name.
- Encourage the children to think of words that contain the /ī/ sound.
- Review the card and the spellings _i_ and _i_e_ and ask how this card can help the children read and write.

✱ **Blending**   Have the children blend the following words and sentences. For additional suggestions for blending, see **Learning Framework Card 3.**

Line 1:	I'm I'll find wild
Line 2:	spider tiger giant gigantic
Line 3:	bike lime smile shine
Line 4:	bit bite hid hide
Sentence 1:	Jill hiked nine miles up <u>the</u> hill.
Sentence 2:	Nick's bike and wagon <u>are</u> inside <u>the</u> shed.
Sentence 3:	<u>The</u> wild tiger cannot escape.

Words   In line 1, point out the contractions and tell the children what they stand for. Explain that the apostrophe is used to take the place of missing letters. Write *I am* under *I'm* and read the words. Ask what letter is missing. Do the same with *I will* under *I'll.*

Blend the words in line 2 syllable by syllable with the *i* at the end of the first syllable. *(spi—der, spider)*

In lines 3 and 4, it is important to write the *i_e* spelling as a unit. For example, write and blend *bike* as follows: Write *b,* then have the children give the sound. Write *i_e,* then have the children give the sound and blend through the vowel (bī). Write *k* between *i* and *e* and blend *bike.* Blend the other words in the same way.

In line 4, contrast the short *i* and long *i* spellings.

To review these words, use them in oral sentences, emphasizing the word from the lines. Ask the children to find, say, and erase the word each time:

- The *spider* crawled on the wall.
- A mosquito *bite* is itchy.
- My friends like to *hide* in the yard.
- The clown has a big *smile.*
- The *giant tiger* ran swiftly.
- *I'll* ride my *bike* today.

Sentences   In sentence 2, review the use of *'s* to show that the bike belongs to Nick. For sentence 3, point out the contraction *can't* and show the children how it is made from *cannot.*

❯ Reading/Writing Connection, pages 92–93, reinforce the /ī/ sound spelled *i* and *i_e.* Help the children complete page 92 and the top of page 93.

✳ READING THE BIG BOOK

Captain Bill Pinkney's Journey

Recommendations

If your class has planned a celebration for the conclusion of *Captain Bill Pinkney's Journey,* set aside time for the celebration.

Name
Lesson 51

Sounds and Spellings

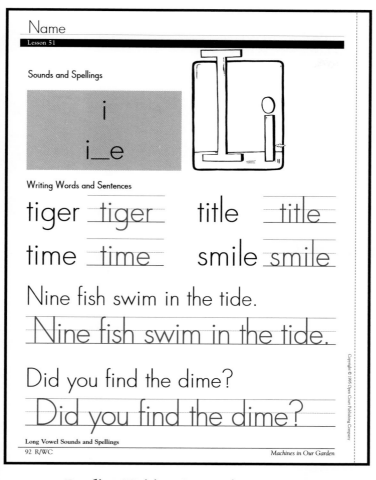

i

i_e

Writing Words and Sentences

tiger _tiger_   title _title_

time _time_   smile _smile_

Nine fish swim in the tide.

Nine fish swim in the tide.

Did you find the dime?

Did you find the dime?

Long Vowel Sounds and Spellings
92 R/WC   Machines in Our Garden

Reading/Writing Connection, page 92

Name
Lesson 51

Completing Sentences

1. I like to _ride_ a bike.   rid / ride

2. Did you _rip_ the page?   rip / ripe

3. Dad made a _fine_ dinner.   fin / fine

4. The man was gentle and _kind_. kin / kind

Dictation and Spelling

Machines in Our Garden   Decoding/Spelling
                                     R/WC 93

Reading/Writing Connection, page 93

✻ READING A STEP-BY-STEP PRACTICE STORY

"A Fine Parade"
Story 28

Getting Ready to Read

Call on a volunteer to read the title of the book aloud. Encourage the children to browse through the book, commenting on any words or illustrations that catch their eye.

Recommendations

- Call on volunteers to read the story aloud as the others follow along. Change readers every two or three sentences.
- Have the children reread the story aloud at least twice, with different children reading. After every two or three sentences, have the children tell what words they have found with the long *i* and the short *i* sound.

Responding

- Ask the children to tell in their own words what happened in the story.

- Have the children point out any words in the selection that were difficult. Have them explain how they figured out these words.
- To help the children focus on the text, have them point out words that answer questions such as the following:

What did Tina ride?

What did Emma ride?

Who pulled April in the wagon?

How does Spike feel about parades?

What did April say about Spike after he found her kite?

Have children reread the story with a partner.

✳ READING ALOUD

Since this is the final lesson dealing with *Captain Bill Pinkney's Journey*, you might review previous lessons for books that you have not yet read to the children. Choose any titles that you think the children might enjoy.

See **Learning Framework Card 5** for suggestions for modeling as you read aloud.

2 WRITING

✳ DICTATION AND SPELLING

Have the children turn to page 93 of their Reading/Writing Connection book. Dictate the following words and sentence, using the suggestions for dictation that appear on **Learning Framework Card 4.**

Line 1:	page stage
Line 2:	ridge bridge
Sentence:	Ginger ate fudge cake.

Help the children proofread each line.

COLLABORATIVE AND INDEPENDENT WRITING

Begin with Seminar, having children share their writing in progress. Any children who drew maps may share them. For children who may still be drawing, take notes on what they talk about during Seminar. Meet with them after Seminar and suggest that they either try to write some of the words they used when they shared their work, or copy some of the words from your notes onto their paper.

Have the children continue working on their pieces. If any children are ready to publish their work, meet with them to revise and proofread their stories. Suggest that they continue preparing their pieces during Workshop.

3 GUIDED AND INDEPENDENT EXPLORATION

WORKSHOP

Remind the children that they may use this time to work on projects of their own or in small groups. Be sure that each child knows what projects he or she may choose and how to complete any independent work. Suggestions for teacher-guided, collaborative, and independent activities follow.

Work with the Teacher

- Assess the children's reading ability, or provide support for those needing it, by listening to children reread Step-by-Step Practice Story 28.
- Play the Word-Building game with individuals or small groups to review the long *i* sound and spellings. Have the children build words on the chalkboard or scratch paper using word lists such as:

kind	mind	find	fine	fin	fan
hid	hide	side	slide	slid	lid
Mike	bike	trike	Spike		

- Play Bingo with small groups of children to review the sounds and spellings they have learned in recent lessons. Prepare Bingo cards and a word list that include the spellings *a_e, i_e, j, _dge, ge, gi_, c, k*, and *_ck*.

Independent Work

- Activity Sheet 51 provides practice with the /ī/ sound spelled *i* and *i_e*. Have the children read each sentence and write *yes* or *no* in the blank depending on whether the sentence correctly describes what is shown in the picture. When they have finished labeling the sentences, the children can work together in pairs to rewrite one of the "no" sentences so that it correctly describes the picture, or they can write a sentence of their own on the back of this sheet.
- Write the following endings on the chalkboard: *-ike, -ide, -ite, -ind, -ine*. Invite children to see how many words they can build by adding different initial letters and letter combinations to these

endings. Tell the children to save their lists for an activity to be completed during tomorrow's Workshop.
- Remind the children that they may use this time to read or browse the books of their choice.
- Some children may want to work on publishing a piece of writing.

Student Collaboration

- Invite pairs of children to reread Step-by-Step Practice Story 28. Encourage peer tutoring. Pair independent readers with less-fluent readers.
- Have pairs of children use small copies of *Animals* or *Look Who's Reading!* and revisit two or three favorite selections. Challenge them to locate and copy all the words in those selections that contain the long *i* sound.
- Cut two sheets of poster board into the shape of eyes. Have small groups of children decorate them with drawings and magazine cutouts of /ī/ items. Encourage them to label as many of the items as they can. When they are done drawing and pasting, the children can adorn the eyes with construction-paper lashes.

TEACHING TIP

Encourage the children to read to each other. You, too, should choose children to read with. As you read with each child, note his or her progress.

Home/School Connection

- Have the children take home Step-by-Step Practice Story 27 to read to their families.

Name

yes / no

1. Mike hides behind a tree.   yes

2. Nine mice ride a bike.   no

3. A chimp licks grape ice.   no

4. The twins ride a slide.   yes

5. Ira flies a kite.   yes

6. A fish smiles at the child.   no

Machines in Our Garden   Activity Sheet 51

Activity Sheet 51

LESSON
52

●●● Lesson Overview

New Learning

- /s/ spelled *ce, ci_*

Materials

- *Machines in Our Garden*
- "Spice Cake," Step-by-Step Practice Story 29
- Sound/Spelling Card 19, Sausages
- Learning Framework Cards 3, 5
- Reading/Writing Connection, pages 94–95
- Outlaw Word Flash Cards
- Activity Sheet 52
- Home/School Connection 12

GETTING STARTED

Choose one or both of the following activities to focus the children's attention and to review some of the concepts they have been learning.

Team Words Have the children sit in teams, making sure that each team has a sheet of paper. Write the word *like* on the chalkboard and have the first member of each team copy the word on the team's paper. The child should then pass the paper to the next person on the team, who should write a new word by changing one sound from the previous word. The paper should be passed until each member of the team has written a word. Have the teams compare their lists, by either writing the lists on the board or by having the first person read the list aloud.

Review /j/ Spellings Write the words that follow on the chalkboard. Then give the clues and have children find and read aloud a word that fits. More than one word may be selected for some clues.

judge	badge	page	just
jam	give	gentle	giggle
stage	giraffe	joke	gum

Which word begins and ends with /j/?
Find a word that has /j/ spelled *dge.*
Which word has /j/ spelled *gi?*
Find a word that has the /g/ sound.
Find a word that has /j/ spelled *ge.*

1 READING

PHONICS

* **Introduce /s/ Spelled *ce* and *ci_*** Point to Sound/Spelling Card 19, Sausages, and ask the children what sound the spelling *s* makes. Tell them that there are other ways to spell the /s/ sound. Uncover or point to the spellings *ce* and *ci_* on the card and explain that when *c* is followed by *e* or *i* it says /s/.

   You might want to tell the children that we call /s/ the soft sound of letter *c.* Ask what other consonant sound is usually changed by *e* and *i.*

* **Blending** Have the children blend the following words and sentences. For additional suggestions for blending, see **Learning Framework Card 3**.

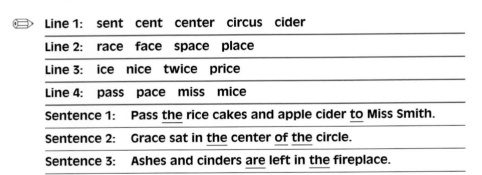

Line 1:	sent cent center circus cider
Line 2:	race face space place
Line 3:	ice nice twice price
Line 4:	pass pace miss mice
Sentence 1:	Pass the rice cakes and apple cider to Miss Smith.
Sentence 2:	Grace sat in the center of the circle.
Sentence 3:	Ashes and cinders are left in the fireplace.

Words In line 1, write each whole word, rather than build the words spelling by spelling, so that the children can see that the *c* in these words will say /s/. Have the children pick out the homophones *sent* and *cent* and use each word in a sentence.

   In lines 2–4, be sure to write the *a_e* and *i_e* spellings as a unit when writing the words.

   After blending the words in lines 2 and 3, ask the children why the vowels in each line make the long *a* or long *i* sound. Point out that the *e* makes the vowel say its name and also makes the *c* say /s/.

   In line 4, contrast the short and long vowel spelling patterns.

   To review the words, point to them one at a time and ask the children to use them in sentences. You may need to explain *cider* and *pace* beforehand.

Reading/Writing Connection, page 94

Reading/Writing Connection, page 95

▶ Reading/Writing Connection, pages 94–95, reinforces the /s/ sound spelled *ce* and *ci_*. Have the children read and copy the words and sentences on page 94. Then, on page 95, help the children write the listed words in the correct column, depending on whether they hear the /s/ or /k/ sound in each word.

✳ **READING THE BIG BOOK**

Machines in Our Garden

About the Selection

Machines in Our Garden tells the story of Ignatz and Olga, two best friends who want to plant a super tomato garden. To accomplish this, they need to lift heavy objects, transport things uphill, post a sign, trim hedges, plant seeds, and water their garden. For all of these tasks, Ignatz and Olga find that they need the help of simple machines. Planting their garden provides them with the opportunity to discover how many of these machines work.

Link to the Unit Concept

Almost everything we do requires work, and work requires effort, or energy. Machines enable people to perform work they would otherwise be unable to do or to perform work with less expenditure of energy. Many of the simple machines people use may not seem to be machines to the children, who are accustomed to seeing high-powered machines bulldozing huge amounts of dirt for road building or other construction projects. In *Machines in Our Garden*, the children will discover along with Ignatz and Olga that many of the tools people use every day are actually simple machines that, in combination, make up complex machines.

About the Author/Illustrator

Jan Adkins is an artist, a storyteller, an explainer, a father, a cook, a sailor, and many other things. He is the author/illustrator of more than 20 books of fiction and non-fiction for children, young adults, and adults. His books for children include *String*, *Workboats,* and the award-winning *Heavy Equipment*. Formerly the art director for *The National Geographic*, he now takes on freelance projects that allow him to illustrate and explain some of his many interests to others.

Activating Prior Knowledge

- Display the cover of *Machines in Our Garden* and read the title aloud, pointing to each word.
- Discuss with the children what they might learn from this book. Make the point that this book gives information. Encourage children to tell about other books they know that give information.

Recommendations for Reading

You will not read from the Big Book in this lesson. Tell the children that you will begin reading tomorrow. Explain that as you read this book together you will learn about machines.

Ask the children to think of machines that are part of their everyday world, for example, cars, washing machines, tools. Make a list of these machines on chart paper to refer to throughout the reading of the book. Tell the children that they will be adding to this list as they read Big Book 4, *Machines in Our Garden*.

TEACHING TIP
Make sure the children know that they can add to this list whenever they wish.

✱ READING A STEP-BY-STEP PRACTICE STORY

"Spice Cake"
Story 29

Getting Ready to Read

- Call on a volunteer to read aloud the title of the book.
- Encourage the children to browse through the book, commenting on any words or illustrations that catch their eye.

Recommendations

- Call on volunteers to read the story aloud as the others follow along. Change readers after every page.

- Have the story read aloud at least three times. After the first reading, vary the oral reading pattern by allowing volunteers to choose whether to read the next page in the selection or to reread the page just read.

Responding

- Have children retell in their own words what happened in the story.
- Ask the children to point out any words that they found interesting or difficult to understand. Discuss the words they indicate.
- To focus the children's attention on the text rather than the illustrations, have the children point out the appropriate words in the text to answer these questions:

  What does the mouse think is wrong with the spice cake?
  How much apple does the mouse put in?
  What does the mouse do when he has added all the ingredients?

Have the children reread the story with a partner.

✴ READING ALOUD

There are many books for children that explain machines. You might want to read one or both of the following aloud:
Simple Machines by Anne Horvatic
The Toolbox by Anne and Harlow Rockwell

See **Learning Framework Card 5** for suggestions for modeling as you read aloud.

> **TEACHING TIP**
>
> Set aside ten minutes for partner reading every day. During this time, you should read with individuals, recording their progress. Reading Assessment Sheets for Phonics Minibooks are available in *Assessment Masters, Grade 1*.

2 WRITING

✴ DICTATION AND SPELLING

Word-Building Game Have the children use pencil and paper for the Word-Building game. Since this exercise focuses on long *i* spellings, you may want to quickly review the Long I card before having the children spell the words. Write the words on the board as the children write on paper. Have the children proofread and correct each word before writing the next word in the list. Use the following words:

hid
hide
ride
rid
rip
ripe
rice
mice
mile
smile

Explain to the children that the author wrote *Machines in Our Garden* to help the reader learn about machines that are part of our daily life. Tell the children that some authors write stories that they make up. Other authors write about real things. Ask what kind of story—real or made up—*Captain Bill Pinkney's Journey* was. Ask if the children know of any other books that give information.

Discuss what things the children know that they could tell someone about. Some children may have information about sports, how to take care of pets, or how to make things. Display chart paper and start a list of some of the children's ideas. Keep the list for Writing in the next lesson.

TEACHING TIP

Based upon the interests of your class, you may want to start collecting books on topics the children have listed to use as resources for Writing and Workshop. Encourage children who have books on these topics or any other interesting topics to bring them in to share with the class.

3 GUIDED AND INDEPENDENT EXPLORATION

W O R K S H O P

Remind the children that they may use this time to work on projects of their own or in small groups. Be sure that each child knows what projects he or she may choose and how to complete any independent work. Suggestions for teacher-guided, collaborative, and independent activities follow.

Work with the Teacher

- Listen to children reread Step-by-Step Practice Story 29.
- Make long *i, i_e, ce, ci,* and *s* word flash cards. Add to them some of the flash cards used to review other spellings in previous lessons. Use the cards to work with children who might benefit from the review.

Independent Work

- Activity Sheet 52 reviews /ī/ and /i/ sounds and spellings. Explain to the children that a kite needs a tail to fly. Often a kite tail has pieces of rag tied to it. Tell the children that they can make their own kite to hang on the wall with this activity sheet. Supply them with a 24" piece of yarn or string, and have them write the word *kite* on the diamond-shaped *body* of the kite. Tell the children to color the ties containing long *i* words yellow, and ties containing short *i* words green. Encourage them to color the body of the kite any way they like. Then have them cut out the ties and body, glue the ties along the yarn, and tape the kite's tail to the back of its body.
- Children who made lists of long *i* words in the previous lesson can circle all the rhyming words, and exchange lists with a partner for proofreading. When all of the rhyming words have been proofread and corrected, the children can copy them as neatly as possible onto index cards and add them to the Go Fish! card decks.

Student Collaboration

- Have pairs of children reread Step-by-Step Practice Story 29. Ask them to copy all the words that contain the sounds /s/, /ī/, or both. Tell them to underline the letter or letters that make the target sounds.
- Children can use flash cards to review outlaw words with a partner. Encourage peer tutoring by pairing a more independent reader with a less fluent reader. Tell the children that when each partner has read every flash card, they should write two or three sentences with outlaw words and underline the outlaw words in each sentence.

Home/School Connection

- Home/School Connection 12 tells about *Machines in Our Garden* and suggests related books that the children and their families might read together. You might want to send it home at this time.

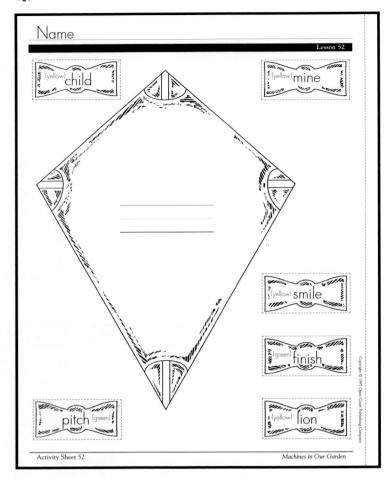

Activity Sheet 52

LESSON 53

Lesson Overview

Materials

- *Machines in Our Garden*, pages 2–32
- Phonics Minibook 9, *The Spider Club*
- Learning Framework Cards 3, 4, 5
- Reading Writing Connection, pages 96–97
- Activity Sheet 53

Prepare Ahead

- Sponge die (see page 212)
- Go Fish! cards (see page 221)

GETTING STARTED

Choose one or both of the following activities to focus the children's attention and to review some of the concepts they have been learning.

Dictate to the Teacher Write the word *mad* on the chalkboard and call on a child to read it. Then have the children tell you how to change the word to make the following series of words:

made	pine
make	pin
Mike	fin
mile	fine
smile	mine
pile	

Substituting a Sound Say the word *race* and have the children repeat it. Ask what vowel sound they hear. Then ask them to say a new word by changing the long *a* sound to long *i (rice)*. Pronounce other words, then have the children make new words by substituting the long *i* sound for the vowel sound in the word. Suggested words follow:

Kate	rode	lake
rope	lone	dune
shone	pan	tame

1 READING

PHONICS

* **Blending** Have the children blend the following words and sentences. For additional suggestions for blending, see **Learning Framework Card 3.**

Line 1:	stable racer mistake awake
Line 2:	lion inside spider bedtime
Line 3:	comet happen rubber pencil
Line 4:	cradle candle diner dinner
Sentence 1:	The small piglets were in the wet mud in the barnyard.
Sentence 2:	An octopus has eight arms.
Sentence 3:	Jack dusted the table until it was spotless.

Words The words in line 1 have two syllables, one with the long *a* sound. Ask the children to identify the syllable that has the long *a* sound. The children may need help blending *awake.* Blend the first syllable as long *a.* The children will adjust their pronunciation when they blend and recognize the word.

The words in line 2 contain two syllables, one with the long *i* sound.

Line 3 reviews two-syllable words with short vowel spellings. Blend *comet* as *com—et.*

The words in line 4 contrast long and short vowel spellings. To demonstrate, say the two words *cradle* and *candle,* passing your hand beneath each word as you say it. Ask which word has the long *a* sound and which has the short *a* sound. Repeat the procedure with the words *diner* and *dinner,* separating the syllables as you say each word. Point out that when the vowel sound occurs at the end of a syllable, it usually makes a long sound; when it occurs in the middle of a syllable, it usually makes the short sound.

To review the words, play a game with a die cut from a sponge. Print the numbers 1–4 on the die, then draw stars on the two empty sides. Tell the children to choose a word line and roll the die. They should read the word in the line that corresponds to the number they roll. If they roll a star, they can choose to read any word in the line, or all the words in the line.

Sentences Introduce outlaw words *were* and *eight* before writing the sentences. Write each outlaw word on the board, read it, and use it in an oral sentence. Have children use the words in oral sentences. Then write sentences 1, 2, and 3 on the board and have the children read them. As the children read the sentences, tell them any outlaw words they have trouble reading.

Point out the word *piglets* in sentence 1. Ask the children what smaller word they see in the bigger one. Then point out *barnyard* and ask the children what two words they notice. Explain that *barnyard* is called a *compound* word because it is made up of two smaller words. Ask whether they can find any other compound words in the lines.

In sentence 2, blend the second syllable of *octopus* as if it were the sound /ō/. Children will adjust their pronunciation when they blend and recognize the word.

Since the sentences are becoming longer and more complex, have volunteers reread the sentences after the whole class has read them.

➤ Reading/Writing Connection, pages 96–97, can be completed at this time. Page 96 provides practice with antonyms and synonyms. Help the children choose the word that means the opposite of each under-lined word on the top half of the page and the word that means nearly the same as each underlined word on the bottom half. On the top part of page 97, help the children name each picture and write a rhyming word in each blank.

Reading/Writing Connection, page 96

Name

Lesson 53

Writing Opposites

| last | finished | soft | off |

1. The girl started the race. **finished**

2. Dad turned the lamp on. **off**

3. Linda is first in line. **last**

4. The bed is too hard. **soft**

Writing Synonyms

| little | ran | cut |

1. Dad will trim the hedge. **cut**

2. Is a gerbil small? **little**

3. Kate raced up the hill. **ran**

Blending

96 R/WC

Machines in Our Garden

Reading/Writing Connection, page 97

Name

Lesson 53

Writing Rhyming Words

| line | mile | ice | cent |

cent　　**line**　　**ice**

Dictation and Spelling

Machines in Our Garden

Sounds and Spellings

R/WC 97

Machines in Our Garden
pages 2–32

Recommendations for Reading

- Display the cover of Big Book 4, *Machines in Our Garden*, and read the title aloud. Slowly turn the pages and browse with the children, encouraging them to notice machines and comment on anything that interests them.
- Wonder aloud about the content—"This doesn't look like a garden. I wonder how there can be a garden among all the trash"—and encourage the children to ask questions and tell what they wonder about.
- Remind the children that many tools in use every day are actually simple machines. Discuss with the children whether or not some of the objects mentioned in the story—such as a wagon, a see-saw, and a shovel—are machines.
- Point out the Glossary at the back of the book. Read aloud the list of entries and ask the children if they know what all of these words mean. Explain that a glossary usually appears at the end of an informational book and gives the meaning of unfamiliar words used in the book. Ask what other glossary they have used.
- Turn to page 24 and point to the word *wedge*. Wonder aloud about what a wedge is and what kind of work it can accomplish. Say, "Maybe the Glossary will tell us what a wedge is." Turn to the Glossary and point to the word *wedge*, then read the definition aloud.

Responding

Have the children name any machines they recognize in the book. Add these to the list you began on chart paper in the previous lesson. Ask volunteers to share any experiences they have had using any of the machines mentioned in the story.

Invite comments about the illustrations.

The Spider Club
Phonics Minibook 9

Getting Ready to Read

- Call on a volunteer to read aloud the title of the book.
- Encourage the children to browse the story, commenting on any words or illustrations that catch their eye.

Recommendations

- Have the selection read aloud. Change readers after each page.
- Tell the children the word *eyes*.
- Have the children reread the story aloud at least two times.

TEACHING TIP

You may want to start a bulletin board where children can put up pictures and descriptions of simple machines and what they do. Encourage children to bring in pictures and label them. Not only is this an easy way to share information, but it may also help some children come up with ideas for writing.

2

"Run, Grace!" yelled Mike. "It's a spider!"

"Run?" said Grace. "What for?"

"Girls hate spiders," said Mike.

3

"Not me," said Grace. "I like spiders. My sister and I have a spider club."

4

"That is a garden spider," said Grace. "It has eight eyes!"

"It has lots of legs, too," said Mike.

"Yes, all spiders have eight legs," said Grace.

5

"Are all spiders alike?" asked Mike.

Grace led Mike to the Spider Club.
Inside the club were lots of spiders.

"No, not all spiders are alike," Grace said.

6

"Here is a spider that jumps," said Grace.

"Jumps? Yikes!" said Mike.

"Not on you," said Grace. "It jumps on insects."

"Can't it spin a web?" asked Mike.

"No," said Grace, "not all spiders spin webs."

7

"This spider makes a trap, not a web," said Grace.
"It digs a trap and hides in it.
Insects fall into the trap."

"Which spider do you like best?" asked Mike.

8

"I like all kinds of spiders," said Grace.
"Crab spiders, pirate spiders, barn spiders,
spiders that fish, and spiders that spit.
But the spiders I like best
are the ones that spin webs.
I bet we can find one outside."

9

"Here's a spider!" called Mike.
"Will it spin a web?"

"Sit still," said Grace, "and we will find out."

"Oh! It fell from the branch!" yelled Mike.
"It made a thread!"

10

"That thread is made of silk," said Grace.

"Isn't silk for shirts?" asked Mike.

"Not spider silk," said Grace.

11

"A spider makes two kinds of silk.
One kind sticks to things," said Grace.
"When an insect hits the web,
it sticks to the silk."

12

"This silk thread is called a dragline.
The spider rides on the end of it.
Then the spider makes two bridges."

"What a trick!" said Mike.

13

"What next?" asked Mike.

"The spider runs from bridge to bridge," said Grace.
"It spins and spins to make a frame for the web."

14

"Next, it fills in the frame," said Grace.
"It spins fast."

"What a wonderful web!" said Mike.
"What will it do next?"

15

"It's time to dine," said Grace.
"The spider will sit still
until an insect hits the web.
It wants a nice snack."

"Me too!" said Mike. "It's time for lunch!"

16

Responding

- After the first reading, have a few children tell what happened in the story.
- Encourage them to comment on anything new and interesting they learned from reading this selection.
- Ask the children to point out any words they found difficult and to explain how they figured them out.
- To focus the children's attention on the text rather than the illustrations, have them point to and read the appropriate words to answer these questions:

     How do girls feel about spiders, according to Mike?
     How many eyes does the garden spider have?
     What is the name of the silk thread from which the spider dangles?
     What does the spider do after the web is finished?

Have the children reread the story with a partner.

✻ READING ALOUD

You might want to continue reading to the children from the list of books about machines given in the previous lesson or from the following books:

An Auto Mechanic by Douglas Florian
The Toolbox by Anne and Harlow Rockwell
Tool Book by Gail Gibbons

See **Learning Framework Card 5** for suggestions for modeling as you read aloud.

2 WRITING

✻ DICTATION AND SPELLING

Have the children turn to the bottom part of page 97 of the Reading/Writing Connection book. Dictate the following words and sentence, using the suggestions for dictation that appear on **Learning Framework Card 4.**

Line 1:   cent   lace

Line 2:   ice   spice

Sentence: Kate rides a nice bike.

In line 1, point out the soft *c* sound. Remind the children that when *c* is followed by either *e* or *i,* it has the soft sound /s/. Help the children proofread their work.

Review the list of topics that the children started yesterday. Talk about other information the children know and could share with the class. If children have brought in books about things they are interested in, have them share some of the information from the books. Machines and vehicles are an interesting topic for children and reading additional books related to the big book may give children new ideas for writing. Some books you might use are

Machines at Work by Byron Barton

An Auto Mechanic by Douglas Florian

Truck and Loader by Helen Haddad

Bikes by Anne Rockwell

Suggest that the children think about what kinds of information they might like to write about to share with others. Remind children that these books—like the stories in *Animals, Captain Bill Pinkney's Journey,* and *Machines in Our Garden*—all contain information that helps us learn about real things.

3 GUIDED AND INDEPENDENT EXPLORATION

WORKSHOP

Remind the children that they may use this time to work on projects on their own or in small groups. Be sure that each child knows what projects he or she may choose and how to complete any independent work. Suggestions for teacher-guided, collaborative, and independent work follow.

Work with the Teacher

- Preread tomorrow's portion of the Big Book, *Machines in Our Garden,* with children who might benefit from a reading.
- Listen to children reread Phonics Minibook 9, *The Spider Club.* Make note of the sounds and spellings with which they have difficulty.
- Using cards prepared for previous lessons, put together a set of flashcards to review the sounds and spellings taught in the last several lessons. Hold a Reading Relay between two teams of children.

Independent Work

- Activity Sheet 53 reviews the various spellings of the sound /s/. Tell the children to circle the letters that make the /s/ sound in each of the newspaper headlines. Remind them to refer to the spellings on the Sausage card if they need help. The children should then draw a picture to go with their favorite headline in the box at the bottom of the sheet.
- The children may write write and illustrate a sentence using one or more of the newly introduced outlaw words.

Student Collaboration

- Encourage pairs of children to reread Phonics Minibook 9, *The Spider Club.* You might want to assign each pair a target sound. Have them copy each word in the story that contains that sound and underline the letter or letters that spell the sound.
- Small groups of children can play Go Fish! Make sure the decks include the long *i* cards children prepared yesterday. You may also want to add cards to cover other new sounds and spellings.

TEACHING TIP
Encourage the children to read to each other. You, too, should choose children to read with. As you read with each child, note his or her progress.

Home/School Connection

Send home Step-by-Step Practice Story 29 for the children to share with their families.

ASSESSMENT Give students the multiple-choice test. See *Assessment Guide: Grade 1* for instructions.

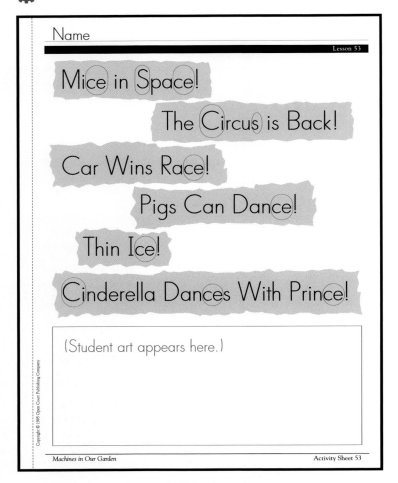

Name

Mi(ce) in (S)pa(ce)!

The (Circus) is Back!

Car Wins Ra(ce)!

Pigs Can Dan(ce)!

Thin I(ce)!

(C)inderella Dan(ce)s With Prin(ce)!

(Student art appears here.)

Copyright © 1995 Open Court Publishing Company

Machines in Our Garden

Activity Sheet 53

Activity Sheet 53

LESSON
54

••• Lesson Overview

New Learning

- /ō/ spelled *o* and *o__e*

Materials

- *Machines in Our Garden*, pages 2–5
- "The Cold Troll," Step-by-Step Practice Story 30
- Sound/Spelling Card 35, Long O
- Learning Framework Cards 3, 5
- Reading/Writing Connection, pages 98–99
- Activity Sheet 54

Prepare Ahead

- Fish for a Spelling game (see page 230)

GETTING STARTED

Choose one or both of the following activities to focus the children's attention and to review some of the concepts they have been learning.

Spelling Challenge Divide the class into three or four teams and be sure each team has a sheet of paper. Explain that you will write a spelling for a long vowel sound on the board and give the teams thirty seconds to one minute to write words that use that spelling. When time is up, call on each team to read and spell its words. Write the words on the board and award one point for each correct word. The team with the most points is the winner. Remind the children to whisper as they suggest words so that the other teams can't overhear their words.

Flip a Sound Game Make a flipper by writing *long* on one side of a plastic lid and *short* on the other side. Place Letter Cards *a* and *i* in a container. One child selects a letter card, while a second child flips the flipper. The first child must give a word that has either the long or the short sound of the vowel chosen, according to the word that is up when the flipper lands. Involve more children by having them work in teams. One team member selects a vowel and another flips the flipper. Each member of the team must give a word with the correct sound, scoring one point for each correct word.

1 READING

PHONICS

Some children may still be having difficulty blending the sounds that have been introduced with others. This is normal. It is very important that you not wait for mastery of each sound before going on to the next. Students will gradually learn the sounds through repetition and practice.

* **Introducing /ō/ Spelled *o* and *o_e*** Turn Sound/Spelling Card 35, Long O. Ask the children what sound they think the card represents and how they know. (The children should recognize the similarity between this and the Long A and Long I cards and be able to predict that the sound of this card will be the letter name.)

Follow the established procedure to introduce the long *o* spellings, *o* and *o__e*. Ask the children to explain the blank in the *o__e* spelling and the function of the *e*. Have the children sing "Apples and Bananas" substituting /ō/ in the verse. The following rhyme contrasts long and short *o*.

> *O*'s my name
> Two sounds I know,
> Short *o* in ***stop***,
> Long *o* in ***go***.

Encourage the children to suggest words with the long *o* sound.

* **Blending** Have the children blend the following words and sentences. For additional suggestions for blending, see **Learning Framework Card 3**.

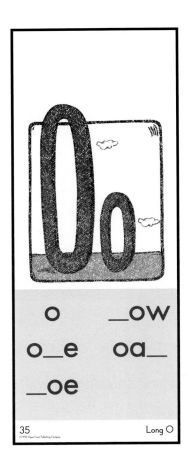

 Line 1: open   robot   protect   program

Line 2: hole   joke   home   throne

Line 3: go   old   cold   most

Line 4: mop   mope   rob   robe

Sentence 1:   Once upon a time an old man sat on a golden throne.

Sentence 2:   I once rode home in a large white car.

Sentence 3:   Blake broke the zipper on his jacket.

Words In line 1, for the word *old* blend the word with a long *o* sound. Point out that for some words you need to try both the long and short sound to determine what a word is. Have the children blend *cold* with you, using both a long and a short sound for the *o*. Have the children tell which way is correct. In line 4, point out the pairs of /o/ and /ō/ words. Ask the children how they know the words *mope* and *robe* contain the /ō/ sound.

To review the words, say a sentence with one of the words and ask the children to find and erase the word you used in the sentence. Some example sentences are:
- Lila told a funny *joke.*
- A *robot* can do jobs that are hard for people.
- The king was wearing a golden *robe.*
- The *old* tree stands deep in a forest.

Sentences Follow the usual procedure to introduce the outlaw word *once.* Then write the sentences on the board and have the children blend and read them. Have the children reread the sentences to increase their fluency. You might ask individual children to read a sentence, then have all the children read it together.

➤ Reading/Writing Connection, pages 98–99, reinforces the /ō/ sound spelled *o* and *o_e*. Help the children read and copy the words and sentences on page 98. Then on page 99, help them read all the words in each box, and mark the word that matches the clue you will give. The clues are:

Box 1: A word that means the opposite of *close.*
Box 2: Mark the word *hold.* Hold the dog's leash tightly.
Box 3: The word that rhymes with *spoke.*
Box 4: Mark the word *acorn.* The little acorn grew into a big tree.
Box 5: A word that means the same as *kind.*
Box 6: The word that rhymes with *hot.*

For the bottom half of page 99, have the children decode the secret word to complete the sentence.

✳ READING THE BIG BOOK

Machines in Our Garden
pages 2–5

Activating Prior Knowledge
Invite comments on anything the children remember from their browsing of *Machines in Our Garden* in the previous lesson. Briefly discuss what children know about planting a garden.

Recommendations for Reading
- Tell the children that today you will read the first part of the book. Read through the main text on pages 2–5 without the captions.

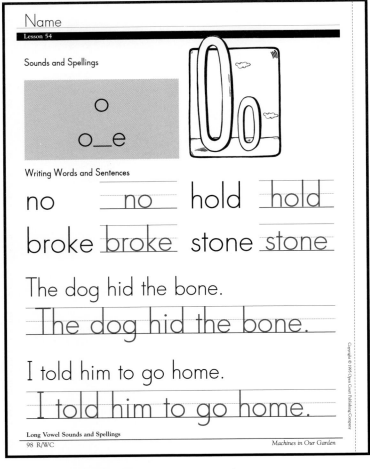

Reading/Writing Connection, page 98

Reading/Writing Connection, page 99

- Return to pages 2–3 and display the pictures of Olga and Ignatz. Read the corresponding captions and reread the text. Display pages 4 and 5 and reread the text. Discuss the area of the garden and have children predict which part of the garden will belong to Olga and Ignatz.
- Encourage the children to ask questions. You may want to pause after reading the second picture caption and ask a child to summarize what has been learned about Olga and Ignatz.

Ignatz and Olga are best friends. They're going to make a garden together. They want to grow big tomatoes.

She's strong. Olga can carry heavy boxes.

2

He's fast. Ignatz can run quick errands. **What a team!**

3

The city lets them use a garden plot.
"Look at these beautiful gardens," Ignatz says, "I'm impressed."
"But," Olga replies, "I'll bet ours will be the best, Ignatz."
"For sure, Olga."

4

5

Responding

- Ask volunteers to tell what has happened so far. Encourage the children to share any comments, questions, and wonderings about the text and pictures.
- Ask the children to discuss what types of machines or tools might be needed for working in a garden. Return to the list of machines that the class began during a previous lesson. Add any new machines that the children mentioned during today's discussion.

TEACHING TIP

In preparation for the next lesson, you might bring in some levers to show to the class. Specific items are suggested in the Prepare Ahead section of the next lesson.

* READING A STEP-BY-STEP PRACTICE STORY

"The Cold Troll"
Story 30

Getting Ready to Read

- Call on a volunteer to read aloud the title of the story.
- Encourage the children to browse the story, commenting on any words or illustrations that catch their eye.
- Have the children find the outlaw word *once*.

Recommendations

- Have children read the selection aloud. Change readers after each page.
- Have the selection reread aloud at least twice. Vary the oral reading pattern by allowing readers to decide whether they wish to reread the page just read or go on to the next page in the selection.
- Model surprise as the children read how cold Troll's home was.

Responding

- After the first reading, ask what the troll's problem was and how he solved it.
- Ask the children to point out any difficult or interesting words.
- To focus the children's attention on the text rather than the illustrations, have them point to and read the words that answer these questions:

    What was the problem with the old troll's house?
    Where did Mole live?
    What did Mole tell Troll?

Have the children reread the story with a partner.

* READING ALOUD

Be sure to set aside time to read to the children. You may want to share one or both of the following books with them:

The Carrot Seed by Ruth Krauss
From Seed to Plant by Gail Gibbons

See **Learning Framework Card 5** for suggestions for reading aloud.

TEACHING TIP

Set aside ten minutes for partner reading every day. During this time, you should read with individuals, recording their progress. Reading Assessment Sheets for Phonics Minibooks are available in *Assessment Masters, Grade 1*.

2 WRITING

✳ DICTATION AND SPELLING

Word-Building Game Have the children use paper and pencil for the Word-Building game. Write the words on the board as the children write them on paper. Encourage the children to ask for help if they need it, especially for long vowel spellings. Have each word proofread and corrected before writing the next word in the list. Use the following words:

so
go
gold
sold
hold
hole
pole
poke
spoke

INDEPENDENT AND COLLABORATIVE WRITING

Most children are interested in learning new information and are eager to share that information with others. In the next several lessons, the children will be encouraged to work on a writing project that shares information. The following books tell about how things are made or how they work. These and others like them may serve as models for the children to use as they work on their writing projects about information they want to share.

Milk by Donald Carrick
My Five Senses by Aliki
How a Book Is Made by Aliki
Lights! Camera! Action! How a Movie Is Made by Gail Gibbons

Children may begin writing about a machine they know about or use, but their writing need not be limited to this. They should feel free to write a piece that gives information about anything that they are interested in. Some may want to write about how to make something, such as a model or a kite; others may prefer to write about how to do something, such as take care of a pet or plant seeds; still others may want to create books of vehicles or machines. The important point is for children to share some information through writing.

Have the children decide on a topic. If several children share a common interest, suggest that they work together to develop a book or mural about that topic. Remind them that a good way to get started is to write a list of the ideas that they want to include in their piece.

Hold conferences with children, helping them decide on an idea for writing. Remind children to put their name and the date on their paper and put it in their writing folders.

TEACHING TIP

You may want to have the children generate a list of ideas first. Add these to the list begun in earlier lessons. This may help children who are not sure about what to write.

3 GUIDED AND INDEPENDENT EXPLORATION

WORKSHOP

Remind the children that they may use this time to work on projects of their own or in small groups. Be sure that each child knows what projects he or she may choose and how to complete any independent work. Suggestions for teacher-guided, collaborative, and independent activities follow.

Work with the Teacher

- Reread and discuss pages 2–5 of *Machines in Our Garden* with small groups of children. You may also want to preteach pages 6–9 for the next lesson.
- Listen to children read Step-by-Step Practice Story 30.
- Use long and short *a, i,* and *o* word flashcards to work with children who need extra help decoding vowel spellings.

Independent Work

- Activity Sheet 54 reviews /ō/ and /o/ sounds and spellings. Explain to the children that in the game of Dominoes, players put the matching ends of the game pieces next to each other. Point out that the dominoes on this sheet are made up of words that have either the /ō/ or /o/ sound. Tell the children to cut out the dominoes and, beginning with any two game pieces, match either the ends with the /ō/ words or the /o/ words. Then they should match the other ends of the dominoes with words that have similar vowel sounds. You might mention to the children that not all of the dominoes have one /o/ and one /ō/ word on them. Explain that they can lay down the game pieces in any pattern they wish, and after using all the dominoes, they can mix them up and play again. If

each child lightly colors the back of his or her dominoes, they can combine sets and play together. Then separate the sets at the end of the game.

- Write the following spellings on the board: *a__e, i__e,* and *o__e.* Challenge children to write as many words as they can for each spelling. When they have finished, they should circle the rhyming words and save their papers for tomorrow's Workshop.
- Encourage children to look at books on their own. Provide a selection of books about machines for this purpose. You may want to include any of books recommended for reading aloud.

Student Collaboration

- Partners may reread "The Cold Troll" or any other previously read Step-by-Step Practice Stories or Phonics Minibooks.
- Introduce the Fish for a Spelling game to a small group of children. Write the following spellings on index cards: *ar, a, a__e, i, i__e, o, o__e.* Place some or all of the cards in a jar. Have the children take out pencils and scratch paper and sit in a circle around the jar. Each child should take a turn drawing a card, pronouncing the spelling on the card, and then writing a word that contains that spelling. If a child has trouble writing his or her word, the other children may help out.

Name

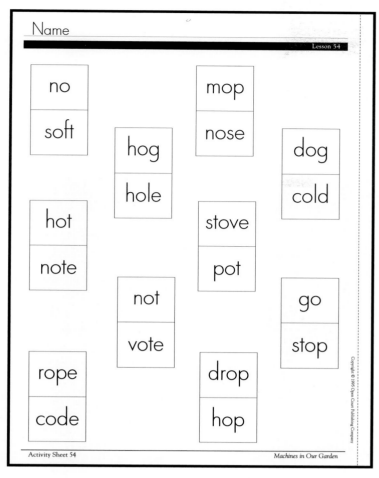

no	mop	
soft	nose	dog
hog		cold
hole	stove	
hot	pot	
note	not	go
	vote	stop
rope	drop	
code	hop	

Machines in Our Garden

Activity Sheet 54

LESSON
55

• • • Lesson Overview

New Learning

- /z/ spelled *s*

Materials

- *Machines in Our Garden*, pages 6–9
- "The Surprise," Step-by-Step Practice Story 31
- Sound/Spelling Card 26, Zipper
- Learning Framework Cards 3, 4, 5
- Reading/Writing Connection, pages 100–101
- Activity Sheet 55

Prepare Ahead

- Scrambled Sentences Game (see page 240 and Games and Songs Teacher Tool Card 8)
- Several examples of levers commonly found at home, such as a boot jack, a bottle opener, a garlic press, a hammer, a nutcracker, a shoe horn, a snow shovel (see page 238)

GETTING STARTED

Choose one or both of the following activities to focus the children's attention and to review some of the concepts they have been learning.

Long Vowel Says Game   Point to the Sound/Spelling Cards Long A, Long I, and Long O and ask the children to give the sound for each. Play a version of Simon Says in which you give directions. If the action contains a long vowel sound, the children should do it. If the action does not have a long vowel sound, they should not do it.

Practice the game with these instructions. Give the word first, then the sentence.

hide: Long Vowel says *hide* your eyes. (Children do.)

make: Long Vowel says *make* a face. (Children do.)

blow: Long Vowel says *blow* on your finger. (Children do.)

hop: Long Vowel says *hop* two times. (Children should not do.)

Other instructions to use in the game include
tap: Long Vowel says *tap* your foot.
hold: Long Vowel says *hold* your toe.
wipe: Long Vowel says *wipe* your feet.
skip: Long Vowel says *skip* around the room.
tie: Long Vowel says pretend to *tie* your shoe.
blow: Long Vowel says *blow* on your thumb.
skate: Long Vowel says pretend to *ice skate.*

Long Vowel Spelling Review Divide the class into two teams. On both ends of the chalkboard, write the following words: *slice, open, April, take, sofa, close, pine, cider, bone, pale,* and *bike.* Add other long *a, i,* or *o* words so that there will be a word for each team member. Tell the children that you will say a sound and that one child from each team should go to the board, circle a word with that sound, and underline the letter or letters that spell that sound. For each sound that the children identify correctly, their team receives a point. At the end of the activity, point to each word and have the children read them aloud together.

1 READING

PHONICS

* **Introduce /z/ Spelled *s*** Direct the children's attention to Sound/Spelling Card 26, Zipper, and ask what sound the *z* spelling makes. Uncover or point to the _*s* spelling and tell the children this is another way to spell the /z/ sound. Some children may already know some words in which the *s* is pronounced /z/. Ask the children if they know what the blank before the *s* means. If necessary, explain that the blank means that this spelling for /z/ never comes at the beginning of a word.

* **Blending** Have the children blend the following words and sentences. For additional suggestions for blending, see **Learning Framework Card 3.**

Line 1:	nose rose hose suppose
Line 2:	chose froze rise prize
Line 3:	base chase trace price
Line 4:	most post fold sold
Sentence 1:	Rosa would like to pose for the artist.
Sentence 2:	I suppose we could ice skate since the lake is frozen.
Sentence 3:	Your prize is a bunch of red roses.

Words In lines 1 and 2 point out that the *s* spelling of the /z/ sound often follows a long *i* or long *o*. Use the words in line 2 to review that the /z/ sound can be spelled with either *z* or *s*. Compare *chose* and *froze*, then *rise* and *prize*. In line 3, remind the children that the /s/ sound can be spelled with *s* or *ce*.

Ask the children what vowel sound they hear in each word in line 4 and how the long *o* sound is spelled in these words.

Review the words by asking the children to find

- a kind of flower
- words with the long *a* sound
- three words that rhyme
- something you use to water your garden
- something you might win

Sentences To encourage fluent reading, have each sentence read several times.

❯ Reading/Writing Connection, pages 100–101, can be completed at this time. Page 100 reinforces the /z/ sound spelled *z* and *_s*. Help the children read each word and write it in the correct column, depending on the sound of the letter *s* in the word. On the top part of page 101, have the children write the pairs of opposite words next to each other.

Reading/Writing Connection, page 100

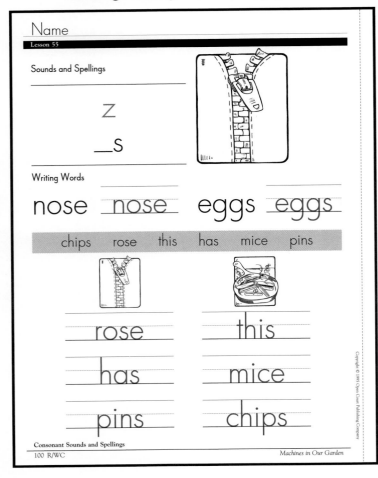

Reading/Writing Connection, page 101

Machines in Our Garden
pages 6–9

Activating Prior Knowledge

Invite the children to tell what they remember from yesterday's reading. Ask the children to name some machines. Then tell them that today they will read about a special kind of machine called a *simple machine.*

Recommendations for Reading

- Display pages 6–7 and ask if this is the kind of garden Olga and Ignatz were planning to have. Then read page 8 aloud.
- Encourage the children to ask questions. Pause once or twice and ask a volunteer to **sum up** what has happened so far.

S T R A T E G I C
R·E·A·D·I·N·G
P R O M P T S
·
These prompts may be used
as guides when working with
reading strategies.

1 You might comment that you don't see any
machines. Ask children to predict what machines
Olga and Ignatz might use.

"What a dump!" Ignatz groans. "How will
we clean this up? We need some big, loud
trash-eating, junk-crushing machines."

"We don't even have a tractor," Olga sighs.
"We'll have to use the machines we have."

1

6

7

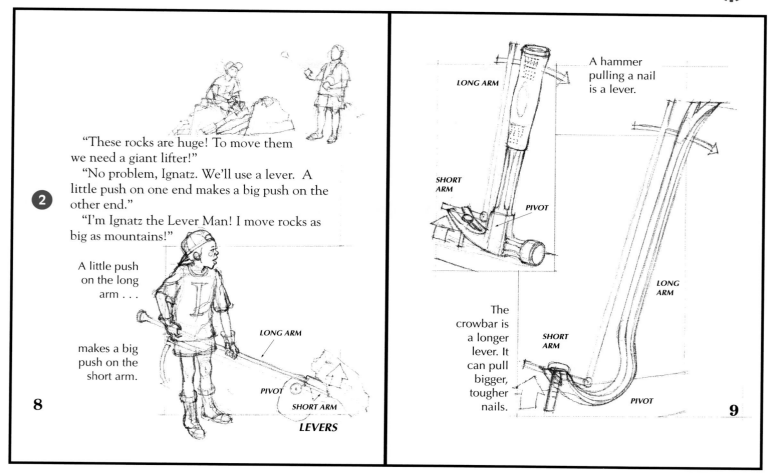

"These rocks are huge! To move them we need a giant lifter!"

2 "No problem, Ignatz. We'll use a lever. A little push on one end makes a big push on the other end."

"I'm Ignatz the Lever Man! I move rocks as big as mountains!"

A little push on the long arm . . .

makes a big push on the short arm.

LONG ARM

PIVOT

SHORT ARM

LEVERS

8

A hammer pulling a nail is a lever.

LONG ARM

SHORT ARM

PIVOT

LONG ARM

SHORT ARM

The crowbar is a longer lever. It can pull bigger, tougher nails.

PIVOT

9

2 If no one questions the meaning of *lever,* wonder aloud about what a lever is and how it will help Olga and Ignatz. Suggest that checking the Glossary might be a good way to find out. Find *lever* in the Glossary and read the definition, then return to page 8.

Responding

- Call on volunteers to **sum up** what they have learned so far about levers and about Olga and Ignatz's plans.
- Share any levers that you brought from home. Ask the children to mention other things that they think might be levers. Point out that boards and sticks can be used as levers.
- Make a chart or a web titled *Machines.* Give the chart or web a sub-heading called "Levers." Under this heading, list all the levers that the children have learned about so far.

✻ READING A STEP-BY-STEP PRACTICE STORY

"The Surprise"
Story 31

Getting Ready to Read

- Call on a volunteer to read aloud the title of the story.
- Encourage the children to browse the story, commenting on any words or illustrations that catch their eye.
- Introduce outlaw words *your, could.*

Recommendations

- Have the children read the selection aloud. Change readers after each page.
- Have the selection reread aloud at least twice. For the second reading, you might assign the parts of Moses and Dad, changing readers after every two pages.

Responding

- After the first reading, ask what Moses' problem was and how it was solved.
- Ask the children's opinions of the father's suggestions.
- Ask the children to point out any words that were difficult or interesting.
- To focus the children's attention on the text rather than the illustrations, have them point to and read the appropriate words to answer these questions:

    Where did Dad think Moses should get roses?
    What did Moses' dad say to him at the end of the story?

Have the children reread the story with a partner.

✻ READING ALOUD

Be sure to set aside time to read to the children. Two books about machines that the children might enjoy follow:

Machines at Work by Byron Barton
Tool Book by Gail Gibbons

TEACHING TIP

Remind the children to read each book twice. When they finish today's book, they should get one from a previous lesson. Reading Assessment Sheets for Phonics Minibooks are available in *Assessment Masters, Grade 1.*

After reading, be sure to ask the children what they learned about levers or other machines.

See **Learning Framework Card 5** for suggestions for reading aloud.

2 WRITING

✳ DICTATION AND SPELLING

Have the children turn to page 101 of their Reading/Writing Connection book. Dictate the following words and sentence, using the suggestions for dictation that appear on **Learning Framework Card 4.** Before you dictate the words, review the long *o* spellings on the Long O Sound/Spelling Card.

✎ **Line 1:** go   hope

Line 2: open   hold

Sentence: Stan told us a joke.

INDEPENDENT AND COLLABORATIVE WRITING

Start with Seminar and have children share their ideas for writing an informational piece. Classmates may want to make suggestions to the Seminar leader about things to include in the piece. Write down these suggestions and share them with the students during writing conferences. You may want to share examples of ways other authors have shared information. For example, in *Ladybug* magazine there are many simple informational pieces, such as "Veterinarian" (March 1992), "Adopting Daisy" (October 1993), "The Panda" (February 1994), "Spring" (April 1993), and "Bedtime" (March 1993), which present considerable information about a topic using pictures and labels.

Encourage the children to work on their pieces. Hold conferences with children who may be having trouble getting started. You may want to remind children about making posters as a way to share information. For those who have begun a project, help them elaborate on their ideas by asking what else they know about the topic and where they might add that information to their piece.

3 GUIDED AND INDEPENDENT EXPLORATION

Remind the children that they may use this time to work on projects on their own or in small groups. Be sure that each child knows what projects he or she may choose and how to complete any independent work. Suggestions for teacher-guided, collaborative, and independent activities follow.

Work with the Teacher

- Reread today's excerpt from *Machines in Our Garden* with those children who might benefit from another reading. You may also want to preteach tomorrow's reading.
- Listen to children reread Step-by-Step Practice Story 31.
- Play an oral spelling game with a group of children to review the long vowel spellings they have learned thus far. Write *cap* on the chalkboard. Ask a volunteer to read the word and then tell you how to make it *cape*. Call on another child to tell you how to change *cape* to *cope*. Proceed through the following:

hope	lid
hose	lad
rose	glad
rode	glade
rod	blade
rid	blame
ride	shame
slide	shape
slid	

Independent Work

- Activity Sheet 55 provides practice with following directions. Tell the children to cut out the pictures at the bottom of the sheet, then read each sentence and paste the pictures where the directions tell them to.
- Encourage children to select books to read on their own. Provide books for them to choose.

Student Collaboration

- Have pairs of children reread Step-by-Step Practice Story 31. Ask them to copy all of the words in the story that contain the /ō/ or /z/ sound. Have them write a sentence with two of the words.
- Partners or small groups can play the Scrambled Sentences game. The children may create scrambled sentences of their own for others to solve.
- Partners can play Dominoes with their sets of domino cards.

TEACHING TIP

Encourage the children to read to each other. You, too, should choose children to read with. As you read with each child, note his or her progress.

Home/School Connection

Send home Step-by-Step Practice Story 30 and encourage the children to read it to their families.

Name

Paste the snake in the crate.

Paste the fish under the crate.

Paste the chicken on top of the crate.

Paste the daffodil to the left of the crate.

Paste the lizard on the side of the crate.

Paste the horse next to the daffodil.

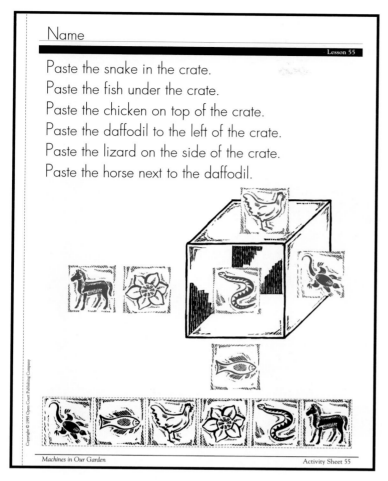

Machines in Our Garden   Activity Sheet 55

Activity Sheet 55

LESSON
56

● ● ● Lesson Overview

New Learning

- /v/ spelled **v**

Materials

- *Machines in Our Garden*, pages 10–13
- Sound/Spelling Card 22, Vacuum
- Learning Framework Cards 3, 5
- Reading/Writing Connection, pages 102–103
- Alphabet Flash Cards
- Activity Sheet 56

Prepare Ahead

- Long Vowel Flash Cards (see page 242)
- Spider Game (see page 249 and Games and Songs Teacher Tool Card 6)

GETTING STARTED

Choose one or both of the following activities to focus the children's attention and to review some of the concepts they have been learning.

Long Vowel Spellings Write each of the words that follow on an index card and place the cards in a container. Write the vowel spellings *a, a__e, i, i__e, o,* and *o__e* on the chalkboard. Have children select a card, read the word, then place it beneath the correct spelling. When all the cards have been placed, have the group read the words for each spelling. Words to use are *table, cave, nice, tiger, no, nose, home, over, lace, hide, giant, final, cold, find, acorn.*

Review Sound/Spelling Cards Using Alphabet Flash Cards, display one letter at a time. The children should name the letter, then pronounce the letter sound and name the corresponding Sound/Spelling Card. When a vowel is displayed, have the children respond with the short sound, then (for *a, i, o*) the long sound.

1 READING

* **Introducing /v/ Spelled *v*** Turn Sound/Spelling Card 22, Vacuum, and tell the children this is the Vacuum card. Read aloud the vacuum story. You can find the procedure for introducing a new sound and spelling on **Learning Framework Card 2.**

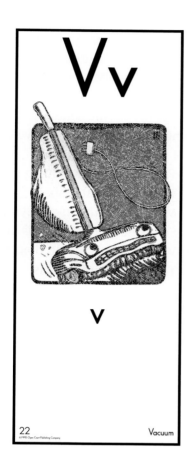

Vinny the Vacuum is cleaning again.
Before visitors visit, he always begins.
This is the sound of his very loud voice: /v/ /v/ /v/ /v/ /v/!
If only that Vinny could clean without noise!

Vinny picks up the crumbs baby Vicki dropped. /v/ /v/ /v/ /v/ /v/!
He visits nearly everywhere except the tabletop. /v/ /v/ /v/ /v/ /v/!
Three vine leaves, two vitamins, part of a vase—
All vanish when Vinny goes over the place! /v/ /v/ /v/ /v/ /v/!

As Vinny vacuums the velvety rug
A van full of visitors starts to drive up.
But Vinny's not done with the very last room!
Will you help Vinny the Vacuum vacuum?
(Ask groups of children to say /v/ in a round to make the continuous sound of a vacuum cleaner.)

Show the children how to form a *v* with their fingers. Tell them that you are going to say some words. If they hear the /v/ sound at the beginning of a word, they signal by holding up a *v*. Use the words that follow.

vacuum	vase	vine
picture	violin	vegetable
vitamin	bubble	visit

Ask the children to suggest other words that begin with /v/. Then have the children listen for /v/ at the end of words and to signal when they hear it. Use these words:

move	have	sing
dove	stove	pave
laugh	skip	drive

* **Blending** Have the children blend the following words and sentences. For suggestions for blending, see **Learning Framework Card 3.**

Line 1: van   vase   vote   visit

Line 2: save   shave   stove   drove

Line 3: dive   drive   driver   alive

Line 4: river   seven   never   clever

Sentence 1: Five men visited the vacant lot with Robert.

Sentence 2: Dave gave his sister a silver bracelet.

Sentence 3: Jessica and Fred drove the van to the cave.

Words In line 2, point out that the spelling *v* is followed by an *e* that is silent in every word. Explain that the spelling *v* is almost never at the end of a word.

In line 4, blend the words syllable by syllable: *riv—er, sev—en, nev—er, clev—er.* Some words, such as *vote* and *clever,* may be unfamiliar to the children. Ask volunteers to use these words in sentences.

To review the words, read aloud the sentences below and ask the children to find and read a word from the board to complete each sentence. Repeat the sentence using their word. If the word completes the sentence appropriately, have the child erase the word.

- I put the flowers in a _____.
- The fish were swimming in the _____.
- The number after six is _____.
- My grandmother is always glad to see us when we _____.
- Someone who is smart is also _____.
- When there is an election, my mother will _____.
- The opposite of dead is _____.

▶ Reading/Writing Connection, pages 102–103, provides additional practice with the /v/ sound spelled *v.* Help the children complete the pages at this time.

Reading/Writing Connection, page 102

Name _____

Lesson 56

Sounds and Spellings

v

v _____
V _____

Writing Words and Sentences

vine vine van van

brave brave five five

Vince has seven valentines.
Vince has seven valentines.

Consonant Sounds and Spellings
102 R/WC   *Machines in Our Garden*

Reading/Writing Connection, page 103

Name _____

Lesson 56

Completing Sentences

| stove | drives | never |
| velvet | saves | vase |

1. My mom drives a van.

2. Jim saves baseball cards.

3. Val has a velvet dress.

4. Lance put the pan on the stove.

5. Put the buds in a vase.

Decoding
Machines in Our Garden   R/WC 103

Machines in Our Garden
pages 10–13

Recommendations for Reading

- Ask the children to recall the problem or challenge that Olga and Ignatz have. Then refer back to the chart (or web) on machines that you began in the previous lesson and review the types of levers you listed. Discuss how these levers make work easier.
- Have the children listen as you read the selection.
- Invite the children to look for any words they might know.
- Encourage the children to ask about any words they don't understand.

STRATEGIC
R·E·A·D·I·N·G
PROMPTS

These prompts may be used
as guides when working with
reading strategies.

❶ If no one mentions that the lever on this page
resembles a see-saw, you might ask the children
whether they have ever lifted anyone the way
Olga is lifting Ignatz in this picture.

"Lever Man can even lift Olga," Ignatz says,
flexing his muscles.
"No way!"

Olga sits on the short arm.
Ignatz pushes the long arm.
Olga goes up!

LONG ARM

SHORT ARM

PIVOT

LEVERS

10

"Let me try my side," Olga says. "To the
moon, Ignatz!"

Ignatz sits on the long
arm. Olga bounces
hard on the short arm.

❶

LONG ARM

SHORT
ARM

PIVOT

11

With a little machine help, Ignatz can become strong Lever Man.

With a lever, Olga can do her work faster. "This crowbar saves me time!"

Pushing down on the shovel's long handle makes the shovel's short blade lift earth easily.

LONG ARM

SHORT ARM   **PIVOT**

LEVERS

Big spikes come out easily with a crowbar.

12

13

Responding

- Discuss the levers that appear in today's reading as well as any other commonly used tools the children can think of that use a lever. Add these levers to the chart.
- Invite the children to tell about any new things they learned about simple machines from today's reading.

✳ READING ALOUD

The following books can be used to introduce the children to other machines that use the same principles the children are being exposed to in this Big Book:

Machines by Fred Wilkins

The Giant Nursery Book of Things That Work by George J. Zaffo

After reading, remember to ask the children what they find interesting and what they like best.

See **Learning Framework Card 5** for suggestions for reading aloud.

2 WRITING

✳ DICTATION AND SPELLING

Word-Building Game Use the following words for the Word-Building game. Have the children use paper and pencil.

no
nose
note
vote
vat
van
vane
vine

COLLABORATIVE AND INDEPENDENT WRITING

Children who have begun a project may continue to work on their informational pieces.

If any children are having problems getting started, you may want to use Phonics Minibook 9, *The Spider Club,* as a model and discuss what kinds of information the book contains. Ask what questions children may have about spiders or what they wonder about spiders, for example, Are all spiders dangerous? What do spiders eat? How do spiders act and live? Suggest that children write in their journals about anything that interested them in this selection. They may want to write a list of things they would like to know about spiders, or write a list of interesting words related to spiders. They can use words from the story and then add their own.

Children can use other books from the library or from the literacy center in your classroom as models for the same types of activities.

Additional ideas for informational writing can be found in the following books. You may want to read one or more of the books or put them in the literacy center for children to look at on their own.

A Dentist's Tools by Kenny De Santis

The Supermarket by Ann and Harlow Rockwell

Fill It Up! All About Service Stations by Gail Gibbons

3 GUIDED AND INDEPENDENT EXPLORATION

WORKSHOP

Remind the children that they may use this time to work on projects on their own or with small groups. Be sure that each child knows what projects he or she may choose and how to complete any independent work. Suggestions for teacher-guided, collaborative, and independent activities follow.

Work with the Teacher

- Reread *Machines in Our Garden* to a small group of children who could use more time with the Big Book. Pause after each page or two and ask a child to retell the page in his or her own words.
- Review Sound/Spelling Card 22 and today's Blending lesson to those children who had difficulty with the new sound, /v/ spelled *v*.
- Invite a small group of students to participate in a spelling challenge. Ask each child to take out scratch paper and pencil. Write a long vowel spelling (*a, i, o, a__e, i__e, o__e*) on the chalkboard and have the children race to use it in a word. Have them hold up their papers as soon as they finish writing. Call on them to read their words one by one.

Independent Work

- Activity Sheet 56 provides practice with antonyms. Tell the children to choose the word that means the opposite of each given word, and write it in the blank provided.
- Invite the children to draw pictures of machines that they use at home. Have them label each machine and write a sentence or brief paragraph telling what it does.

Student Collaboration

- Invite pairs of children to revisit *Machines in Our Garden* on their own, using the small copies if they are available. Have them look for words and sentences that they can read on their own. They may want to choose favorite words to use in an original sentence.
- Ask a group of children to search the classroom for machines. Provide them with scratch paper and tape and have them affix a label to each item telling what it is and what it does.
- Suggest that children play the Spider Game. (See Games and Songs Teacher Tool Card 6.) You may want to prepare some *v* word flashcards for them to use. Refer to today's Blending exercise for word ideas.

Home/School Connection

Send home Step-by-Step Practice Story 31 and encourage the children to read it to their families.

Name

stop	open	save	under
sit	hot	hide	plump

spend __save__   go __stop__

find __hide__   shut __open__

stand __sit__   over __under__

cold __hot__   thin __plump__

Machines in Our Garden

Activity Sheet 56

LESSON 57

Lesson Overview

New Learning

- /ū/ spelled *u* and *u_e*

Prepare Ahead

- Fish for a Spelling Cards (see page 257)

Materials

- *Machines in Our Garden*, pages 2–13
- "Cupid the Mule," Step-by-Step Practice Story 32
- Sound/Spelling Card 36, Long U
- Learning Framework Cards 3, 4, 5
- Reading/Writing Connection, pages 104–105
- Letter Cards *a, i, o*
- Activity Sheet 57

GETTING STARTED

Choose one or both of the following activities to focus the children's attention and to review some of the concepts they have been learning.

Add a Sound Game Move rapidly through the following list, making sure you pronounce the clues clearly and distinctly.

Start with *mōō* then add /v/. What do you get?
Start with *spā* then add /s/. What do you get?
Start with *clō* then add /z/. What do you get?
Start with *sā* then add /v/. What do you get?
Start with *lōō* then add /s/. What do you get?
Start with *rī* then add /z/. What do you get?
Start with *prōō* then add /v/. What do you get?

Flip a Sound Game Use a plastic lid—with the word *long* on one side and *short* on the other side—for the flipper. Place Letter Cards *a, i, o* in a container. Have one child select a letter and a second child flip the flipper. The child with the letter must say a word with either the long or short sound of the vowel as dictated by the flipper. To involve more children, have them work in teams of four or five. One team member chooses a letter and another flips. Then each person on the team must write a word for the vowel sound. Have the team members read their words.

1 READING

✱ **Introduce /ū/ Spelled *u* and *u_e*** Display Sound/Spelling Card 36, Long U and introduce the long vowel sound. Have the children sing "Apples and Bananas," substituting long *u* in the verse.

Contrast the long and short sounds of *u* by pointing to the Tugboat card and asking the children to pronounce the short *u* sound. Then teach the children this rhyme to contrast the two sounds.

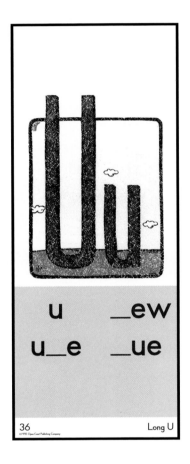

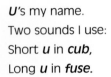
U's my name.
Two sounds I use:
Short *u* in **cub**,
Long *u* in **fuse**.

Point to the spellings *u* and *u_e* on the Long U card and have the children say the /ū/ sound with you. Have the children tell what they know about the *u_e* spelling and if necessary point out that a consonant goes in the blank while the *e* helps the *u* say its name. Have the children listen to the following words and signal when they hear the long *u* sound.

human	silly	wish	stare
desk	**fuse**	**cute**	**music**
step	horse	question	bake
violin	**mule**	cub	**fuel**

Have the children review the Long U card, telling how they can use it to help them with reading and writing.

✱ **Blending** Have the children blend the following words and sentences. For additional suggestions for blending, see **Learning Framework Card 3.**

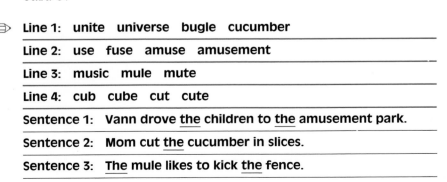
Line 1: unite universe bugle cucumber
Line 2: use fuse amuse amusement
Line 3: music mule mute
Line 4: cub cube cut cute
Sentence 1: Vann drove the children to the amusement park.
Sentence 2: Mom cut the cucumber in slices.
Sentence 3: The mule likes to kick the fence.

Words As the children blend the words in lines 1 and 2, ask what spellings make the sound /ū/. In line 3, point out that /ū/ in *music* is spelled *u*, while the /ū/ in *mule* and *mute* is spelled *u_e*.

Line 4 contrasts the /u/ and /ū/ sounds. Ask the children why the /u/ in *cub* changes to /ū/ in *cube*. Elicit that the *e* at the end makes the vowel say its name. Repeat with *cut* and *cute*.

The children may not be familiar with some of the words, such as *unite, universe, bugle, fuse,* and *mute*. Encourage children who are familiar with these words to use them in oral sentences.

Review the words by telling the children to look at a particular line such as line 3. Say a sentence with a word from the line, then have the children point to the word, read it, and erase it.

Sentences Point out the *nn* spelling in the name *Vann*. Ask how many *n*'s they see and how many /n/ sounds they hear. If necessary, remind the children that two of the same consonant together make only one sound. You might also tell the children that the word *van,* meaning a kind of automobile, is spelled with only one *n*.

To encourage fluency, have the children read the sentences several times.

▶ Reading/Writing Connection, pages 104–105, reinforce the /ū/ sound spelled *u* and *u_e*. Help the children complete page 104 and the top part of page 105.

✳ READING THE BIG BOOK

Machines in Our Garden
pages 2–13

Recommendations for Reading

- Discuss with the children what machine Olga and Ignatz have used.
- You might want to perform the following experiment with the children, so that they can experience for themselves how levers work.

Have the children work in pairs. Each pair will need a hard cover book and two pencils or a craft stick and one pencil. Place one end of a pencil or the craft stick under a hard cover book and press down on the other end. Point out that this action does nothing to make the book move. Next have the pairs position a second pencil under the first pencil or under the craft stick, near the book. The pencil just added acts as a pivot. Press down on the exposed pencil end again, raising the book, and invite the children to indicate which side of the pivot is the short arm and which is the long arm. Have the children experiment with the lever by moving the pivot farther from the book. Continue to have the children point out the short and long arms of the lever.

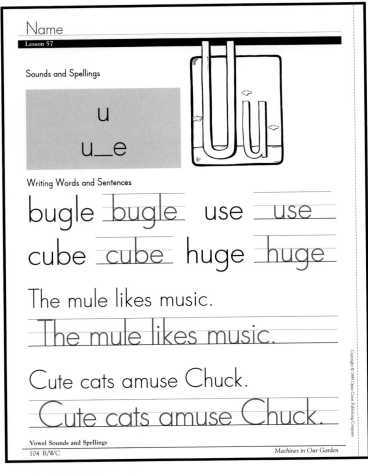

Reading/Writing Connection, page 104

Reading/Writing Connection, page 105

Responding
- Discuss with the children which location of the pivot makes the book easiest to lift.
- Display chart paper and tell the children that you can write about the experiment you just did. Have them help you compose several sentences to write. Draw a picture to illustrate the lever lifting the book. The children will be asked to do this on their own in Writing.

✱ READING A STEP-BY-STEP PRACTICE STORY

"Cupid the Mule"
Story 32

Getting Ready to Read
- Have the children assemble the Step-by-Step Practice Story.
- Discuss with the children what they noticed about the story in browsing it as they put it together.
- Encourage children to **predict** what the story will be about. If they simply say, "It's about a mule," ask them what else they think the story might be about or say, "Tell me more." Then invite the children to find out if their predictions are right as they read the story.

Recommendations

- Call on a volunteer to read the title.
- Call on different children to read each page of the story aloud. Feel free to stop and discuss with the class anything of interest on a page, then have another child reread the page before going on. Help the children blend any words they have difficulty with or remind them of the pronunciation of outlaw words.
- Invite the entire class to reread the story a third time, choosing new readers for each page.

Responding

- Ask the children if they had any questions about what they just read, such as problems with recognizing outlaw words, sounding and blending, or understanding vocabulary. Allow the class to try to clear up the problem areas.
- To determine whether the children are focusing on the words in the story rather than simply on the pictures, have them answer questions such as those that follow, by pointing to a word and then calling on two or three children to say the word. Repeat the word. Then call on children to point to any word they choose and say it.

   What is the name of the mule?
   What did the mule like?
- Ask the children to tell anything they can about the story, and ask them what they liked about it. Keep this discussion brief, but if the children's answers are sparse, ask, "What else?"

Have the children reread the story with a partner.

✳ READING ALOUD

You may want to share with the children part of one or both of the following books:

Fun with Simple Science: Machines and How They Work by
   Barbara Taylor
An Auto Mechanic by Douglas Florian

Remember to ask what the children find interesting and what they learned about levers or other machines from these books.
   See **Learning Framework Card 5** for suggestions for reading aloud.

2 WRITING

✳ DICTATION AND SPELLING

Have the children turn to page 105 of their Reading/Writing Connection book. Dictate the following words and sentence, using the suggestions for dictation that appear on **Learning Framework Card 4**.

Remind the children to check the Sound/Spelling Cards and to ask for help if they need it.

Line 1:	nose rise
Line 2:	velvet drive
Sentence:	Dave dove in the waves.

Have the children proofread their work.

COLLABORATIVE AND INDEPENDENT WRITING

Tell the children that when scientists do an experiment they write down what happens, as you did after the experiment. Briefly discuss the lever experiment the children did with books and pencils and what they learned about the pivot and the arms of the lever. Ask the children to illustrate and write about their experiment. They may want to return to their partner to work. Provide a bulletin board where the scientists can post and share their findings.

Have children continue writing on their independent projects. You may want to hold conferences with individuals or small groups as they work. Select samples of children's writing to use in the next Revising Minilesson. Be sure to ask the children's permission. Make a transparency of the samples if possible.

TEACHING TIP

As you hold conferences with students, note where they are in terms of their developing spelling. By now most children will be writing something. Some may be using just initial consonants, or some combination of initial, medial, and final consonants to represent words. Encourage these children to think about the vowel sound they hear, to check the Sound/Spelling Cards, and to write the spelling in the word. Do not be concerned if children are not using vowels consistently or correctly. It takes time for vowels to be accurately represented in children's writing. Children have also learned a number of outlaw words in their reading. If you have been keeping a chart of these, remind the children to check the chart for the spellings of these words.

3 GUIDED AND INDEPENDENT EXPLORATION

WORKSHOP

Remind the children that they may use this time to work on projects on their own or in small groups. Be sure that each child knows what projects he or she may choose and how to complete any independent work. Suggestions for teacher-guided, collaborative, and independent activities follow.

Work with the Teacher

- Play an oral spelling game to review long vowel spellings. Write the word *cape* on the chalkboard. Ask a volunteer to read the word and tell you how to change it to *cap.* Ask the next volunteer how to change cap to cab. Proceed through the following list of words:

  cub
  cube
  cute
  cure
  care
  scare
  scan
  plan
  plane

- Listen to children reread Step-by-Step Practice Story 32. Make note of those children who are having trouble decoding words with long vowels and plan to spend some extra time with them.
- Repeat today's Dictation lesson with children who had difficulty.

Independent Work

- Activity Sheet 57 provides practice with the long vowel sounds that the children have learned thus

far. Tell the children they can complete this page by changing the long vowel sound in each word to form a new word and by drawing a picture of the new word in the box.
- Circle the word *nose* in line 1 of today's Dictation. Invite the children to copy the word onto a sheet of paper. Challenge them to form as many new words as they can by changing one letter of the previous word. Have them write a sentence using one or more of the new words.
- Encourage children to read on their own. You might want to provide a selection of books from which to choose. You may want to include some books of very simple experiments.

Student Collaboration

- Ask partners to reread Step-by-Step Practice Story 32. Have them make a list of all the long vowel words in the story and underline the letters that spell each vowel sound.
- Invite the children to play Fish for a Spelling. Add *u* and *u_e* to the Fish for a Spelling cards.

TEACHING TIP

Encourage the children to read to each other. You, too, should choose children to read with. As you read with each child, note his or her progress.

Name

Lesson 57

a i o u

(Student art appears here.)

bake	bike
cone	cane
pane	pine
mile	(Possible answers:) (mule, male, mole)
Kate	kite

Machines in Our Garden Activity Sheet 57

Activity Sheet 57

LESSON
58

••••
Lesson Overview

New Learning

- /ē/ spelled *e* and *e_e*
- Revising

Materials

- *Machines in Our Garden*, pages 14–17
- "Steve's Secret," Step-by-Step Practice Story 33
- Sound/Spelling Card 37, Long E
- Learning Framework Cards 3, 5
- Reading/Writing Connection, pages 106–107
- Activity Sheet 58

Prepare Ahead

- Go Fish! Cards (see page 267 and Games and Songs Teacher Tool Card 7)

GETTING STARTED

Choose one or both of the following activities to focus the children's attention and to review some of the concepts they have been learning.

Who Am I? Game Ask the children Who Am I? questions that focus their attention on long vowel sounds. As the children respond, write their answers on the board. Have children identify the long vowel spelling in each word. Some questions to use are:

- I'm a color with the long *i* sound. Who am I? (white)
- I'm the opposite of *low*. I have the long *i* sound. Who am I? (high)
- I'm someone who makes cakes. I have a long *a* sound. Who am I? (baker)
- You find me in the freezer and put me in a drink. I have long *i* and long *u.* Who am I? (ice cube)
- I'm something you hear on the radio. I have the long *u* sound. Who am I? (music)

Quick Change Teams Have the children work in teams and make sure each team has a sheet of paper. Write the word *cut* on the chalkboard and have the first member of each team copy the word at the top of the team's paper. Tell that person to change the word to *cute* and to write the new word under *cut.* The paper should then be passed to the next person to write a new word according to your directions. Continue giving directions until each member of the team has written a word. Then write the list of words on the board for the teams to check their lists. Call on children to use the words in sentences. The complete list follows:

cut
cute
cube
cub
rub
rob
robe
rode
ride
hide
hid

1 READING

PHONICS

* **Introduce /ē/ Spelled e and e_e** Display Sound/Spelling Card 37, Long E. Follow the usual procedure for introducing a long vowel Sound/Spelling Card, calling attention to the picture of the letters on the card as a reminder that the spellings on this card say /ē/. Sing "Apples and Bananas," adding a long *e* verse.

Contrast long *e* and short *e* by pointing to the Hen card and reviewing its sound and spelling. Then teach the children the following rhyme.

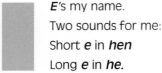

E's my name.
Two sounds for me:
Short *e* in **hen**
Long *e* in **he.**

Point to the spellings *e* and *e_e* on the Long E card and explain that these are two of the ways to spell /ē/. Have the children review the Sound/Spelling Card and tell how they can use it to help them read and write. Ask what the children know about ways to spell long vowel sounds. They should be aware that the letter *e* at the end of a word can make the vowel before it long, and that a vowel by itself can be long.

e   ea
e_e   _y
ee   _ie_

37   Long E

✱ **Blending** Have the children blend the following words and sentences. For additional suggestions for blending, see **Learning Framework Card 3.**

Line 1:	be he she we
Line 2:	even fever meter regal
Line 3:	elect behind decide eleven
Line 4:	these Steve Pete pet
Sentence 1:	Can she be related <u>to</u> Beth?
Sentence 2:	Gene is sick with a fever and a cold.
Sentence 3:	A cute little kitten hides behind <u>the</u> bushes.

Words Blend the words in line 2 by breaking them into syllables: *e—ven, even; fe—ver, fever; me—ter, meter;* and *re—gal, regal.*

In line 3, the /ē/ in the first syllable of each word may become a schwa sound in natural speech. Blend the words with the sound /ē/ and the children will make any adjustments when they pronounce the words naturally.

In line 4, ask the children why two of the words begin with a capital letter. Then ask how the word *pet* is different from the other words in the line.

Review the words using a sponge die marked with the numbers 1–4 and two stars on its sides. Children pick a line and toss the die, reading the word that corresponds to the number that shows on the die. If a star is tossed, the child may read any word in the line or all the words in the line.

Sentences Point to the punctuation at the end of each sentence. Ask what the punctuation tells about the sentence and how the sentence should be read.

➤ Reading/Writing Connection, pages 106–107, reinforce the /ē/ sound spelled *e* and *e__e*. Have the children complete page 106 by reading and copying the words and the sentences. On page 107, the children should write the sentence that describes each picture on the lines provided.

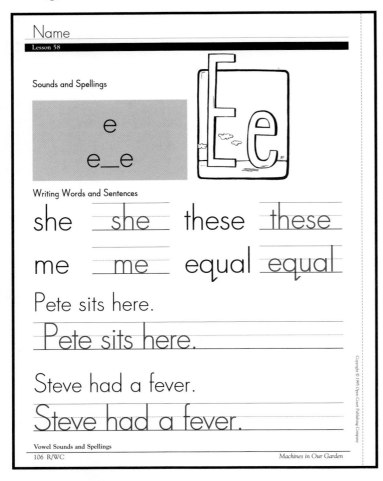

Reading/Writing Connection, page 106

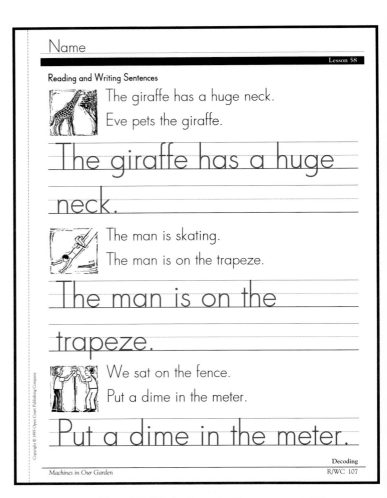

Reading/Writing Connection, page 107

✳ READING THE BIG BOOK

Machines in Our Garden
pages 14–17

Recommendations for Reading

- Ask for volunteers to tell what has happened in the story so far.
- Wonder aloud with the class, "Now that the children have moved all of the trash out of their garden, what do you think will be their next problem?"
- Read the text (not the caption) on page 14. Ask the children for ideas about how the wheel might be helpful at this point in the story.
- Next, read the captions on pages 14 and 15. Discuss with the children where to find wheels in everyday life.
- Read the text (not the caption) on page 16. Ask a volunteer to review for the class how a lever works. Wonder aloud how a wheelbarrow is a lever.
- Read the captions on pages 16 and 17. Point out the various ways that wheels assist us and ask the children if they can think of other ways in which wheels are helpful.

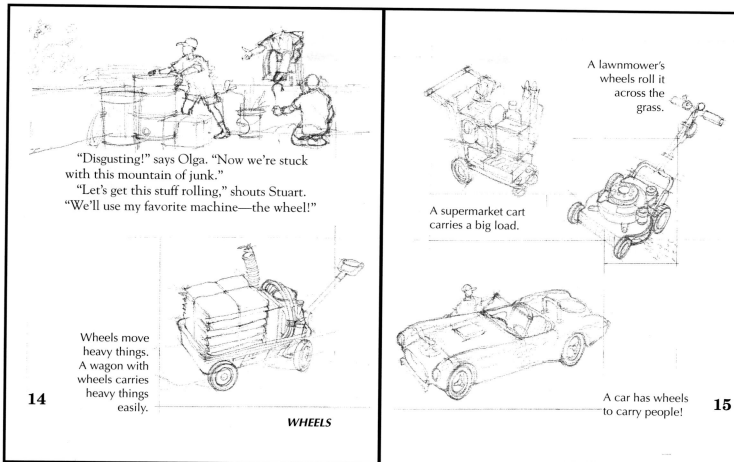

"Disgusting!" says Olga. "Now we're stuck with this mountain of junk."

"Let's get this stuff rolling," shouts Stuart. "We'll use my favorite machine—the wheel!"

Wheels move heavy things. A wagon with wheels carries heavy things easily.

14

WHEELS

A lawnmower's wheels roll it across the grass.

A supermarket cart carries a big load.

A car has wheels to carry people!

15

A wheelbarrow is two machines. It is a wheel and a lever. It lifts things and rolls things. "This junk is out of here!" they cry.

A wheelbarrow's long arms help lift the load. Its wheel rolls the load along.

16

WHEELS

Wheels on luggage make trips easier.

Skate wheels make Ignatz faster.

Little wheels carry Skateboard Olga.

17

Responding

- Talk with the children about how wheels work and add a wheel category to your class list of simple machines.
- Ask the students to name objects that use wheels and add these items to your chart. Children will almost certainly name cars and trucks, but they might overlook other familiar items, such as bicycles, roller skates, and skateboards.
- Children may be surprised to discover some of the common machines that require wheels to operate. You may want to mention some less obvious examples, such as bicycle gears, pulleys, and can openers, to get the children thinking more broadly about wheels.

TEACHING TIP

Showing the class how a hand-operated can opener works would be an excellent example of how wheels and levers can be used as parts of a more complex machine.

✻ READING A STEP-BY-STEP PRACTICE STORY

"Steve's Secret"
Story 33

Getting Ready to Read

- Have the children assemble the Step-by-Step Practice Story.
- Discuss with the children what they noticed about the story in browsing it as they put it together.

Recommendations

- Call on a volunteer to read the title.
- Call on different children to read each page of the story aloud. Feel free to stop and discuss with the class anything of interest on a page; then have another child reread the page before going on. Help the children blend any words they have difficulty with or remind them of the pronunciation of outlaw words.
- Invite the entire class to reread the story a third time, choosing new readers for each page.

Responding

- Ask the children whether they had any questions about what they just read, such as problems with recognizing outlaw words, blending, or understanding vocabulary. Allow the class to try to clear up the problem areas.
- To determine whether the children are focusing on the words in the story rather than simply on the pictures, have them answer questions such as the following by pointing to a word. Call on two or three children to say the word. Then call on children to point to any word they choose and say it.

    What is the boy's name in the story?
    What did he have?
    Where did Steve hide his secret?

- Ask the children to discuss what the story was about and what they liked about it. Keep this discussion brief, but if the children's answers are sparse, ask, "What else?"

Have the children reread the story with a partner.

TEACHING TIP

Set aside ten minutes for partner reading every day. During this time, you should read with individuals, recording their progress. Reading Assessment Sheets for Phonics Minibooks are available in *Assessment Masters, Grade 1.*

✳ READING ALOUD

You may want to select one of the following books about machines to read aloud:

Monster Trucks and Other Machines on Wheels by Jerry Bushey
Big Wheels by Anne Rockwell

Remember to ask the children what they find interesting and what they like best.

See **Learning Framework Card 5** for suggestions for reading aloud.

2 WRITING

✳ DICTATION AND SPELLING

Word-Building Game Have the children use pencil and paper to spell the words that follow. After dictating each word and allowing a moment for the children to write it on their own, write each word on the board as a model. Be sure to have each word proofread and corrected before having the children write the next word. You may want to review the spellings on the Long U card before dictating the words. Use the following list of words:

cub
cube
cure
cute
mute
mule
muse
use

Minilesson

Revising

Some of the children may have completed their informational pieces. Discuss what authors do when they have completed a piece—they reread it to see if it makes sense. Authors also make sure that they have included all the important information about the topic. Remind the children that they can add information by including new sentences or by extending ones that they have already written. If you have selected student pieces to use for revising examples, write them on the board or on an overhead projector.

First read through the example piece with the children. Then go back through the piece, asking its author at logical points what else he or she knows that could be added to the sentence or that might be added as a separate sentence. Write the information down, using a caret to show where the information belongs in the sentence. Do not worry about spelling or mechanics at this point. If you prefer, you may use the following example or a piece of your own to illustrate revising.

> I have a cat. My cat is named Funny. I feed him. Sometimes
> I give him a treat.

Using the example, you may want to suggest questions that the author might have answered that would give the reader more information. For example, the author might have told about what the cat eats, the fact that cats need water, what kind of special treat the cat likes, where the cat sleeps, or what the cat does. Since many children know about cats, have them tell you some of the information that this author could have included in the piece.

Have the children continue to work on their informational pieces. As children finish their work, remind them to reread the piece to see whether it makes sense and to see whether any additional information should be added. This is a good opportunity to hold small-group conferences with children who are ready to revise. Remind the children to put their names on their work and to keep the pages in their writing folders.

3 GUIDED AND INDEPENDENT EXPLORATION

WORKSHOP

Remind the children that they may use this time to work on projects on their own or in small groups. Be sure that each child knows what projects he or she may choose and how to complete any independent work. Suggestions for teacher-guided, collaborative, and independent activities follow.

Work with the Teacher

- Repeat today's Blending lesson with children who would benefit from additional practice. You may want to have the children return to the Step-by-Step Practice Story to locate /ē/ words and tell how /ē/ is spelled in each word.
- Listen to children reread Step-by-Step Practice Story 33.
- Play the Word-Building game with children who need extra help with spelling. Repeat today's list, or devise a list based on the children's areas of need.

Independent Work

- Activity Sheet 58 reviews the sounds and spellings of long e and long u. Point out the color key at the top of the page and tell the children that they can use it to help them color the candies. Explain that they should read each word and color those candies having the long e sound red and those having the long u sound green. You might also mention that there will be some candies left uncolored because they have neither the long e nor the long u sound.
- Remind the children that they may use this time to read the books of their choice. Some children may enjoy revisiting small copies of the first two Big Books to see how many more words they can now read.

Student Collaboration

- Have the children reread Step-by-Step Practice Story 33 with a partner. Encourage peer tutoring by pairing more-independent readers with less-fluent readers.
- Children might want to draw pictures of machines. At the top of each drawing, the artist should write the machine's name. At the bottom of each drawing, the artist should write a brief description of what the machine does. Tomorrow, the children can put all the drawings together to make a collage or bulletin board display.
- Add rhyming long u and long e words to the collection of Go Fish! cards. Remove some of the easiest-to-read cards if the deck or decks are becoming too large. Invite the children to play Go Fish! or a memory game.

TEACHING TIP

Encourage the children to read to each other. You, too, should choose children to read with you. As you read with each child, note his or her progress.

Home /School Connection

Send home Step-by-Step Practice Story 32 and encourage the children to read it to their families.

Name _____

red= **Ee**   green= **Uu**

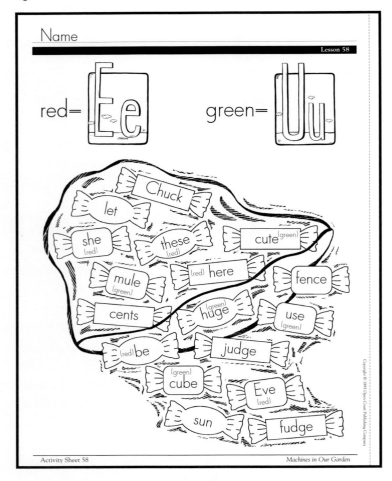

Activity Sheet 58

LESSON
59

••• Lesson Overview

Materials

- *Machines in Our Garden*, pages 14–17
- Phonics Minibook 10, *Eva Uses Her Head*
- Learning Framework Cards 3, 4, 5, 6
- Reading/Writing Connection, pages 108–109
- Letter Cards
- Activity Sheet 59

Prepare Ahead

- Large cardboard box, small wagon or dolly (see page 271)
- Plastic lid (see page 269)

GETTING STARTED

Choose one or both of the following activities to focus the children's attention and to review some of the concepts they have been learning.

Flip a Sound Game Place Letter Cards *a, e, i, o, u* in a container. With a marker, write *long* and *short* on opposite sides of a plastic lid. Children should take turns flipping the lid and choosing a card. Then they must say a word with the chosen vowel's long or short sound as indicated by the lid.

Spelling Challenge Have the children work together in teams of four or five. Write the word part *ake* on the chalkboard and give the teams several minutes to write as many words as they can that contain this spelling. Have each team read its list as you write the words on the board. Award a point for each correct word.

1 READING

✻ **Blending** Have the children blend the following words and sentences. For additional suggestions for blending, see **Learning Framework Card 3.**

✏️ | | |
|---|---|
| **Line 1:** | health breath weather sweater |
| **Line 2:** | crate Pete kite note cute |
| **Line 3:** | beside hotel broken potato |
| **Line 4:** | exercise surprise secret predict |
| **Sentence 1:** | Pete could tap on the drum to make music. |
| **Sentence 2:** | Shane ate a baked potato for dinner. |
| **Sentence 3:** | Rose used a hose to water the tomato plants in the garden. |

Words Line 1 reviews the *ea* spelling for the short *e* sound. Remind the children that this spelling occurs only in the middle of words and never at the beginning or end.

In line 2, be sure to write the vowel spelling and have the children blend through the vowel before writing the spelling for the final consonant sound. (For example, for *crate* write and blend cra_e and then write the *t* and blend the whole word.) Have the children repeat each word and tell what vowel sound they hear. Have them point to the Sound/Spelling Card that shows the vowel spelling used in each word.

Lines 3 and 4 provide practice in blending words with more than one syllable. After the children have blended the words, have them clap each one to determine the number of syllables in it.

Review the words by having the children find and read words that
- have the sound /e/
- have the sound /ā/
- have the sound /ī/
- have the sound /ū/
- have the sound /ō/

Sentences Sentence 2 reinforces the long *a* sound. *Shane, ate,* and *baked* all form /ā/ with *a_e*. Say *potato*, breaking it into syllables and ask the children why *a* says /ā/ (last sound in the syllable). You may wish to compare *tomato* in sentence 3 with *potato*.

▶ Reading/Writing Connection, pages 108–109, reviews words with long and short vowel spellings. On page 108, help the children choose the word that has a different vowel sound from the others in the group, and write it on the blank. For the top part of page 109, the children should label each picture with the correct word.

Name _____
Lesson 59
Listening for Vowel Sounds

cake   cape   cap   cap

help   here   hen   here

kitchen   kitten   kite   kite

rope   robber   rocket   rope

cute   cub   cube   cub

crane   crash   crate   crash

trapeze   tape   tap   tape

Vowel Sounds and Spellings
108 R/WC   *Machines in Our Garden*

Name _____
Lesson 59
Word Study

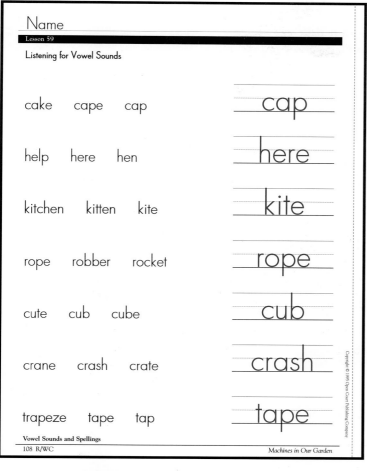

cake   cap
              cake
              make

kite   bike
              kitten
              kite

cube   cube
              cute
              cut

hose   nose
              hose
              rose

Dictation and Spelling

_____   _____
_____   _____
_____   _____
_____   _____
_____   _____
_____   _____

Machines in Our Garden   Decoding/Spelling
                                      R/WC 109

Reading/Writing Connection, page 108   **Reading/Writing Connection,** page 109

✳ R E A D I N G   T H E   B I G   B O O K

Machines in Our Garden
pages 14–17

Recommendations for Reading

- Ask the children to tell what they learned about wheels from the previous lesson.
- To help the children understand how wheels help us accomplish work, you might want to perform the following experiment:
  1. Place a cardboard box on the floor at the front of the class.
  2. Have each child deposit a book (preferably a heavy one) inside the box.
  3. When the box is full of books, ask the children for ideas about how to move the box across the room without carrying it.
  4. Allow the children to take turns trying to push and pull the box. Ask them to describe how difficult it was to move it.
  5. Next, lift the box onto a wagon or dolly and invite the same students to move the box now that it is on wheels. Ask them whether the box is easier or harder to move than before.

Responding

- Explain to the children that when things rub together, we call it friction. For example, when they tried to push and pull the box across the floor, there was friction between the box and the floor. Tell the children that friction slows things down and that one of the ways wheels work is to help reduce friction. That is why the box could move faster on wheels than it could on the floor; the wheels created less friction with the floor than the box did.
- Tell the children that all work requires energy. Discuss with them whether it required more energy to move the box with or without wheels.
- Return to pages 14–17 of *Machines in Our Garden*. As you browse each page with the students, ask them to point out those machines that use wheels to reduce friction (move faster).
- Review the wheel section of the class list of simple machines with the children. Ask them to identify which of the machines listed use wheels to reduce friction.

✳ READING A PHONICS MINIBOOK

Eva Uses Her Head
Phonics Minibook 10

Getting Ready to Read

Reading the Title   Read the book's title and point out that it contains two stories whose titles are also on the cover. Then have the children turn to the first page of the first story and invite them to read the story's title, "The Step Problem," silently. Call on two or three volunteers to read the title aloud.

Repeat this procedure for story 2, "The Bug Problem."

Browsing the Story   Allow the children to page through the book, commenting on what they see in the illustrations and what they think the story will tell them. Ask them if they notice anything about the words.

Recommendations

Follow the procedures for reading a Phonics Minibook. See **Learning Framework Card 6** for procedures on reading Phonics Minibooks.
- Call on a different child to read each page of the story aloud. Clarify any difficulties the children may have while reading. Then have a different child reread the page before going on.
- Reread the story at least twice, calling on different children to read.
- Repeat these steps for story 2.

The Step Problem

2

3

Hugo sat on his front step
and moped.
"Such a sad face, Hugo!" said Nana.
"What has made you so sad?"

4

"I want to invite Eva over,"
said Hugo, "but even if she came,
she wouldn't be able
to get up these steps."

5

"Do not mope, Hugo," said Nana.
"Use your head. Talk to Eva.
She is used to this kind of problem."

6

Hugo talked to Eva.
"No problem!" said Eva.
"Let's go!"

7

"I'm glad you came," said Hugo.
"But these steps are huge.
Will we be able to get inside?"

8

Eva smiled.
"This is not a hard problem," she said.
"I just use my head!"

9

The Bug Problem

10

11

Hugo and Eva sat in Eva's yard.
"Let's go inside," said Hugo.
"These bugs make me itch!"

"I have an idea!" said Eva.

12

"Take these," Eva said.
She held out two poles.

"What are these for?" asked Hugo.

13

"These poles go here," said Eva,
"and those go next to you."

"Then what is the rope for?" asked Hugo.

14

"I will pull on this end of the rope,"
said Eva, "and you pull on that end."

Eva and Hugo pulled on the rope.

15

"We made a tent!" said Hugo.

"Yes, we used our heads,"
said Eva, "but let's be quick
and get inside!
These bugs make me itch!"

16

Responding

- Ask the children to talk about any hard words they came across in their reading and how they figured out the words.
- To make sure the children are focusing on the words in the story rather than on the pictures, have them answer questions such as the following by pointing to and reading the words aloud.

  Who was feeling sad?

  Who did Hugo want to invite over?

  Who told Hugo to use his head?

  What did Eva come over in?

  How does Hugo describe the steps?

  What did Eva say she used?

- Call on volunteers to point out any words they can read well.
- Invite the children to tell what they liked best about the story.
- Repeat the procedure for the second story. Have them answer questions such as the following by pointing to and reading the words aloud.

  Where did Hugo and Eva sit?

  What did the bugs make Hugo do?

  What did Eva say she had?

  What did Eva and Hugo use to solve the problem?

Have the children reread the story with a partner.

* READING ALOUD

Be sure to set aside time for reading aloud. Many books about machines have been written for children. You may want to share one or both of the following books.

The Science Book of Machines by Neil Ardley

The ABC of Cars, Trucks, and Machines by Adelaide Hall

Remember to ask what the children find interesting and what they like best.

See **Learning Framework Card 5** for suggestions for reading aloud.

> **TEACHING TIP**
>
> Remind the children to read each book twice. When they finish today's book, they should get one from a previous lesson. Reading Assessment Sheets for Phonics Minibooks are available in *Assessment Masters, Grade 1*.

2 WRITING

* DICTATION AND SPELLING

Have the children turn to page 109 of their Reading/Writing Connection book. Dictate the following words and sentences, using the suggestions for dictation that appear on **Learning Framework Card 4.** Review the *e* and *e__e* on Sound/Spelling Card 36, Long E, before dictating the words.

> **TEACHING TIP**
>
> Do not be concerned if the children have not yet mastered all the long vowel spellings that have been introduced. Encourage them to ask which spelling to use. The children will have many more opportunities to write words with long vowels and will gain confidence with the spellings through practice.

Line 1: be   behind

Line 2: these   use

Sentence: Pete has a secret.

Have the children proofread their work. For the sentence, discuss what kind of letter should be at the beginning of a sentence and what should be at the end.

COLLABORATIVE AND INDEPENDENT WRITING

Remind the children that scientists write about their experiments. Briefly discuss what the children learned about wheels in the wheel experiment. Suggest that they draw and write about the experiment to tell others what they learned. You may want to provide bulletin board space where the "scientists" can display their work.

For children who are ready to proofread their writing projects, have them work in small groups. Remind them to check for beginning capitalization and ending punctuation. They should also look for words that contain short vowel sounds and check their spelling.

Have other children continue working on ongoing projects. If children prefer they can begin a new piece or work in their journals. Children may want to write about places where they see wheels, levers, screws, ramps, and other machines used in everyday life.

TEACHING TIP

Participate in these small groups. This is a good opportunity to observe children.

3 GUIDED AND INDEPENDENT EXPLORATION

WORKSHOP

Remind the children that they may use this time to work on projects on their own or in small groups. Be sure that each child knows what projects he or she may choose and how to complete any independent work. Suggestions for teacher-guided, collaborative, and independent activities follow.

Work with the Teacher

• Review the spellings that have been introduced so far for the sounds /ā/, /ō/, /ū/, and /ē/. You may want to hold a long vowel Reading Relay between two teams of children. Prepare new cards to review long vowel spellings that do not appear on any previously used flash cards.
• Listen to children reread Phonics Minibook 10.
• Repeat today's Dictation lesson with children who would benefit from additional help.

Independent Work

• Activity Sheet 59 is a crossword puzzle that reviews various sounds and spellings. Tell the children to choose words from the box to complete each sentence, then write the answers in the corresponding boxes of the crossword puzzle.
• Using at least one or two words from today's Blending exercise, children can write and illustrate sentences about their favorite machines, real or imaginary.
• Children may want to continue working on their writing projects.

Student Collaboration

• Have partners reread Phonics Minibook 10. Encourage peer tutoring by pairing independent readers with less fluent readers.
• Invite pairs of children to review outlaw words with flash cards. Again, pair confident readers with children who need extra practice.
• Invite the children to form small reading circles, in which one or two children read aloud to the others. You may want to provide some books for them to choose from.

ASSESSMENT During partner reading, workshop, or other times during the day, listen to students individually read one of the stories in one of the Phonics Minibooks introduced so far. Using a Reading Assessment Sheet, record your observations and add them to each student's folder.

Home/School Connection

Send home Step-by-Step Practice Story 33 and encourage the children to read it to their families. A letter to accompany this story can be found in the book of Step-by-Step Practice Stories.

Name

| Perfume | umpire | vote | November | athlete | ate |

→ 1. An ___umpire___ referees a game.

→ 2. ___November___ is a month.

→ 3. The ___athlete___ runs fast.

↓ 4. I ___ate___ an apple for a snack.

↓ 5. We ___vote___ for a president.

↓ 6. ___Perfume___ can smell like lilacs.

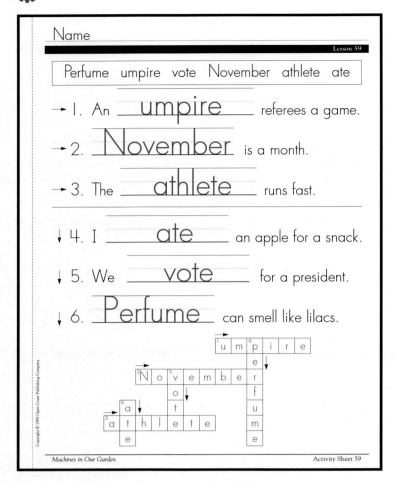

Activity Sheet 59

LESSON

60

Lesson Overview

New Learning

- /ē/ spelled *ee*, *ea*

Materials

- *Machines in Our Garden*, pages 18–21
- "Dragons Don't Get Colds," Step-by-Step Practice Story 34
- Sound/Spelling Card 37, Long E
- Learning Framework Cards 3, 5
- Reading/Writing Connection, pages 110–111
- Outlaw Word Flash Cards
- Activity Sheet 60

Prepare Ahead

- *ee* and *ea* cards for Go Fish! (see page 289)

GETTING STARTED

Choose one or both of the following activities to focus the children's attention and to review some of the concepts they have been learning.

Outlaw Word Review Place the following Outlaw Word Flash Cards in a container: *one, two, three, four, would, should, out, wants, where, water, thing, today, eight, were, eyes, once, your, could.* Choose two cards from the container. As you show the cards to the children, have them read the words aloud with you. Ask one child to make up a sentence containing both words. When the child gives the sentence, invite him or her to choose two new words. Have the child show the new words for the class to read aloud and select a volunteer to use them in a single sentence. Repeat with other pairs of words. Place all the flash cards on the chalkboard ledge. As you call out the words, have individual children find, read aloud, and replace them in the container.

Quick Change Write the word *nap* on the chalkboard and blend it with the children. Then print the word *shave* and blend it. Tell the children that today they are going to solve a puzzle. Together, you will turn the word *nap* into the word *shave* by changing only one sound at a time. Use the following instructions for changing the letters. You may wish to invite children to make the changes at the chalkboard.

- Change the *n* to *str.*
- Change *str* to *t.*
- Add *e* to the end of *tap.*
- Change *tape* into *shape.*
- Change *shape* into *shave.*

After each change, have the children say the new word and use it in a sentence.

1 READING

PHONICS

✱ **Introduce /ē/ Spelled *ee* and *ea*** Tell the children that they are going to learn two more spellings for the long *e* sound. Point to the Long E Sound/Spelling Card and review the spellings *e, e_e.*

Remind the children that vowels often need help from other letters to say their names. Touch the spellings *ee* and *ea* on the Sound/Spelling Card and have the children say the sound /ē/. Since the children have been introduced to the *ea* spelling for short *e,* you might want to point out that most of time *ea* says /ē/ in words. The *ea* spelling for long *e* can be found at the beginning, the middle, or the end of a word.

Encourage the children to think of words with the long *e* sound. Write the children's suggestions on the board. If the children have difficulty thinking of words, you might challenge them to think of words that rhyme with *eat* or *sleep,* for example, or words with /ē/ that begin with /s/, /t/, or other consonant sounds.

Review the Long E card and the four spellings the children have learned.

✱ **Blending** Have the children blend the following words and sentences. For additional suggestions, see **Learning Framework Card 3.**

Line 1:	eat each scream beneath
Line 2:	see sea meet meat
Line 3:	tree street sleep green
Line 4:	sell seal bet beat
Sentence 1:	Does Jane need to feed the sheep?
Sentence 2:	Please teach Dean to use clean sheets to make the bed.
Sentence 3:	Did you feel the cold breeze at the beach?

Words Write the *ee* and *ea* spellings as a unit before having the children give the sound /ē/. If the children are having trouble with the long vowel spellings, you might want to write the vowel spellings in a different color from the consonants.

After the children blend line 2, say the words *see* and *sea* and ask the children what they notice about them. After discussing the meanings of the words, have a volunteer use each word in a sentence to illustrate its meaning. Repeat with *meet* and *meat*. If you have used the term *homophone* with the children, remind them, or have them tell you, that words that sound alike but have different spellings are called homophones.

In line 4, ask the children which words have a short *e* sound and which have a long *e* sound.

To review the words, ask the children to find and erase
- a word that rhymes with *stream*
- a pair of homophones
- a color
- an animal that swims

Continue the review by having the children give clues.

Sentences After the children blend the sentences, draw attention to the question marks in sentences 1 and 3 and ask what these marks tell them about the sentences.

For the word *please* in sentence 2 and *breeze* in sentence 3, explain that the final *e* is silent.

▶ Reading/Writing Connection, pages 110–111, reinforces the /ē/ sound spelled *ee* and *ea*. Have the children read and copy the words and sentences on page 110. Then on page 111, the children should write words with opposite meanings next to each other.

✳ **READING THE BIG BOOK**

Machines in Our Garden
pages 18–21

Activating Prior Knowledge

Ask the children to tell what they have learned about levers and wheels. Ask them to share anything that they are wondering about and to keep their wonderings in mind as you read the next part of the book.

Recommendations for Reading
- Read pages 18–21, pausing at the end of each page to display the pictures and to read the caption that accompanies each picture.
- Encourage the children to ask questions. Have volunteers **sum up** each page, in their own words.

Reading/Writing Connection, page 110

Reading/Writing Connection, page 111

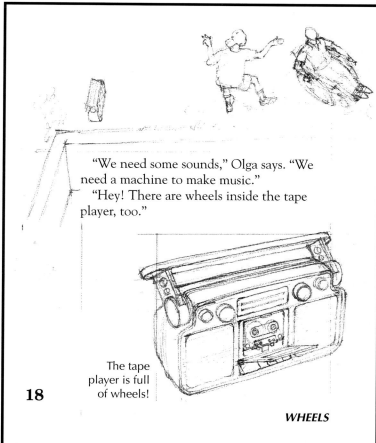

"We need some sounds," Olga says. "We need a machine to make music."

"Hey! There are wheels inside the tape player, too."

The tape player is full of wheels!

WHEELS

18

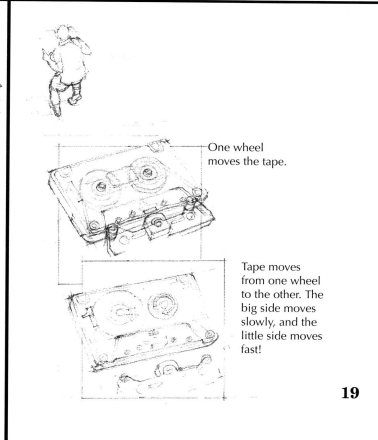

One wheel moves the tape.

Tape moves from one wheel to the other. The big side moves slowly, and the little side moves fast!

19

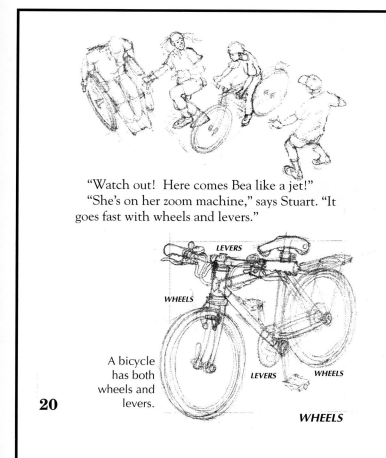

"Watch out! Here comes Bea like a jet!"

"She's on her zoom machine," says Stuart. "It goes fast with wheels and levers."

LEVERS

WHEELS

A bicycle has both wheels and levers.

LEVERS

WHEELS

WHEELS

20

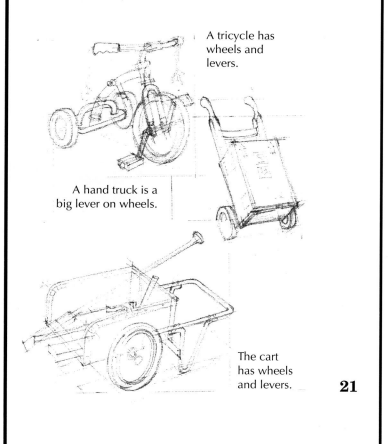

A tricycle has wheels and levers.

A hand truck is a big lever on wheels.

The cart has wheels and levers.

21

Responding

- Encourage the children to share their questions and wonderings. The children may be curious about how so many different bicycle parts can be levers. You may need to explain that handle *brakes* are levers that, when squeezed, activate the braking mechanism of the bike. The *handlebars* serve as a lever that allows the rider to turn the bike with ease. When you pull on the right arm of the lever, your bike turns right. When you pull on the left arm, your bike turns left. Finally, the *pedal arms* serve as a lever that allows you to turn the chain that turns the back wheel of your bicycle. (Your bike is a rear-wheel-drive vehicle; the force of the moving rear wheel sets in motion the front wheel.) To help the children understand how these levers make the rider's work easier, you might ask them to think about how much harder it would be to stop a bike by dragging your feet than by using brakes. Ask them to imagine what it would be like to steer a bike with a knob instead of handlebars. FInally, ask them to think about how difficult—or impossible—it would be to ride a bike if you had to push the wheels or pull on the bike chain yourself instead of simply pushing down on the pedal arms with your feet.

- Some children may wonder why a hand truck is called a lever on wheels. You may need to explain that the handles of a hand truck act as the long arms of a lever, while the platform acts as the short arm. The wheels of the hand truck act not only as wheels but as the pivot of the lever. When you slide the platform of the hand truck under a heavy box and then push down on the handles—or levers—you can lift the box much more easily than you could on your own. Then the wheels roll away the box much more easily than you could carry it or drag it away.

- Add new information to the Machines chart or web. Invite the children to tell you in which section of the chart their suggestions should be listed. For example, the children should now be able to tell you that a bicycle belongs under both the heading Wheel and the heading Lever.

✱ READING A STEP-BY-STEP PRACTICE STORY

"Dragons Don't Get Colds"
Story 34

Getting Ready to Read

- Have the children assemble the Step-by-Step Practice Story.
- Discuss with the children what they noticed about the story as they put it together.
- Encourage the children to **predict** what the story will be about. If they simply say, "It's about a dragon," ask them what else they think the story might be about or say, "Tell me more." Then invite the children to find out whether their predictions are right as they read the story.

Recommendations

- Call on a volunteer to read the title.
- Call on different children to read each page of the story aloud. Feel free to stop and discuss with the class anything of interest on a page, then have another child reread the page before going on. Help the children blend any words they have difficulty with or remind them of the pronunciation of outlaw words.
- Have the class reread the story. Alternate having individuals and groups read each page.

Responding

- Ask the children whether they have any questions about what they have just read, such as problems with recognizing outlaw words, blending, or understanding vocabulary. Allow the class to try to clear up the problem areas.
- To determine whether the children are focusing on the words in the story rather than simply on the pictures, have them answer questions such as the following by pointing to and saying the word. Then call on children to point to any word they choose and say it.

    What is the name of the dragon?
    What hurts the dragon?
    What do dragons breathe?
- Ask the children to discuss what the story is about and what they like about it.

Have the children reread the story with a partner.

* READING ALOUD

Be sure to set aside time to read to the children. Both of the following books relate particularly well to the concepts in *Machines in Our Garden.* You may want to locate one or both books to read to your class.

Big Wheels by Anne Rockwell
Bikes by Anne Rockwell

Remember to ask the children what they found most interesting about the reading and what they have learned.

See **Learning Framework Card 5** for additional suggestions for reading aloud.

TEACHING TIP

Set aside ten minutes for partner reading every day. During this time, you should read with individuals, recording their progress. Reading Assessment Sheets for Phonics Minibooks are available in *Assessment Masters, Grade 1.*

2 WRITING

Word-Building Game Have the children use paper and pencil to write the words for the Word-Building game. Write the words on the chalkboard or overhead transparency as a model. Review the *e, e_e, ee,* and *ea* spellings on the Long E Sound/Spelling Card. Remind the children that they can ask for help if they are unsure of what spelling to use in the words. Have the children proofread and correct each word before they write the next word on the list. Use the homophones in sentences so that the children will know the meaning of the word you want them to write. Dictate the following list of words:

she
see (Use in a sentence)
seed
seem (Use in a sentence)
seam (Use in a sentence)
cream
scream

Discuss with the children what they have learned about simple machines and how machines helped Ignatz and Olga plant their garden. For example, Ignatz and Olga used machines to move rocks, remove trash, and so on. Have the children imagine a machine that they would like to create to help them do something. This machine may be something that could actually work or something that is make-believe. You may want to model this. For example, "I wish that I had a machine that would make my bed for me every day. I wonder what such a machine would look like." (It could be a robot that makes the bed.) Children should come up with other ideas, such as machines for cleaning their rooms, doing their homework, walking the dog, making breakfast, or brushing their teeth. Make a list of these ideas and save them for use in the next lesson. You may want to write the children's initials next to their suggestions. Suggest to children that they think of other ideas while they are at home and out at play this afternoon. Reading the book *The Berenstain Bears' Science Fair* by Stan and Janice Berenstain, particularly the section in which Brother Bear makes a special machine, may help children come up with some fantastic ideas of their own. As you are reading this story, point out how Brother Bear uses simple machines to make his contraption.

3 GUIDED AND INDEPENDENT EXPLORATION

WORKSHOP

Remind the children that they may use this time to work on projects on their own or in small groups. Be sure that each child knows what projects he or she may choose and how to complete any independent work. Suggestions for teacher-guided, collaborative, and independent activities follow.

Work with the Teacher

- Play Tic-Tac-Toe with two teams of children. Place the clusters *shr, str, scr,* and *spl* on the grid. You might use the following patterns:

shr	str	scr	spl	str	spl
str	spl	str	spl	shr	scr
spl	scr	shr	str	scr	shr

Read a word. Have a child from each team go to the board and write the word by filling in its final letters next to the appropriate cluster. The first team to complete a horizontal line of words wins. Erase the words and play again.

- Listen to children reread Step-by-Step Practice Story 34.
- Reread pages 18–21 of *Machines in Our Garden* with children who seemed confused during today's lesson.

Independent Work

- Activity Sheet 60 reviews the spellings for the /ē/ sound. The children are asked to use story context to complete the picture. Tell the children to read the sentences and draw in anything mentioned in the description that is missing from the picture.

- Write the word *wheel* on the chalkboard. Challenge children to make as many new words as they can by changing, adding, or erasing a letter at a time. Ask them to write a sentence containing one or more of their words.

> **ASSESSMENT** Listen to the next several students individually read one of the stories in one of the Phonics Minibooks introduced so far. Using a Reading Assessment Sheet, record your observations and add them to each student's folder.

Student Collaboration

- Challenge pairs of children to write and illustrate sentences that tell about ways a person might use a wheel or a lever. Display their finished papers in the classroom.
- Invite the children to play Go Fish! Prepare some new cards with words that contain /ē/ spelled *e_e, ee,* and *ea.* Check today's Blending lesson for word ideas.

Home/School Connection

Send home the take-home version of Phonics Minibook 9 for the children to share with their families.

Name

At the Park

Steve needs sneakers for his feet.
He has a purple popsicle to eat.
A man reads a map on his lap.
Eve stands by the tree. The
chimpanzee has a banana.

Activity Sheet 60   Machines in Our Garden

Activity Sheet 60

LESSON
61

●●● Lesson Overview

New Learning

- /kw/ spelled *qu*

Prepare Ahead

- Bingo cards and Bingo word list (see page 298)

Materials

- *Machines in Our Garden*, pages 22–23
- "Queen Squid and Her Sea Pals," Step-by-Step Practice Story 35
- Sound/Spelling Card 17, Quacking ducks
- Learning Framework Cards 2, 3, 4, 5
- Reading/Writing Connection, pages 112–113
- Activity Sheet 61

GETTING STARTED

Choose one or both of the following activities to focus the children's attention and to review some of the concepts they have been learning.

Long Sound/Short Sound Review long *e* and short *e* spellings by writing one word on the chalkboard at a time. Have the children read the word to themselves. If the word contains a long *e* sound, they should hold their arms out from their sides. If the word contains a short *e* sound, they should hold their hands close together in front of them. After the children have indicated whether the *e* is long or short, ask them to read the word aloud together. Use the following words:

seem	web	steam	weed
these	even	eat	splendid
me	pest	feet	fever

Find a Word Write words with long vowel spellings on the chalkboard. Name a long vowel sound and have a child go to the board and touch any word that contains the sound. Give a signal for the whole class to read the word. Then have the child identify and circle the spelling of the long vowel. Continue until all the words have been read. Words to use are

eagle	lion	five	state
cable	music	stone	fuse
fever	see	donut	here

1 READING

PHONICS

* **Introduce /kw/ Spelled qu** Turn Sound/Spelling Card 17, Quacking ducks, and ask the children what animals they see on the card and what sound they make. Tell the children this is the Quacking ducks card and that its sound is /kw/. Point to the spelling *qu* and tell the children that the letters *q* and *u* together make the /kw/ sound. Ask what the blank after the *qu* spelling means. If necessary, explain that it means that the *qu* spelling does not usually occur at the end of a word. Then read aloud the Quacking ducks story.

You can find the procedure for introducing a new sound on **Learning Framework Card 2.**

17
©1995 Open Court Publishing Company   Quacking ducks

Quincy the Duck couldn't quite quack
Like all the other quacking ducks.
Oh, he could say /kw/ /kw/ /kw/ /kw/,
But it never seemed just right.

When Quincy tried to quack quietly (**softly**) /kw/ /kw/ /kw/ /kw/
His quack came out loudly (**loudly**) /kw/ /kw/ /kw/ /kw/!
When he tried to quack slowly (**slowly**) /kw/ . . . /kw/ . . . /kw/ . . . /kw/
His quack came out quickly (**quickly**) /kw/ /kw/ /kw/ /kw/!
Quincy just couldn't quack right!

One day Quincy was practicing quacks.
His friend Quip quacked along with him.
"Repeat after me," said Quip (**quietly**) /kw/ /kw/ /kw/ /kw/.
But Quincy quacked back, (**in normal voice**) /kw/ /kw/ /kw/ /kw/ /kw/!
Quincy still couldn't quack quite right.

But Quincy kept quacking. He said, "I won't quit
Until I quack like the best quackers around."
Can you show Quincy how quacking ducks quack?
(**Have the children join in**) /kw/ /kw/ /kw/ /kw/ /kw/ /kw/ /kw/ /kw/!

Tell the children to listen to some words and to signal when they hear a word that begins with the /kw/ sound. Example words are

quiet	question	quit
queen	cookies	quarrel
quick	washer	quilt

Have the children review Sound/Spelling Card 17 and the information on it.

✱ **Blending** Have the children blend the following words and sentences. For additional suggestions for blending, see **Learning Framework Card 3.**

✎ Line 1: quilt   quick   quit   quite

Line 2: quack   quake   queen   quiet

Line 3: squeal   squeak   squeeze   squirrel

Line 4: creep   cream   scream   screen

Sentence 1: Hugo heard the quick squirrel run up the tree.

Sentence 2: The queen lived quite far from the princess.

Sentence 3: Peter likes to sleep under a huge quilt.

Words In writing the words, be sure to write the *qu* spelling as a unit before having the children give the sound /kw/.

Contrast the words *quit* and *quite* in line 1. Point out that the *e* at the end of *quite* makes the *i* a long vowel. In line 3, blend *squirrel* as follows: /s/ /qu/ /ir/ /r/ /e/ /l/, *squirrel.* The children will adjust their pronunciation as they recognize the word.

Review the words by asking the children to find and read words in which they hear the following sounds. More than one word may be used.

- short *i*
- long *e*
- short *a*
- /ir/
- long *i*

Ask children to identify each long vowel spelling.

Sentences Introduce the outlaw words *heard* and *lived* before writing the sentences. Write the words on the board, pronounce them, and have the children repeat them. Be sure that the children understand the meanings of the words and have them use the words in oral sentences. Then write sentences 1–3 on the board and have children read them.

❯ Reading/Writing Connection, pages 112–113, provides additional practice with the /kw/ sound spelled *qu.* Have the children read and copy the words and sentence on page 112. Then help the children read all the words on the top of page 113 before giving the following clues. The children should fill in the circle in front of the correct word.

Box 1: The word that means the opposite of *loud.*

Box 2: The sound a duck makes.

Box 3: Mark the word *licked.* The cat licked her kitten.

Name

Lesson 61

Sounds and Spellings

qu_

qu _____   Qu _____

Writing Words and Sentences

queen queen   quack quack

quiet quiet   quit quit

The quilt is made of squares.

The quilt is made of

squares.

Consonant Sounds and Spellings

112 R/WC   Machines in Our Garden

Reading/Writing Connection, page 112

Name

Lesson 61

Listening for Words

○ quit	○ cake	○ liquid
○ quite	○ quake	● licked
● quiet	● quack	○ liked

Dictation and Spelling

_____   _____

Machines in Our Garden   Decoding/Spelling
                                          R/WC 113

Reading/Writing Connection, page 113

✳ READING THE BIG BOOK

Machines in Our Garden
pages 22–23

Activating Prior Knowledge

Invite the children to share anything they remember from yesterday's reading.

Recommendations for Reading

Display pages 22–23 of *Machines in Our Garden.* Read the story line on page 22. Before reading the picture captions on pages 22–23, pause to discuss the meaning of *ramp.* Encourage the children to ask questions and to share their ideas about ramps.

STRATEGIC R·E·A·D·I·N·G PROMPTS

These prompts may be used as guides when working with reading strategies.

1 If no one asks what a ramp is, wonder aloud about the meaning of this word. Ask the children where one might find the meaning of *ramp*. If none of them suggests it, remind the children that the Glossary might be a good place to look.

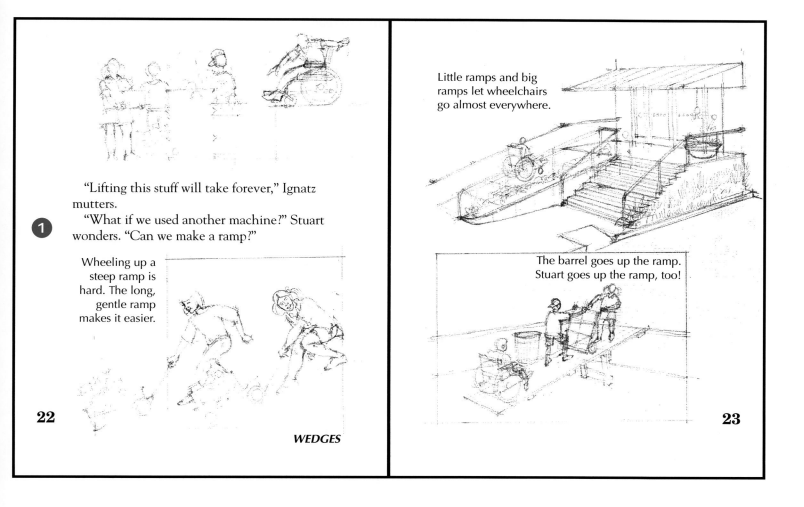

1 "Lifting this stuff will take forever," Ignatz mutters.

"What if we used another machine?" Stuart wonders. "Can we make a ramp?"

Wheeling up a steep ramp is hard. The long, gentle ramp makes it easier.

22

WEDGES

Little ramps and big ramps let wheelchairs go almost everywhere.

The barrel goes up the ramp. Stuart goes up the ramp, too!

23

Responding

- Call on volunteers to tell what Ignatz and Stuart's problem is and how Stuart proposes to solve it. Ask the children to discuss how they think a ramp will help Ignatz and Stuart.
- Invite the children to discuss ramps they may have seen. Some of the children might point out that a playground slide is a ramp. Discuss with the children how machines not only make work easier but can also be used for fun.

✳ **READING A STEP-BY-STEP PRACTICE STORY**

"Queen Squid and Her Sea Pals"
Story 35

Getting Ready to Read

- Have the children assemble the Step-by-Step Practice Story.
- Discuss with the children what they noticed about the story in browsing it as they put it together.
- Encourage the children to **predict** what the story will be about. If they simply say, "It's about a squid," ask them what else they think the story might be about or say, "Tell me more" or "What else did you notice when you browsed?" Then invite the children to find out whether their predictions are right as they read the story.

Recommendations

- Call on a volunteer to read the title. Call on a different child to read each page of the story aloud. Feel free to stop and discuss with the class anything of interest on a page, then have another child reread the page before going on. Help the children blend any words they have difficulty with or remind them of the pronunciation of outlaw words.
- Reread the story. Select a different child to read each page.

Responding

- Ask the children whether they had any problems as they were reading, such as recognizing outlaw words, blending, or understanding vocabulary. Allow the class to try to clear up the problems areas.
- To determine whether the children are focusing on the words in the story rather than simply on the pictures, have them answer questions such as the following and point to the word or words that give the answer. Call on two or three children to say the word. Then allow children to point to any word they choose and read it.

    What kind of animal is the queen?
    What did the queen need?
    What black stuff did the queen squirt?

- Ask the children to tell anything they can about the story, including what they liked about it. Keep this discussion brief, but if the children's answers are sparse, ask, "What else?"

Have the children reread the story with partners.

* READING ALOUD

Be sure to set aside time to read aloud to the children. You may want to read one or both of the following machine-related books:

Machines at Work by Byron Barton

Farm Machinery by R. J. Stephen

After reading, remember to ask what the children liked best and how the reading added to their knowledge of machines. See **Learning Framework Card 5** for suggestions for reading aloud.

2 WRITING

* DICTATION AND SPELLING

Have the children turn to the bottom of page 113 of their Reading/Writing Connection book. Dictate the following words and sentence, using the suggestions for dictation that appear on **Learning Framework Card 4.**

Line 1:   mean   stream

Line 2:   see   need

Sentence: The seal eats fish.

To help the children spell the words, tell them that the words in line 1 have the *ea* spelling for long *e* and that the words in line 2 have the *ee* spelling for long *e*.

COLLABORATIVE AND INDEPENDENT WRITING

Review the list of suggestions that the students generated in the previous lesson. Have the children begin drawing pictures of their imaginary machines or inventions. Have them write about their machines to tell what they are, and what they do.

Leave ample time for Seminar. Children should enjoy seeing and hearing about one another's fantastic machines. They should ask questions about each machine, its intended use, and the way it works.

3 GUIDED AND INDEPENDENT EXPLORATION

W O R K S H O P

Remind the children that they may use this time to work on projects on their own or with small groups. Be sure that each child knows what projects he or she may choose and how to complete any independent work. Suggestions for teacher-guided, collaborative, and independent activities follow.

Work with the Teacher

- Review the Blending activity with children who may benefit from additional practice.
- Listen to individuals or pairs of children reread Step-by-Step Practice Story 35.
- To review *qu, squ, ee, ea,* and *e_e,* play Bingo with a small group of children. Include the above spellings on the Bingo cards and in the words on the Bingo word list. Words you might use include those that appear in the last four Blending exercises.
- Ask children to read aloud to you from any books of their choice. Invite others who are interested to join you.

Independent Work

- In Activity Sheet 61 the children are asked to build new words by changing one or two letters at a time. Tell the children to follow the instructions on the sheet and to write each new word on the blank provided. On the last lines, the children can decide which letters to change and write new words of their own choosing.
- Children who have not finished drawing or writing about imaginary machines or inventions may continue their work at this time.

Student Collaboration

- Ask partners to reread Step-by-Step Practice Story 35. Challenge them to make a list of all the words in the story that contain the /kw/ sound, the long *e* sound, or both sounds.
- Invite the children to work in pairs to review *ea* and *ee* homonyms. Before Workshop begins, write the following word pairs on the chalkboard:

  see   sea
  beet   beat
  meat   meet
  tea   tee
  heal   heel
  peek   peak
  steel   steal

Illustrate the first pair with drawings of a pair of eyes and ocean waves. The children can read and illustrate the remaining pairs.

> **ASSESSMENT** Listen to individuals read one of the stories in a Phonics Minibook to you. Use a Reading Assessment Sheet to record your observations and add these to the students' folders.

Home/School Connection

Send home Step-by-Step Practice Story 34. Encourage the children to read it to their families.

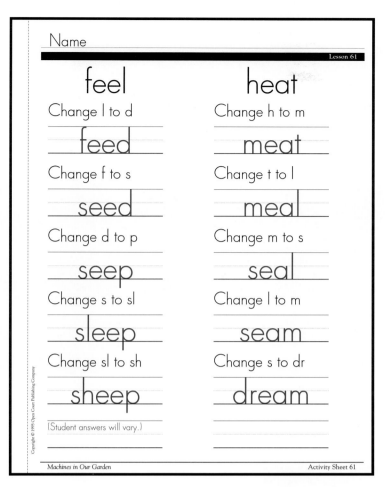

Name

feel
Change l to d

feed

Change f to s

seed

Change d to p

seep

Change s to sl

sleep

Change sl to sh

sheep

(Student answers will vary.)

heat
Change h to m

meat

Change t to l

meal

Change m to s

seal

Change l to m

seam

Change s to dr

dream

Machines in Our Garden

Activity Sheet 61

Activity Sheet 61

LESSON
62

Lesson Overview

New Learning

- Long vowels followed by *r*

Materials

- *Machines in Our Garden*, pages 24–25
- Learning Framework Cards 3, 5
- Reading/Writing Connection, pages 114–115
- Activity Sheet 62

GETTING STARTED

Choose one or both of the following activities to focus the children's attention and to review some of the concepts they have been learning.

Spelling Challenge   Divide the class into three or four teams. Explain that you will write a spelling for the long *e* sound on the board and give the teams thirty seconds to one minute to think of words that contain that spelling. When time is up, call on each team to read and spell its words. Write the words on the board and award one point for each correct word. Remind the teams to whisper so that those on other teams cannot overhear their words.

Quick Change Teams   Divide the group into several teams and give each team a sheet of paper. Write the word *heat* on the chalkboard. Then give the following directions, having each team member write a word and then pass the paper to the next person.

Take off the *h*. (eat)
Add *s* at the beginning. (seat)
Take off the *t*. (sea)
Add *m* at the end. (seam)
Change the *s* to *t*. (team)
Change the *t* to *dr*. (dream)

Write the list of words on the board for the teams to check their words. Have children use each word in a sentence.

1 READING

PHONICS

* Long Vowels Followed by *r* Write the word *file* on the chalkboard and have the children blend and read the word. Ask what new word they would get if they changed the letter *l* to *r*. Write *fire* beside *file* and have the children blend and read the new word. Continue having the children blend and read other words in which the long vowel is followed by the letter *r*. Use the following word pairs:

cute	cure	tone	tore	cape	care
date	dare	heat	hear	race	rare
mole	more	deep	deer		
time	tire	wide	wire		

* Blending Have the children blend the following words and sentences. For additional suggestions for blending, see **Learning Framework Card 3.**

Line 1:	**fire tire wire inquire**
Line 2:	**deer dear here hear**
Line 3:	**care share scare square**
Line 4:	**for more store explore**
Sentence 1:	**Did <u>you</u> hear <u>the</u> siren <u>from</u> <u>the</u> fire truck?**
Sentence 2:	**It is a short ride <u>to</u> <u>the</u> seashore.**
Sentence 3:	**We used a huge square crate <u>to</u> make a pretend fort.**

Words In line 1, write and blend *inquire* as follows: *in—qu—i_e—r, inquire*. Ask the children if they know another word for *inquire*.

In line 2, help the children differentiate between the meanings for *deer dear* and *here hear*. Use each pair of words in sentences to show their meanings.

The vowel sounds in lines 2, 3, and 4 approximate long *e*, long *a*, and long *o*, respectively. The children will adjust their pronunciation as they recognize the words.

Play a game to review the words. Write the numbers 1 to 4 on separate pieces of construction paper and place the pieces in a container labeled Lines. Write the numbers again on four pieces of construction paper of a different color and place these in a container labeled Words. Students select a number from each container and use the two numbers to locate the word to read. For example, if the child chooses 4 and 4, the word to find and read is *explore*. Return the numbers and repeat with other volunteers.

Sentences Before the children blend and read the sentences, review the underlined outlaw words.

TEACHING TIP

In some cases, the pronunciation of the long vowel changes slightly when it is followed by an *r*. The children will adjust their pronunciation naturally as they blend the word.

➤ Have the children turn to pages 114–115 of their Reading/Writing Connection books. On page 114, they can complete the sentences by writing the appropriate words in the blanks. On page 115, help the children choose the homophone that completes each sentence, and correctly label each picture.

✳ READING THE BIG BOOK

Machines in Our Garden
pages 24–25

Recommendations for Reading

- Invite children to retell what they learned about ramps in the previous lesson.
- Display pages 24–25 of the Big Book and read the first two lines of text on page 24, using the think-aloud prompt. Help the children use the Glossary to expand their understanding of the new term.
- Continue by reading the captions on the spread, in which different kinds of wedges are described.

Reading/Writing Connection, page 114

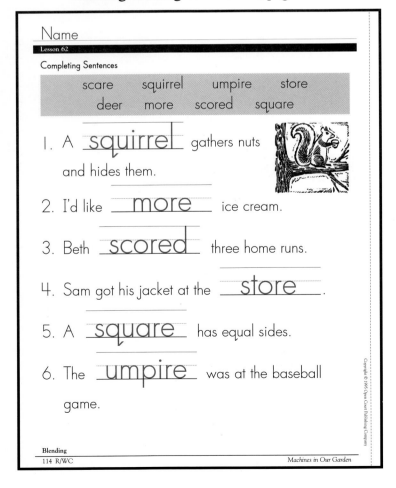

Reading/Writing Connection, page 115

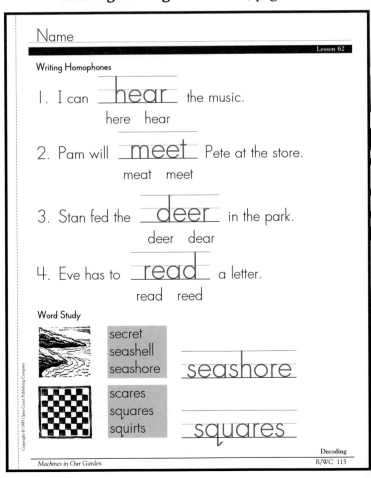

STRATEGIC R·E·A·D·I·N·G PROMPTS

These prompts may be used as guides when working with reading strategies.

1 You might model responding to the word *wedge* by saying something like, *I **wonder** how we could find out more about a wedge. Maybe we could look in the Glossary.*

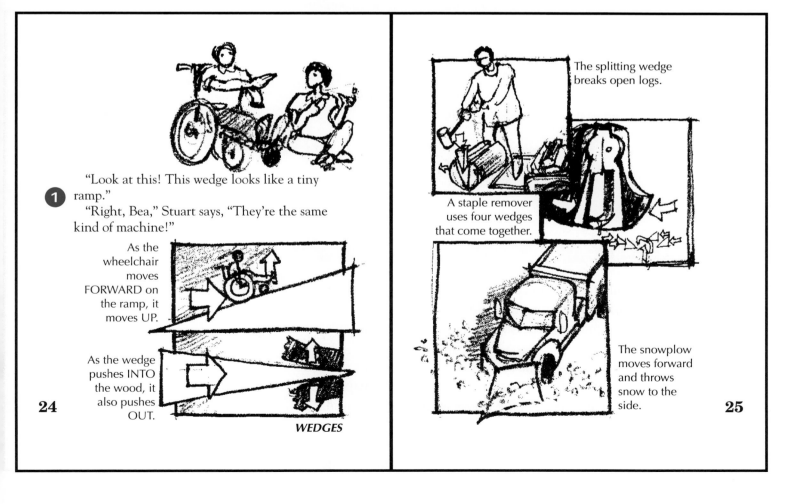

1 "Look at this! This wedge looks like a tiny ramp."

"Right, Bea," Stuart says, "They're the same kind of machine!"

As the wheelchair moves FORWARD on the ramp, it moves UP.

As the wedge pushes INTO the wood, it also pushes OUT.

24

WEDGES

The splitting wedge breaks open logs.

A staple remover uses four wedges that come together.

The snowplow moves forward and throws snow to the side.

25

Responding

- Ask the children to name the wedges that were mentioned on these pages.
- Discuss with the children other familiar wedges that are not usually thought of as wedges. You might draw a wedge or V-shape on the chalkboard and ask the children what kind of things have this shape and push other things apart. If the children need help thinking of wedges, you might suggest the following: knives, axes, shovels, airplanes, cars, needles, combs.
- Add the category Wedges to the Machines Chart and list the examples you have discussed.

✳ READING ALOUD

The following books tell about machines that include wedges. You may want to share one or both books with the children.

Katie and the Big Snow by Virginia Lee Burton

If I Drove a Tractor by Miriam Young

See **Learning Framework Card 5** for suggestions for reading aloud.

2 WRITING

✳ DICTATION AND SPELLING

Word-Building Game Have the children use their own paper for the Word-Building game. After allowing the children a few moments to write each word on their own, you should write the word on the chalkboard or the overhead transparency. Two word lists are provided—one to practice *qu* and one to practice long vowels followed by *r*.

quiet	here
quite	hire
quit	care
quick	scare
quack	score

INDEPENDENT AND COLLABORATIVE WRITING

The children should feel free to continue creating and writing about other fantastic machines and inventions. Some children may want to work on other writing projects. The suggestions that follow are related to the unit theme.

Machines are everywhere—in the supermarket, the dentist's office, the school office, the gas station, and so on. Some children may want to create a catalogue of machines, and the places where they are used. For example, computers are used in many places—offices, homes, department stores, airports. For children who still prefer to draw pictures and write labels, this is a good project. Other children may want to write about their favorite machine and tell why they feel as they do. Some children may prefer writing about how some machine actually works. The machine could be as simple as a lamp. To make a lamp work, a person puts in a bulb, plugs in the cord, and turns on the switch. A more challenging project would be to write a humorous story about a malfunctioning machine.

The children should feel free to write about whatever interests them. The subject need not be related to machines.

Hold conferences with children to help them decide on a topic. For children who have trouble getting started, recommend that they draw their ideas first.

3 GUIDED AND INDEPENDENT EXPLORATION

WORKSHOP

Remind the children that they may use this time to work on projects independently or in small groups. Make sure that all the children know what projects they may choose and how to complete any independent work. Suggestions for teacher-guided, collaborative, and independent activities follow.

Work with the Teacher

- Review long vowels followed by *r* with children who might benefit from extra help. Write the word *file* on the chalkboard, ask a volunteer to read the word aloud, and have him or her tell you how to change it to *fire*. Continue, using sequences of words such as *wire, tire, tile; for, more, store, stole; cute, cure, care, scare, square; date, dare, share, stare; deer, deep, steep, steel, steer.*
- Ask some independent readers to read aloud to you from books of their choice. Invite other children to listen in.

Independent Work

- Activity Sheet 62 requires the children to choose the correct word to complete each sentence.
- Challenge children to copy a word from the Blending exercise and to make as many new words as they can by changing one letter at a time.
- Children may continue working on writing projects.
- Suggest that the children might draw their own picture for "Queen Squid and Her Sea Pals," Step-by-Step Practice Story 35. Have them write a sentence to tell about it.

Student Collaboration

- Pairs of children might like to draw pictures showing different examples of wedges or ramps. Refer them to the Machines chart for drawing ideas. Ask each pair to write a sentence about the drawing at the bottom of their paper. If possible, display the drawings in the classroom.
- Invite pairs or groups of children to play the classroom game of their choice. Provide a selection of games for them to choose from.

TEACHING TIP

Encourage the children to read to each other. You, too, should choose children to read with. As you read with each child, note his or her progress.

Home/School Connection

Have the children take home Step-by-Step Practice Story 35 to read aloud to their families.

Name _____

Lesson 62

1. See the ___deer___ run.
   | deer |
   | dean |

2. Dad ___rakes___ leaves.
   | racks |
   | rakes |

3. A whale swims in the ___sea___.
   | sea |
   | seal |

4. I eat ___meat___ for dinner.
   | meat |
   | mean |

5. The ___tea___ is hot.
   | team |
   | tea |

6. The dog does a ___flip___.
   | flea |
   | flip |

Activity Sheet 62   *Machines in Our Garden*

Activity Sheet 62

LESSON 63

Lesson Overview

New Learning

- /ē/ spelled _y, _ie_

Materials

- *Machines in Our Garden*, pages 26–27
- "The Fancy Party," Step-by-Step Practice Story 36
- Sound/Spelling Card 37, Long E
- Learning Framework Cards 3, 4, 5
- Reading/Writing Connection, pages 116–117
- Activity Sheet 63

GETTING STARTED

Choose one or both of the following activities to focus the children's attention and to review some of the concepts they have been learning.

Stop Sign Prepare a set of cards with action words and phrases and one card with the word *stop*. Have the children stand. Hold up one card at a time and have the children perform the action in place until you hold up the "stop sign." Use these action words and phrases (add others if you wish):

hop	hands on head	hands behind back
hands on knees	whisper	sneeze
hold ears	stamp feet	wiggle nose
snore		

Sound Review Name a Sound/Spelling Card and call on a child to say the sound the card represents. The child should then give a word that contains the sound and identify where the sound is heard in the word. That child then names a new card and calls on another child to say the new sound and a new word. Continue in the same manner.

TEACHING TIP

You may prefer to write the actions on an overhead transparency and uncover one at a time.

1 READING

PHONICS

⁕ **Introducing /ē/ spelled _y and _ie_** Point to Sound/Spelling Card 37, Long E, and ask the children what sound this card represents. Review the *e, e_e, ee,* and *ea* spellings for the sound /ē/. Explain that there is another spelling for /ē/ and point to the _y spelling. Ask the children what the blank in front of the *y* means. Explain, if necessary, that the *y* spelling of the long *e* sound occurs only at the end of a word or syllable. Write the following words on the chalkboard: *baby, bunny, candy, lady.*

Blend each word with the children. Ask how many parts or syllables each word has. Point out that /ē/ spelled as *y* appears at the end of words with two or more syllables. Many words of two or more syllables that end with a long *e* sound have this _y spelling. If some of the children's names end with this spelling invite them to write their name on the board.

Point to the spelling _ie_ on the Sound/Spelling Card. Tell the children that this is one more spelling for the long *e* sound. Explain that the blanks with this spelling mean that this spelling does not usually come at the beginning or end of a word. Instead, there is usually a consonant before and after the *ie* with a long *e* sound.

To demonstrate that the *ie* spelling and the *y* spelling for long *e* are often related to each other write the word *pony* on the chalkboard. Have the children blend the word and use it in a sentence. Tell them that *pony* means just one animal. Ask what word they would use to talk about two or more animals. Write the word *ponies* on the board and have the children blend it. Tell the children that often when you change words ending in *y* to mean more than one you change the *y* to *ie* and add *s.* Teach the children the following rhyme:

> For more than one, no need to guess—
> Change *y* to *i* and add *es.*

Review the Long E card and all the spellings.

⁕ **Blending** Have the children blend the following words and sentences. For reference and additional suggestions for blending, see **Learning Framework Card 3**.

✐ Line 1: field   thief   chief   brief

Line 2: baby   babies   lady   ladies

Line 3: shady   pony   tiny   speedy

Line 4: party   dirty   funny   happy

Sentence 1: Did they see the tiny bunnies run across the street?

Sentence 2: They ran in the muddy field.

Sentence 3: The lazy little puppy slept on the sunny porch.

TEACHING TIP

Changing *y* to *i* before adding *es* is a spelling pattern, more than a decoding strategy. However, it may be beneficial for children to understand this principle as it affects words they will encounter in reading.

TEACHING TIP

Do not be concerned if the children have not yet mastered all the long vowel spellings that have been introduced. Encourage them to ask which spelling to use. The children will have many more opportunities to write words with long vowels and will gain confidence with the spellings through practice.

Words Be sure to write the _ie_ spelling as a unit as the children sound and blend the words.

In line 2, ask the children where they hear the sound /ē/ in each word. Explain that a final _y_ in a word with more than one syllable is usually pronounced /ē/. Remind the children of the rhyme for forming plurals that was taught above. Point out how the _y_ to _ie_ spelling change is used in these words to form plurals (with the addition of _s_).

In line 3, blend the first three words as follows: sha—dy, po—ny, ti—ny so that the children blend the first syllable with a long vowel sound. Remind the children that when a syllable ends in a vowel, that vowel is usually long.

Use the following sentences to review the words. Have a child point to and read the word that is emphasized in each sentence.

- The police _chief_ is the best hockey player on the team.
- The _thief_ ran away.
- There are two _babies_ in the stroller.
- The clown was riding a _tiny_ bike.
- Jessica is going to have a birthday _party_.

Have a child choose a word, say it, and use it in a sentence.

Sentences Follow the usual procedure to introduce the outlaw word _they_. Have the children use the word in oral sentences. Then write the sentences as the children blend the words. Point out the new word in sentences 1 and 2. To encourage fluent reading, call on individuals to reread the sentences after the whole group has read them. This would be a good time to return to the poem "Babybuggy" in the Big Book _Look Who's Reading!_ Have the children look through the poem for words with the _y_ and _ie_ spellings. Then have them read the poem with you.

➤ Reading/Writing Connection, pages 116–117, reinforces the /ē/ sound spelled _y_ and _ie_. Work with the children to complete page 116 and the top of page 117.

✳ READING THE BIG BOOK

Machines in Our Garden
pages 26–27

Recommendations for Reading

- Review with the children what they have already learned about machines. Be sure to refer them to the chart of machines.
- Display pages 26–27 of the Big Book and read the text and captions to the children.

Name

Lesson 63

Sounds and Spellings

e	ea
e_e	_y
ee	_ie_

Writing Words and Sentences

shiny shiny   chief chief

pony pony ponies ponies

Betty saves her pennies.

Betty saves her pennies.

Sally fed the bunnies.

Sally fed the bunnies.

Vowel Sounds and Spellings
116 R/WC

Machines in Our Garden

Reading/Writing Connection, page 116

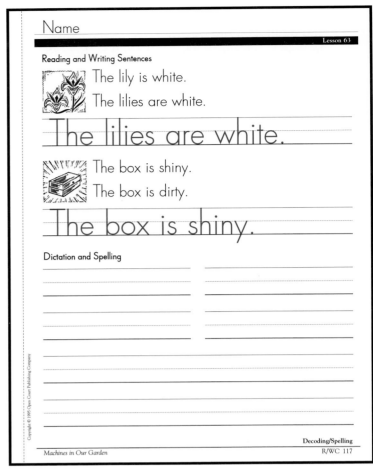

Name

Lesson 63

Reading and Writing Sentences

The lily is white.
The lilies are white.

The lilies are white.

The box is shiny.
The box is dirty.

The box is shiny.

Dictation and Spelling

Machines in Our Garden

Decoding/Spelling
R/WC 117

Reading/Writing Connection, page 117

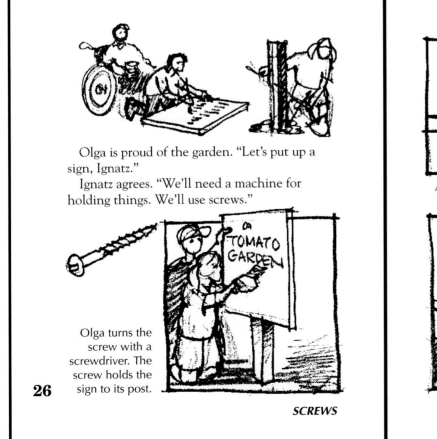

Olga is proud of the garden. "Let's put up a sign, Ignatz."

Ignatz agrees. "We'll need a machine for holding things. We'll use screws."

Olga turns the screw with a screwdriver. The screw holds the sign to its post.

26

SCREWS

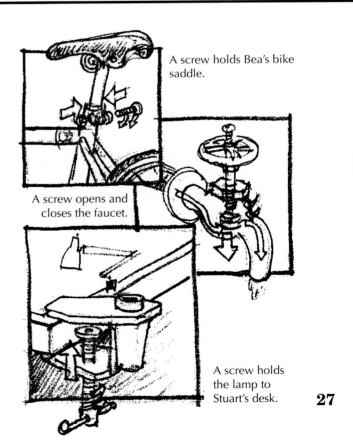

A screw holds Bea's bike saddle.

A screw opens and closes the faucet.

A screw holds the lamp to Stuart's desk.

27

Responding

- Discuss the screws that are presented in the story.
- Help the children to think of other examples of screws, such as on the base of lightbulbs, the tops of jars, corkscrews, and drills.
- Add the category *screws* to the *Machines* chart along with the examples you have discussed.

✳ **READING A STEP-BY-STEP PRACTICE STORY**

"The Fancy Party"
Story 36

Getting Ready to Read

Have the children put together Step-by-Step Practice Story 36. Call on a child to read the title. Ask what children might do at a party.

Recommendations

Call on a different child to read each page of the story aloud. If a child has difficulty with a word, help her or him blend the word. Tell the children any outlaw words they do not know. Reread the story at least twice, calling on different children to read each time.

Responding

After reading, ask the children to tell in their own words what happened in the story and to discuss any difficulties they had in reading it. To check that the children are paying attention to the words, ask the following questions, having the children point to the word or words that answer each question.

Whom did Nelly and Willy invite to their party?
What did Nelly make for the party?
What did the puppies do after the party was over?

Have the children reread the story with a partner.

TEACHING TIP

Remind the children to read each book twice. When they finish reading today's book, they should get one from a previous lesson. Reading Assessment Sheets for Phonics Minibooks are available in *Assessment Masters, Grade 1*.

✳ **READING ALOUD**

You may want to share the following books with your class:
Simple Machines by Anne Horvatic
The Science Book of Machines by Neil Ardley

See **Learning Framework Card 5** for suggestions for reading aloud.

2 WRITING

✳ **DICTATION AND SPELLING**

Have the children open their Reading/Writing Connection books to page 117. Dictate the following words and sentence, using the

suggestions for dictation that appear on **Learning Framework Card 4.**
Be sure to use *dear* in a sentence. Help children with vowel spellings as
necessary.

Line 1:	dear	share
Line 2:	tire	more
Sentence:	The store was quite large.	

INDEPENDENT AND COLLABORATIVE WRITING

Select children who are working on pieces about different types of
machines. Have them share their pieces during Seminar. Children may
get ideas for their own writing from these authors.

Have the children continue their writing on whatever they please.
Remind them to put their names and dates on their work before they
put it in their writing folders.

3 GUIDED AND INDEPENDENT EXPLORATION

WORKSHOP

Remind the children that they may use this time to work on projects independently or in small groups.
Make sure that all the children know what projects they may choose and how to complete any independent
work. Suggestions for teacher-guided, collaborative, and independent activities follow.

Work with the Teacher

- Use the Sound/Spelling Cards to review the various spellings of long vowels.
- Listen to individuals or pairs of children reread Step-by-Step Practice Story 36, "The Fancy Party."
- Review today's Blending exercise with children who need extra help with the various spellings of /ē/.

Independent Work

- Activity Sheet 63 reviews the /ē/ sound and spellings. Tell the children to cut out the presents at the bottom of the page and paste the ones with the /ē/ words to the party table. They can then color the table and gifts any way they like.
- Children may continue working on machine stories or on other unfinished pieces. Remind them to write their names on any pieces they complete and to place those papers in their writing folders.

Student Collaboration

- The children may wish to work in pairs to create Scrambled Sentences. When they have finished printing each word on an index card, they may place the cards in an envelope and trade Scrambled Sentences with another pair. Remind each pair to print an answer key on the inside flap of their envelope.
- Suggest that the children work with a partner to draw a picture of one way a screw is used and to write a sentence telling about their picture. If space permits, display their work in the classroom.
- Invite the children to form read-aloud groups. One or two children from each group can read the books of their choice to the other group members.

Name

tree

cheap

Eve

each

squeeze

cream

Eve

each

Fred

bread

cream

head

tree

cheap

squeeze

Machines in Our Garden

Activity Sheet 63

Activity Sheet 63

LESSON 64

Lesson Overview

Materials

- *Machines in Our Garden*, pages 26–27
- Phonics Minibook 11, *Dog Dreams*
- Learning Framework Cards 3, 5, 6
- Reading/Writing Connection, pages 118–119
- Activity Sheet 64

Prepare Ahead

- Containers with plastic press-on lids, containers with screw-on tops (see page 317)
- Reading Relay Flash Cards (see page 324 and Games and Songs Teacher Tool Card 9)

GETTING STARTED

Use one or both of the following activities to focus the children's attention and to review some of the concepts they have been learning.

Sound Review Place a set of Letter Cards in a container. Have children choose a card, then name the Sound/Spelling Card, say the sound, and give the spelling(s). If a vowel is chosen, the child may choose to tell about either the long or short sound.

Dictate to the Teacher Write the word *mule* on the chalkboard and call on a child to read it. Then have the children tell you how to change the word to make the following words:

mile

mole

more

mare

care

cure

pure

1 READING

Review the Long E Sound/Spelling Card. Have the children tell you the sound, the spellings, and anything special about the spellings. Pay particular attention to the *y* and *_ie_* spellings.

Blending Have the children blend the following words and sentences. For additional suggestions for blending, see **Learning Framework Card 3**.

Line 1:	city cities shine shiny
Line 2:	thirsty sadly hurry hazy
Line 3:	memory story fifty thirty
Line 4:	leave dream sneeze seaweed
Sentence 1:	The silly man juggles three shiny balls.
Sentence 2:	We visited thirty cities this summer.
Sentence 3:	We wore fancy hats at the party.

Words In line 1, after the children blend the word *city*, ask them what word tells about more than one city. Blend *cities* with them. Point out that the *y* is changed to *i* before adding *es*. Compare *shine* and *shiny*. Have a volunteer tell you how the words are the same.

As you blend the words in lines 2 and 3, remind the children that a final *y* in a word with more than one syllable usually indicates /ē/. Clap the words to confirm that each one has two or more syllables.

Use line 4 to review other spellings for /ē/. Note that the final *e* in the word *sneeze* is silent.

Review the words using a sponge die labeled with the numbers 1–4 and two stars. Tell the children to choose a word line, roll the die, and read the word in the line that matches the number they roll. If they roll a star, they can choose to read any word in the line or all the words in the line. If they roll a number that has already been rolled, they roll again.

Sentences As you blend the sentences, pay special attention to words with more than one syllable and that end with *y*. Remind the children that *y* in this position makes the sound /ē/.

❯ Have the children turn to pages 118–119 of their Reading/Writing Connection book. For the top part of page 118, they should write the words from the list on the blanks next to the words that have almost the same meaning. For the bottom half of the page, have the children read all the words before giving the following clues to mark the target words.

Name _____

Lesson 64

Writing Synonyms

| tiny | funny | muddy | unhappy |

dirty **muddy** silly **funny**

little **tiny** sad **unhappy**

Listening for Words

Box 1	Box 2	Box 3
● water	● grass	○ story
○ winter	○ glass	● stories
○ whisper	○ grab	○ study

Box 4	Box 5	Box 6
● dirty	○ quack	○ sheep
○ dizzy	● quake	● shore
○ distance	○ quick	○ shape

Decoding

118 R/WC

Machines in Our Garden

Reading/Writing Connection, page 118

Name _____

Lesson 64

Completing Sentences

| ponies | thirsty | twenty |
| emergency | stories | cherries |

1. Popcorn can make you **thirsty**.

2. Call 911 in an **emergency**.

3. Jerry likes to eat red **cherries**.

4. Thirty is more than **twenty**.

5. The **ponies** were nice to ride.

6. There are many **stories**
to read in the library.

Decoding

R/WC 119

Machines in Our Garden

Reading/Writing Connection, page 119

Box 1: Something you swim in.

Box 2: Something green that grows in a yard.

Box 3: Mark the word *stories*. Dad read us three stories.

Box 4: A word that means the opposite of clean.

Box 5: The word that rhymes with bake.

Box 6: Mark the word *shore*. I found seashells on the shore.

The children can complete the sentences on page 119 by writing the correct word in each blank.

✳ READING THE BIG BOOK

Machines in Our Garden
pages 26–27

Recommendations

- Display pages 26–27 and ask the children to recap what they know about screws.
- To give the children a better understanding of how screws help to hold things together, you might want to perform the following experiment:

Divide the class into small groups. Give each group two containers, one with a plastic, press-on lid, and one with a screw-on lid. Ask the children to take turns trying to pull the two lids off of their respective containers.

Responding

- Discuss with the children which lid was easier to remove, the press-on lid or the screw top. Ask for volunteers to explain how the screw top holds the lid onto the jar.
- Add *screw-on lid* to your class list of simple machines. Discuss any other examples of screws the children can think of and add them to the *screws* category of the Machines chart.
- Review the entire list of simple machines with the children. As you finish reading through each category, ask the children if they have thought of other machines to add to the list.

✳ READING A PHONICS MINIBOOK

Dog Dreams
Phonics Minibook 11

Getting Ready to Read

Reading the Title Ask the children to read the title of the book. If any children have dogs as pets, ask what dogs often do when they dream. (Most dogs will move their feet or sometimes bark as they sleep.)

Browsing the Story Invite the children to page through the book, commenting on the illustrations and predicting what the book will be about. Ask what they think a dog might dream about.

Recommendations

Follow the standard procedure for reading a Phonics Minibook:

- Call on a different child to read each page of the story aloud using the procedures shown on **Learning Framework Card 6**. Then have a different child reread the page before going on.
- Reread the story at least twice, calling on different children to read.

2

Quincy the duck was out for some sun.

3

"Quack, quack, quack,"
Quincy said as he went.
"Quack, quack, quack, quack."

4

Quincy came to a tree
with big green leaves.
A dog was asleep under the tree.

5

It was Harry!
"Quack!" said Quincy.
But Harry did not wake up.

6

Harry was deep in a dream.
Harry's feet ran in his sleep.

7

Harry spoke in his sleep.
Quincy heard Harry repeat,
"Hurry, Harry, hurry!
Hurry, Harry, hurry!"

8

"Harry!" Quincy quacked.
"Wake up! You do not have
to hurry in your sleep!"

9

"Fire!" barked Harry.
"Hurry, Harry, hurry!"

"I've got to wake him up!"
said Quincy. "Wake up, Harry!
Quack, quack, quack, quack, quack!"

10

Harry woke up. He was all out of breath.
"I had a dream," said Harry.
"I had three dreams."

"Tell me your dreams," said Quincy.
"I like dream stories."

11

"In one dream, fleas and bees
were after me. I had to hurry.
Hurry, Harry, hurry!"

12

"In the next dream,
a queen had me chase a rabbit.
Hurry, Harry, hurry!
I had to chase the rabbit away."

13

"In the last dream, a fire trapped
three sheep. I had to hurry.
Hurry, Harry, hurry!
I had to lead the sheep
away from the fire!"

14

"You hurry too much, Harry.
You even hurry in your sleep,"
quacked Quincy.
"You make me feel tired.
I need a little nap."

15

But Harry did not hear Quincy.
Harry was in a hurry.
He had to run off.
Hurry, Harry, hurry!

16

Responding

- Ask the children to talk about any difficult words they came across in their reading and to tell how they figured out those words.
- To make sure the children are focusing on the words in the story, rather than simply on the pictures, have them answer questions such as the following by pointing to and reading aloud the appropriate words:

  What is the name of the duck in the story?

  What did Quincy see under the tree?

  What did Quincy say to Harry?

  What did Harry say in his sleep?

  Why was Harry hurrying in his first dream?

  Why was Harry hurrying in his second dream?

  Why was he hurrying in his third dream?

- Invite children to tell what they like best about the story.

Have the children reread the story with a partner.

✽ READING ALOUD

You may want to share one or more of the following books about machines with your class:

Dig, Drill, Dump, Fill by Tana Hoban

Machines as Tall as Giants by Paul Stickland

Click, Rumble, Roar: Poems About Machines by Laura Geringer

After reading, remember to ask the children questions such as "Did anything in the book surprise you? What?" and "Did this book answer any questions you had?"

For additional suggestions for reading aloud, see **Learning Framework Card 5.**

TEACHING TIP

Set aside ten minutes for partner reading every day. During this time, you should read with individuals, recording their progress. Reading Assessment Sheets for Phonics Minibooks are available in *Assessment Masters, Grade 1*.

2 WRITING

✽ DICTATION AND SPELLING

Word-Building Game Have the children use their own paper. As you dictate each word, remind the children to check the Sound/Spelling Cards to help them write the words. Provide help with the vowel spellings as needed. Write the words on the chalkboard or an overhead transparency as a model. Have the children proofread and correct each word before writing the next word in the list. Use the following words:

sandy

sand

land

lad

lady

INDEPENDENT AND COLLABORATIVE WRITING

Discuss what the children learned about screws in the experiment they did. Suggest that they illustrate and write about this experiment. They may want to work in the groups in which they did the experiment. Have them display their papers.

Children may want to continue working on their writing in progress. If children are finished, encourage them to select a recent piece from their writing folders that they would like to revise, proofread, and perhaps publish. Review with the children what they need to think about as they revise their work: Does it make sense? Is there anything else I can add? How can I extend my sentences? For proofreading, children should remember to check for capitals, end punctuation, and the spelling of short vowel words and outlaws. If any children are ready, meet with small groups to help them revise and edit their work.

TEACHING TIP

You might want to gather sets of student illustrations and explanations of their experiments into books. Put a piece about each experiment in each book and make several books to keep in the classroom library.

3 GUIDED AND INDEPENDENT EXPLORATION

WORKSHOP

Remind the children that they may use this time to work on projects on their own or in small groups. Make sure each child knows what projects he or she may choose and how to complete any independent work. Suggestions for teacher-guided, collaborative and independent activities follow.

Work with the Teacher

- Listen to children reread Phonics Minibook 11. Use this opportunity to assess their progress.
- To review the spellings of long *e,* hold a Reading Relay between two teams of children. Prepare new flash cards to cover the various spellings of long *e.* Mix them up with some of the Reading Relay Flash Cards used in previous lessons.
- Repeat one or more of the experiments from today's Reading lesson with children who seemed confused during the initial teaching. If you did not have time to perform all of the experiments, you might want to use this time to try out a new experiment with those children who seem particularly interested.

Independent Work

- Activity Sheet 64 provides practice with writing plurals. Tell the children to write the words in their plural forms, then illustrate the sentence at the bottom of the page.
- The children may continue revising and proofreading their writing projects. Encourage them to exchange papers with classmates for help with proofreading.

- Remind the children that they may use this time to read on their own. Provide a selection of books for them to choose from.

Student Collaboration

- Encourage pairs of children to reread Phonics Minibook 11. Facilitate peer tutoring by pairing independent readers with less fluent readers.
- Write several long vowel spellings, such as *i_e, ea,* and *a_e* on the chalkboard. Have pairs of children look through books to find and list as many words as they can for each spelling. Have them use several words in sentences.

TEACHING TIP

Encourage the children to read to each other. You, too, should choose children to read with. As you read with each child, note his or her progress.

Home/School Connection

Send home Step-by-Step Practice Story 36 and encourage the children to read it to their families.

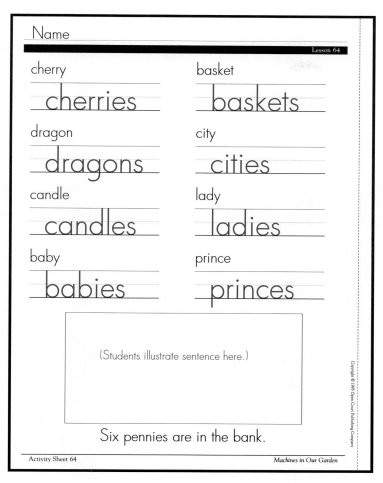

Name

cherry

cherries

basket

baskets

dragon

dragons

city

cities

candle

candles

lady

ladies

baby

babies

prince

princes

(Students illustrate sentence here.)

Six pennies are in the bank.

Copyright © 1995 Open Court Publishing Company

Machines in Our Garden

Activity Sheet 64

LESSON
65

Lesson Overview

New Learning

- /ā/ spelled *ai_* and *_ay*

Materials

- *Machines in Our Garden*, pages 28–31
- "Sail Day," Step-by-Step Practice Story 37
- Sound/Spelling Card 33, Long A
- Learning Framework Cards 3, 4, 5
- Reading/Writing Connection, pages 120–121
- Activity Sheet 65

GETTING STARTED

Choose one or both of the following activities to focus the children's attention and to review some of the concepts they have been learning.

Sound Card Review Name a vowel Sound/Spelling Card and have the children say the sound the card represents. Then call on several children one by one to give a word that contains the sound and to identify where the sound is heard in the word. Continue reviewing other cards in this fashion.

Which Doesn't Belong? Write the words *map*, *tam*, and *mat* on the chalkboard. Blend all three words, then ask the children which is different and why. Repeat with other sets of words, such as *lake, bake, bike*; *hop, hope, hip*; *cup, mug, pup*.

TEACHING TIP

Accept any response the children can justify. Some may say that *tam* is different because it doesn't start with *m*. Others may decide that *mat* and *tam* have the same letters, so *map* is different.

1 READING

PHONICS

* **Introduce /ā/ Spelled *ai_* and *_ay*** Point to Sound/Spelling Card 33, Long A, and have the children tell what they know about the spellings. Explain that there are other ways to spell the sound /ā/. Uncover or

point to the *ai_* spelling. Ask what the blank after this spelling means. Explain, if necessary, that the blank indicates that this spelling may appear at the beginning or middle of a word or syllable but not at the end of a word or syllable.

Next point to the *_ay* spelling and explain that this is another way of spelling the /ā/ sound. Ask the children what the blank in front of this spelling means. Explain, if necessary, that this spelling usually occurs at the end of a word or syllable.

Review the sound and the spellings on the Long A card. You may want to point out that a vowel often needs the help of another letter or letters to say its name.

* **Blending** Have the children blend the following words and sentences. For additional suggestions for blending, see **Learning Framework Card 3.**

Line 1:	say stay pay play
Line 2:	crayon payment daydream yesterday
Line 3:	pail mail nail snail
Line 4:	train chair afraid raise
Sentence 1:	The mailman comes with letters everyday.
Sentence 2:	The art center contains crayons, paints, and paper to use.
Sentence 3:	May hurries to the computer to play a game.

Words Remember to write the *ai_*, *_ay*, and other vowel spellings as a unit for the children to sound and blend. Blend the words in line 2 syllable by syllable (for example, *cray—on, crayon*). Ask the children what spelling pattern is repeated in the line.

Some children may be unfamiliar with the word *payment* in line 2. Have a child who is familiar with the word use it in a sentence.

In line 4, tell the children that the final *e* in *raise* is silent.

To review the words, say sentences with missing words and have the children point to, read, and erase the words that will complete each sentence.

- A _____ hides in its shell.
- A letter from grandmother came in the _____.
- The old _____ clickety clacks down the tracks.
- I like to sit in a comfortable _____.
- We play in the sand with a shovel and _____.

Have the children give clues for the remaining words.

Sentences Introduce the outlaw word *comes* in the usual manner: write it on the board, read it, and use it, or have children use it, in oral sentences. Then write sentence 1 and underline the word.

Reading/Writing Connection, page 120

Name

Lesson 65

Sounds and Spellings

a   ai_
a_e   _ay

Aa

Writing Words and Sentences

pail   _pail_   snail   _snail_

pay   _pay_   stay   _stay_

The raisins are stale.

The raisins are stale.

Kay's birthday is in May.

Kay's birthday is in May.

Vowel Sounds and Spellings

120 R/WC   Machines in Our Garden

Reading/Writing Connection, page 120

Reading/Writing Connection, page 121

Name

Lesson 65

Writing Homophones

pale   pail   sail   sale   tale   tail

pail   _sail_   _tail_

Dictation and Spelling

Machines in Our Garden

Decoding/Spelling

R/WC 121

Reading/Writing Connection, page 121

➤ Reading/Writing Connection, pages 120–121, reinforces the /ā/ sound spelled *ai_* and *_ay*. Have the children complete page 120 by reading and copying the words and sentences. Then help them choose the correct homophone to label each picture on the top of page 121.

✳ READING A BIG BOOK

Machines in Our Garden
pages 28–31

Activating Prior Knowledge
Ask volunteers to review what has happened so far in the story.

Recommendations for Reading
Finish reading *Machines in Our Garden* (pages 28–31). Encourage the children to share any questions and wonderings they may have about the gardening tools presented on these pages.

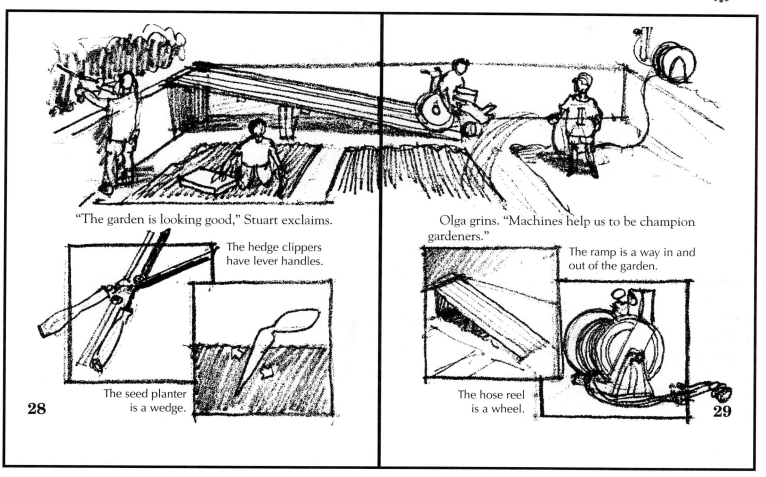

"The garden is looking good," Stuart exclaims.

The hedge clippers have lever handles.

The seed planter is a wedge.

28

Olga grins. "Machines help us to be champion gardeners."

The ramp is a way in and out of the garden.

The hose reel is a wheel.

29

"Party time!" Bea giggles.
"Machines helped us grow these tomatoes. Machines even help us at the Big Tomato Picnic!" Ignatz says.

The flip top of a juice can is a lever.

A juice squeezer has a lever.

30

A nutcracker can be a lever or a screw.

A screw cap holds a soda bottle tightly closed.

31

Responding

- Ask volunteers to list all of the machines that were discussed in the Big Book (lever, wheel, wedge, ramp, screw) and to **sum up** what they remember about each machine.
- Ask the children if they thought of any additonal examples of these machines during today's reading. Invite them to share each example and tell what it is used for.
- List any new examples and information on the Machines chart or web.

✳ **READING A STEP-BY-STEP PRACTICE STORY**

"Sail Day"
Story 37

Getting Ready to Read

Call on a volunteer to read aloud the title of the story. Encourage the children to browse the story, commenting on any words or illustrations that catch their eye.

Call attention to the outlaw word *comes*.

Recommendations

Have the children read the selection aloud. Change readers after each page. Have the selection reread aloud at least twice. For the second reading, you might assign the parts of Mrs. Fay and Ray, changing readers after every two pages.

Responding

- Ask what Ray's main thoughts were about. What was Mrs. Fay thinking about? Ask the children to tell about the problems that Mrs. Fay and Ray had during the sailing lesson. Allow the children to point out any words that were difficult or interesting.
- To focus the children's attention on the text rather than the illustrations, have children point to and read the appropriate words to answer these questions:

  What does Ray say when Mrs. Fay warns him that it might start to rain?

  What are the names of the sails in this story?

  What does Mrs. Fay tell Ray to do after it begins to rain?

Have the children reread the story with a partner.

✳ **READING ALOUD**

Ignatz and Olga grew tomatoes in their garden. The following books tell about how some other foods grow. You may want to share one or both of these books with your class.

Apples: All About Them by Alvin and Virginia B. Silverstein

Eat the Fruit, Plant the Seed by Millicent Selsam and Jerome Wexler

TEACHING TIP

Remind the children to read each book twice. When they finish today's book, they should get one from a previous lesson. Reading Assessment Sheets for Phonics Minibooks are available in *Assessment Masters, Grade 1*.

After reading, invite the children to tell what they found most interesting about the book and to discuss the new information they learned from it.

See **Learning Framework Card 5** for suggestions for modeling as you read aloud.

2 WRITING

✱ DICTATION AND SPELLING

Have the children turn to page 121 of their Reading/Writing Connection book. Dictate the following words and sentence, using the procedure for dictation on **Learning Framework Card 4.** Encourage the children to ask for help if they are unsure which vowel spelling to use. Help them try to figure out which spelling to use. For example, if a two syllable word ends with the long *e* sound, the children should realize that the correct spelling is most likely *y*.

Remind the children of the rhyme they learned about changing *y* to *i*:
For more than one, no need to guess—
Change *y* to *i* and add *es.*

Line 1:   funny   silly

Line 2:   lady   ladies

Sentence: Patty pets the bunnies.

As you help the children proofread line 1, point out the pattern of a short vowel followed by a double consonant. In line 2, point out that the long vowel in the first syllable is followed by a single consonant and another vowel.

MONITORING DICTATION Collect students' Reading/Writing Connection books. Scan them for spelling and proofreading skills. Add notes about your observations to students' portfolios.

INDEPENDENT AND COLLABORATIVE WRITING

Today should be a time for as many children as possible to share what they have written about machines. This might be a whole group Seminar, or you might have small groups hold their own Seminars. If some children have published books, tell the class that the books will be in the literacy center for everyone to enjoy.

ASSESSMENT Observe as students share their books and as they ask and respond to questions. Record your observations. Send the books home with a Family Response Form. When the books and the completed forms are returned, add them to the student portfolios. Family Response Forms can be found in *Assessment Masters, Grade 1.*

3 GUIDED AND INDEPENDENT EXPLORATION

WORKSHOP

Remind the children that they may use this time to work on projects of their own or in small groups. Be sure that each child knows what projects he or she may choose and how to complete any independent work. Suggestions for teacher-guided, collaborative, and independent activities follow.

Work with the Teacher

- Assess the children's reading ability or provide support by rereading aloud "Sail Day" with small groups of children.
- Review the Phonics lesson with additional long *a* words: *mail, fail, tail, trail, airmail; play, say, spray, way, stay; lake, able, apron, tame, came.*
- Encourage individuals or small groups to share their writing projects with you. Work with individuals to revise and proofread their work.

Independent Work

- Activity Sheet 65 reviews the /ā/ sound spelled *ai_* and *_ay*. Tell the children to cut out the letters at the bottom of the page and rearrange them to form as many words as they can. They should write each word in the appropriate column, depending on its spelling, and draw a picture of one or more of the words in the box.
- The children may copy any interesting words from "Sail Day" into their notebooks. They may want to write a sentence or begin a story that uses one or more of these words.
- Children who are ready to publish a writing piece may work on it at this time.

TEACHING TIP
You may want to reuse the format of Activity Sheet 65 in the future, substituting new spellings as the children learn them.

Student Collaboration

- Partners may reread "Sail Day." Have them find and list all the words with an *ai_* or *_ay* spelling. Have them use several of the words in sentences.
- Some children may enjoy making a mural or collage depicting the machines they have learned about during this unit. You might suggest that they complete a playground scene including at least one example of each machine discussed in the Big Book. Have them write a label next to each machine.
- The children may wish to work together on writing projects, commenting on and proofreading each other's writing in preparation for a future sharing time. Remind them to check the capital letters, punctuation, and short vowel spellings.

TEACHING TIP
Encourage the children to read with a partner. You, too, should choose children to read with. As you read with each child, note his or her progress.

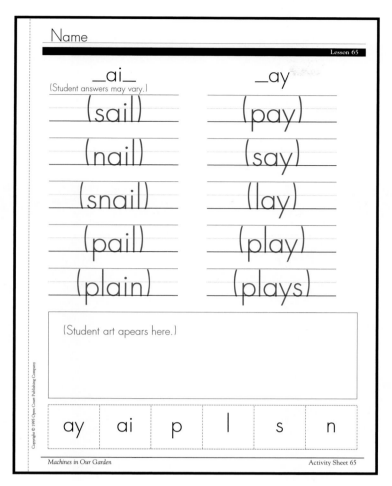

Name ___

Lesson 65

_ai_
(Student answers may vary.)

(sail)
(nail)
(snail)
(pail)
(plain)

_ay

(pay)
(say)
(lay)
(play)
(plays)

(Student art apears here.)

| ay | ai | p | l | s | n |

Machines in Our Garden   Activity Sheet 65

Activity Sheet 65

LESSON
66

Lesson Overview

New Learning

- /ī/ Spelled *igh*

Prepare Ahead

- Scrambled Sentences game (see page 339 and Games and Songs Teacher Tool Card 8)

Materials

- "The Opossum," Step-by-Step Practice Story 38
- Sound/Spelling Card 34, Long A
- Learning Framework Cards 3, 5
- Reading/Writing Connection, pages 122–123
- Activity Sheet 66

GETTING STARTED

Choose one or both of the following activities to focus the children's attention and to review some of the concepts they have been learning.

Opposites   Write these words on the chalkboard or on an overhead transparency:

hard	happy	go
neat	cold	sweet
huge	late	whisper
girl	day	giggle

Then say a word and have children find and read its opposite on the chalkboard. Use these words:

come	soft	messy
sad	shout	night
early	hot	cry
tiny	boy	sour

Long Vowel Spelling Review   This activity will review some of the spellings of long vowel sounds the children have learned so far. Divide the class into two teams. On both ends of the chalkboard, write the following words: *clay, sleep, cube, hear, stain, oval, fire, bone, ice, stare, use.* Tell the children that you will say a sound and that one child from each team should go to the board, circle a word with that sound, and underline the letter or letters that spell that sound. For each sound that the children identify correctly, their team receives a point. At the end of the activity, point to each of the words one by one and have the children read them aloud in unison.

1 READING

PHONICS

* **Introduce /ī/ Spelled *igh*** Point to Sound/Spelling Card 34, Long I, and review the *i* and *i_e* spellings that have been introduced by having the children tell what they know about the long *i*. Point to the *igh* spelling and tell the children this is another way to spell the long *i* sound. Write *igh* on the board. Touch the spelling, and have the children say /ī/. Add letters *n* and *t* to make *night* and help the children read the word. Tell the children that when letters *gh* come together in words they are often silent. When the letters *gh* follow *i*, they help the *i* say its long sound. Review the Long I card and the spellings that have been introduced so far.

* **Blending** Have the children blend the following words and sentences. For additional suggestions for blending, see **Learning Framework Card 3.**

Line 1:	high sigh right light
Line 2:	fight tight sight bright
Line 3:	frighten mighty tightness lightly
Line 4:	tightrope daylight
Sentence 1:	The bright light from the lamp shines in my eyes.
Sentence 2:	The baby eats his meals in the high chair.
Sentence 3:	Did the thunder frighten Ray last night?

Words Remember to write the spelling *igh* as a unit when writing the words. To help the children blend the words in line 3, ask them to look for a small word in each one, for example, *fright* in *frighten* and *might* in *mighty*. Have them use the words in sentences.

Tell the children that the words in line 4 are made up of two smaller words—they are compound words. Have children find and blend the two smaller words, and then blend them together to read the longer word.

TEACHING TIP

For the compound words, you may want to write the first word and have children blend it, add the second word, and have children blend it, then have them blend the whole word.

Review the words by having the children point to and read
- the one-syllable word that begins with the sound /br/
- the two-syllable word with the sound /ā/ in the middle
- the word that means the opposite of low
- the word that means the opposite of wrong
- the word that means "to scare"
- two words that end with the long *e* sound

Sentences Before the children blend and read the sentences, review the underlined outlaw words.

➤ Reading/Writing Connection, pages 122–123, provides practice with the long *i* sound spelled *igh.* Have the children read and copy the words and sentences on page 122. Then help them read the words at the top of page 123 and join one word from each column to form a new compound word. The children should write these new words on the lines provided, then use them to complete the sentences at the bottom of the page.

Reading/Writing Connection, page 122

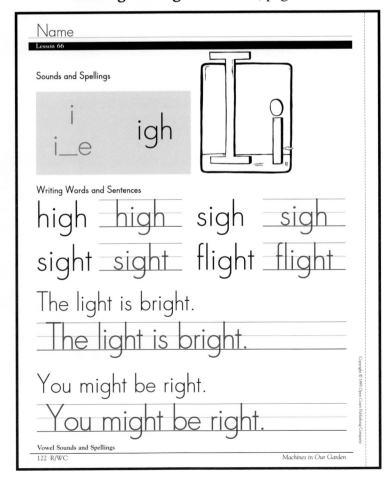

Reading/Writing Connection, page 123

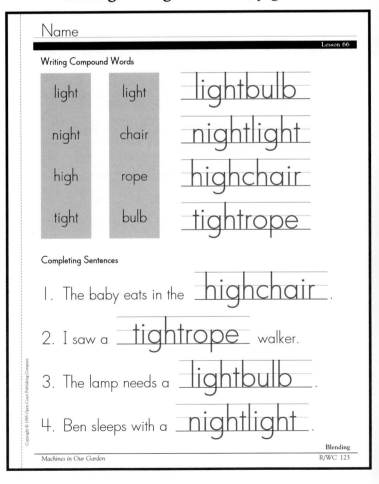

"The Opossum"
Story 38

Getting Ready to Read

Have the children put together Step-by-Step Practice Story 38. Call on a child to read the title of the selection. Ask if any of the children have ever seen an opossum. If children are not familiar with an opossum, tell them they will learn about this animal when they read this book.

Recommendations

Call on a different child to read each page of the story aloud. If a child has difficulty with a word, help her or him blend it. Pronounce the word if it is an outlaw. Reread the story at least twice, calling on different children to read each time.

Responding

- Ask the children to tell in their own words what happened in the story and to discuss any difficulties they had in reading it.
- To make sure that the children are paying attention to the words in the story, ask the following questions, having children point to the word in the story that answers each question.

  What do the birds call?

  What does the opossum feed her babies?

  What does the opossum tell her babies?

Have the children reread the story with a partner.

TEACHING TIP

Set aside ten minutes for partner reading every day. During this time, you should read with individuals, recording their progress. Reading Assessment Sheets for Phonics Minibooks are available in *Assessment Masters, Grade 1*.

Be sure to set aside time later in the day to read aloud to your class. You may want to share one or more of the following books, which depict a variety of machines in action:

Farming Today Yesterday's Way by Cheryl Walsh Belville

Grand Constructions by Gian Paolo Cesarani

In the Driver's Seat by Ron Goor and Nancy Goor

After reading, ask the children to discuss what they liked best about the book or books and what the books told them that they did not know before.

See **Learning Framework Card 5** for additional suggestions for reading aloud.

2 WRITING

✳ DICTATION AND SPELLING

Word-Building Game Have the children use a sheet of paper for the Word-Building game. With the children, write each word on the chalkboard or overhead transparency, but allow a few moments for them to write the word on their own. Proofread each word before moving to the next. Encourage the children to think about when to use each vowel spelling. You may want to remind them, for example, that they can tell from the Long A card that _ay is usually at the end of a word or syllable, and that the spelling ai_ is usually at the beginning or middle of a word or syllable. Dictate the following words:

pail

pain

main

may

mate

might

light

late

EXPLORING THE WRITER'S CRAFT

In Step-by-Step Practice Story 29, *Spice Cake,* children read about a baking experience. This may remind them of cooking experiences they have had. Encourage children to talk about any times they have helped prepare foods. Ask children who have used recipes to tell the class what a recipe is. If necessary, explain that a recipe tells how to prepare food. Recipes include a list of ingredients (all the things necessary to make something) and directions for what to do. If you wish, share a recipe with the children. This can be something simple, like a recipe for tuna fish salad. Ingredients might include a can of tuna fish, an onion, celery, and mayonnaise. List these on the board. If children wish to add other ingredients that they put in their tuna fish, add them to the list. Then give the children the directions, or have them suggest what to do. For example, open the can of tuna, drain the water and put the tuna in a bowl. Chop the onion and celery and put them in. Then add mayonnaise and stir.

Have children talk about some of their favorite recipes. For young children this may be as simple as a recipe for peanut butter sandwiches or making tortilla chips and salsa. Make a list of recipes your children might like to put in a class recipe book. Tell the children that tomorrow they will start writing their recipes. They may want to talk about their recipes at home and make a list of the ingredients they will need.

3 GUIDED AND INDEPENDENT EXPLORATION

WORKSHOP

Remind the children that they may use this time to work on projects independently or in small groups. Make sure each child knows what projects he or she may choose and how to complete any independent work. Suggestions for teacher-guided, collaborative, and independent activities follow.

Work with the Teacher

- Reread pages 2–13 of *Machines in Our Garden* with children who could use an additional review. Be sure to pause so that the children can read the words they know with you. Pause after every couple of pages and ask a child to **sum up** the reading.
- Listen to individuals or pairs of children reread Step-by-Step Practice Story 38.
- Play Guess My Word to review long *a* spelled *ai* and *ay* and long *i* spelled *igh*. Write _*ay* on the chalkboard. Say that this word is something you do with toys. When they guess *play,* ask them what letters you should add to _*ay*. Write the letters and blend the word. Have a child use the word in a sentence. Repeat with these mystery words:

  _*ay:* something a horse eats *(hay)*
  _ _*ain:* the place where the water goes out of a bathtub *(drain)*
  *igh:* when the sun goes down *(night)*
  _ _*ay :* the opposite of go away *(stay)*
  _*ai_:* what you do with a letter *(mail)*
  _*igh:* The opposite of low *(high)*

Independent Work

- Activity Sheet 66 is a crossword puzzle that reinforces the various /ī/ spellings the children have learned thus far. Tell the children to choose words from the box to complete each sentence, then write the answers again in the corresponding boxes of the crossword puzzle. Remind the children to use the arrows to help them write their answers correctly in the puzzle.
- Challenge children to write and illustrate a nonsense sentence using two or more rhyming words from the Blending exercise.
- Encourage the children to read on their own. Provide a number of books for them to choose.

Student Collaboration

- Encourage partners to reread Step-by-Step Practice Story 38. Challenge them to list all the words in the story that contain the long *i* sound and to underline the letters in each word that spell long *i*.
- Suggest that the children play Scrambled Sentences. Prepare some new sentences that include words with the spellings *igh, ai,* and *ay*.
- Children who have begun work on a Machines mural or collage may complete their work today.

Home/School Connection

Send home Step-by-Step Practice Story 37, "Sail Day," for children to read aloud to their families. A letter to accompany this story can be found in the book of Step-by-Step Practice Stories.

Name

| pie | kite | spider | dive | bike | night |

→ 1. A __spider__ has 8 legs.

→ 2. You can ride on a __bike__ .

→ 3. You go to bed at __night__ .

↓ 4. A __kite__ flies on a string.

↓ 5. A __pie__ can be apple or cherry.

↓ 6. You can __dive__ into the water.

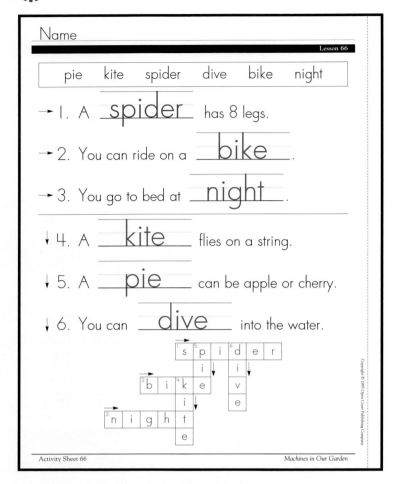

Copyright © 1995 Open Court Publishing Company

Machines in Our Garden

Activity Sheet 66

LESSON 67

LESSON

••• Lesson Overview

New Learning

- /ī/ Spelled _y and _ie_

Prepare Ahead

- Stop Sign Cards (see page 342)

Materials

- "Why, Bly?," Step-by-Step Practice Story 39
- Sound/Spelling Card 34, Long I
- Alphabet Flash Cards
- Learning Framework Cards 3, 4, 5, 6
- Reading/Writing Connection, pages 124–125
- Outlaw Word Flash Cards
- Activity Sheet 67

GETTING STARTED

Choose one or more of the following activities to focus the children's attention and to review some of the concepts they have been learning.

Before and After Game Have the children sit in a circle. Shuffle the Alphabet Flash Cards and go around the circle, showing a different card to each child. The child should name the letter shown, then tell which letter follows it in the alphabet. Vary the game by having the children name the letter that comes before the one shown, or the letters that come before and after.

Find a Word Game Write words on the chalkboard that contain various vowel sounds and spellings. Use at least fifteen words, such as *night, train, peace, store, play, cube, smile, apron, free, kite, hay, poke, music, sigh, plain*. Name a vowel Sound/Spelling Card and have a child find and read a word that contains that sound. Have the children identify the spelling used in the word.

TEACHING TIP

Some children may have difficulty blending words that have long vowel spellings. This is normal. It is very important that you not wait for mastery of each spelling before going on to the next. Proficiency will come through repetition and practice.

Stop Sign Prepare a set of cards or an overhead transparency with action words and phrases and one card with the word *stop*. Have the children stand. Hold up one card at a time and have the children perform the action in place until you hold up the "stop sign." Use the following action words and phrases and add others if you wish:

hop	snore	stamp feet
wiggle your nose	hands on knees	hands on head
hands behind back	hold ears	whisper
sneeze	jump	raise your left hand
say your name	go to your seat	

1 READING

PHONICS

* **Introduce /ī/ Spelled _y and _ie** Point to Long I card, and ask the children to tell what they know about the sound and the spellings. Uncover or point to the spellings _y and _ie on the card and tell the children that these are other spellings for long *i*. Discuss what the blanks before the spellings mean. Explain that the blank before the *y* spelling indicates that this spelling never occurs at the beginning of a word. In fact, this spelling is almost always found at the end of a word or syllable. The blank in front of the *ie* spelling again indicates that this spelling of long *i* does not occur at the beginning of a word. The *ie* spelling can, but does not always, occur at the end of a word or syllable. Write some example words on the chalkboard, read them, and point out where the spellings occur. Some example words are *my, sky, tie, flies*.

* **Blending** Have the children blend the following words and sentences. For additional suggestions for blending, see **Learning Framework Card 3.**

Line 1:	cry cried try tried
Line 2:	dry dried fry fries
Line 3:	pie lie tied tide
Line 4:	by shy fly why
Sentence 1:	The shy puppy tries to hide under the bed.
Sentence 2:	Birds can fly high in the sky.
Sentence 3:	We ate French fries, hamburgers, and lime pie at the diner.

Words In lines 1 and 2, compare the spelling changes that occur when endings are added to the base word. You may wish to remind the children about similar changes that occur with the long *e* spellings _y and _ie_. Tell the children that *ies* may say /īs/ or /ēs/ and *ied* may say /īd/ or /ēd/. If the word has only one syllable, the *ies* or the *ied* has the long *i* sound.

In line 3, compare the homophones *tied* and *tide*. Help the children use each word in a sentence.

After the children blend the words in line 4, discuss where the spelling *y* occurs and what sound it spells. Explain that when *y* occurs at the end of a word with one syllable, it makes the /ī/ sound. Invite the children to find other words in the lines that follow this pattern. You may wish to compare the *y* spelling for long *i* to the *y* spelling for long *e* at the end of a word with two or more syllables. Example words are *by, baby; sky, pesky.*

Review the word lines by having one child say any word from any line and having another child find and erase the word.

Sentences If the children have difficulty blending *hamburger* in sentence 3, have them blend one syllable at a time, then blend the syllables together. Blend *diner* in syllables as follows: *di—ner.*

➤ Reading/Writing Connection, pages 124–125, reinforces the long *i* sound spelled *_y* and *_ie.* Help the children complete page 124 and the top part of page 125.

Reading/Writing Connection, page 124

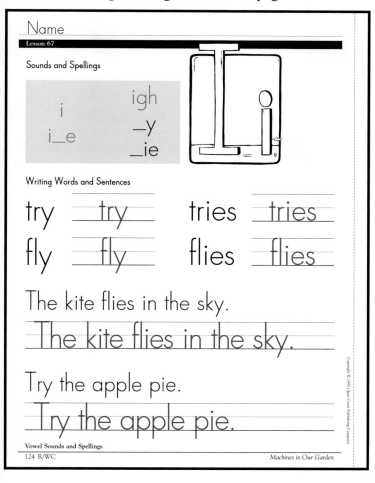

Reading/Writing Connection, page 125

Name

Lesson 67

Completing Sentences

fly   tie   tries   pie   sky

1. The ___fly___ buzzes by my head.

2. I ate the cherry ___pie___ all by myself.

3. Tyrone ___tries___ to do a trick.

Dictation and Spelling

Machines in Our Garden

Decoding/Spelling

R/WC 125

"Why, Bly?"
Story 39

Getting Ready to Read

Ask the children to assemble Step-by-Step Practice Story 39, "Why, Bly?" Call on a child to read the title. Encourage discussion of anything the children noticed about the story as they put it together.

Recommendations

Follow the standard procedure for reading a Step-by-Step Practice Story, shown on **Learning Framework Card 6.** Have the story reread at least twice, calling on different children to read.

Responding

- Invite the children to tell what the story is about and to discuss any questions they have about it.
- To ensure that the children are focusing on the words in the story rather than simply on the pictures, have them answer the following questions by pointing to and reading aloud the words that answer the question:

  What kind of a bird do the animals feel Bly is?
  What size head does Bly have?
  Who thinks Bly should lie in the sun?
  Why can't Bly fly in the sky?

- Call on volunteers to read entire sentences.
- Finally, have the children discuss what the story is about and what they like about it.

Have the children reread the story with a partner.

The following are some of the many books about gardens. You might want to share one or more of these with your class:

Johnny Crow's Garden by L. Leslie Brooke
Linnea in Monet's Garden by Christina Bjork
Your First Garden Book by Marc Brown

Remember to ask the children what they found most interesting about the reading, and what it told them that they did not already know.

See **Learning Framework Card 5** for suggestions for reading aloud.

TEACHING TIP

Remind the children to read each book twice. When they finish today's book, they should get one from a previous lesson. Reading Assessment Sheets for Phonics Minibooks are available in *Assessment Masters, Grade 1*.

2 WRITING

✳ DICTATION AND SPELLING

Have the children turn to page 125 of their Reading/Writing Connection book. Dictate the following words and sentence, using the suggestions for dictation that appear on **Learning Framework Card 4.**

Line 1:   high   bright

Line 2:   paint   stay

Sentence: It rained day and night.

As you help the children proofread, call attention to the *-ed* spelling at the end of *rained*.

TEACHING TIP

Remind the children to check the Long A card. Ask what clues on the card may help them determine which long *a* spelling to use for *stay* and *day*.

INDEPENDENT AND COLLABORATIVE WRITING

Children's cookbooks usually show a combination of pictures and text. Pictures are numbered, with a brief statement about what to do. You may want to share some children's cookbooks before children start writing today. *Cook and Learn* by Thelma Harms, et al., is a good example.

Remind the children of some of the recipes they talked about yesterday. There are several important things and steps to remember as they write their recipes. First, they need to write the name of the recipe. Then they must remember to include all the ingredients. Write the word *Ingredients* on the board. Then tell the children that next they need to remember to write the directions. Add the word *Directions* to the board.

Have children start writing out their favorite recipes. Take time to write one of your own to include in the class recipe book.

Hold conferences with children. Remind them to include both ingredients and directions. Many of the recipes may be less than conventional. A recipe for chicken noodle soup may consist of opening a can of soup, pouring the soup into a bowl, heating it in the microwave, and then eating it. This is fine!

Hold Seminar and have several of the children share the recipes they have begun writing. Remind the children who are listening that this is this particular cook's recipe, and therefore they may make the same food in a different way. They need to listen for three things: the name of the recipe, the ingredients, and the directions.

3 GUIDED AND INDEPENDENT EXPLORATION

WORKSHOP

Remind the children that they may use this time to work on projects on their own or with small groups. Be sure that each child knows what projects he or she may choose and how to complete any independent work. Suggestions for teacher-guided, collaborative, and independent activities follow.

Work with the Teacher

- Work with children to practice decoding long and short vowel words. Write sentences containing both long and short vowel words on the board and have children read the sentences. Ask them to identify the long vowel words and the vowel spellings used, and the short vowel words. Some sentences to use are

   An ant ate a bit of cake.
   Pat broke the light switch.
   The ship sails over high waves.
   My cat tries to catch mice.

- Use flash cards to review outlaw words with those children who are having trouble remembering them.

Independent Work

- Activity Sheet 67 reviews long *i* spellings. Tell the children that only one word in each sentence has the long *i* sound. They should circle that word, then draw a picture of the word in the corresponding box at the bottom of the page.
- Some children might like to write sentences using words from the Blending exercise and illustrate them.
- Encourage children to read on their own. Provide a selection of books from which they may choose. Any of the books listed for reading aloud would be appropriate for the children to explore.

Student Collaboration

- Encourage pairs of children to reread Phonics Minibook 11 or any of the Step-by-Step Practice Stories from previous lessons.
- Have the children play the Stair Steps game in pairs or small groups. One student begins by writing a word on a piece of paper. The next student in turn must spell a word that begins with the last letter of the first student's word, and write that word using the last letter of the first word and going down. The next child writes a new word going across from the last letter. For example:

   p a i n t
            r
            a
            i
   n a p k i n

TEACHING TIP

Encourage the children to read to each other. You, too, should choose children to read with. As you read with each child, note his or her progress.

Home/School Connection

Send home Step-by-Step Practice Story 38, "The Opossum," for children to read aloud to their families.

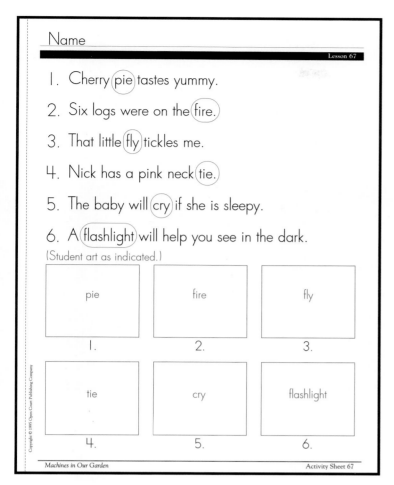

Name

1. Cherry (pie) tastes yummy.

2. Six logs were on the (fire.)

3. That little (fly) tickles me.

4. Nick has a pink neck (tie.)

5. The baby will (cry) if she is sleepy.

6. A (flashlight) will help you see in the dark.

(Student art as indicated.)

pie	fire	fly
1.	2.	3.

tie	cry	flashlight
4.	5.	6.

Machines in Our Garden   Activity Sheet 67

Activity Sheet 67

LESSON
68

•••• Lesson Overview

New Learning

- /ng/ spelled _**ng**_
- words with **nk**

Materials

- *Machines in Our Garden*, pages 2–13
- Sound/Spelling Card 38, Gong
- Learning Framework Cards 2, 3, 5
- Reading/Writing Connection, pages 126–127
- Activity Sheet 68

GETTING STARTED

Choose one or both of the following activities to focus the children's attention and to review some of the concepts they have been learning.

Categories Write the words that follow on the chalkboard. Then name a category and have the children find and read all the words that belong. Categories are *animals, food,* and *tools.*

lion	nail	ponies
candy	drill	beaver
hammer	raisins	peanuts
ostrich	vice	wheat bread

Dictate to the Teacher Write the word *light* on the chalkboard and have children read it. Ask how to change this word to *night,* write the new word, and have children read it. Continue having children tell how to make these words:

right
bright
sight
sigh
high
might
mighty

1 READING

PHONICS

✳ **Introduce /ng/ Spelled _ng_** Turn Sound/Spelling Card 38, Gong, and tell the children that this is the Gong card. Tell them that today's story is about a gong used to wake up a young king.

You can find the procedure for introducing a new sound/spelling on **Learning Framework Card 2.**

The young king has slept much too long.
Let's go and awaken the king with a gong.

A pinging gong? It makes a quiet song: **(softly)** /ng/ /ng/ /ng/ /ng/ /ng/.

That gong is wrong. **(softly)** /ng/ /ng/ /ng/ /ng/ /ng/.
We need a louder gong!

A dinging gong? It makes this song: **(a bit louder)** /ng/ /ng/ /ng/ /ng/ /ng/.

That, too, is wrong. **(as before)** /ng/ /ng/ /ng/ /ng/ /ng/.
We need an even louder gong!

A clanging gong? It makes this song: **(loudly)** /ng/ /ng/ /ng/ /ng/ /ng/!

That's just the thing! /ng/ /ng/ /ng/ /ng/ /ng/!
That's the gong we needed all along!

Now, which gong should we bring to awaken the king?
(Have children make the /ng/ sound loud enough to wake the king.)
/ng/ /ng/ /ng/ /ng/ /ng/

Point to the _ng_ spelling on the card. Ask the children to say the sound this spelling makes. Ask the children what the green box before the spelling means. Have the children point out other spellings on other cards that have the green box. Have the children recall any words from the story with this sound.

✳ **Blending** Have the children blend the following words and sentences. For reference and additional suggestions for blending, see **Learning Framework Card 3.**

Line 1:	king bring finger single
Line 2:	sink drink think shrink
Line 3:	rang bang bank thank
Line 4:	sinking winking singing swinging
Sentence 1:	Hank and Jake are flying a kite with a long string.
Sentence 2:	The singer sang three songs at the concert.
Sentence 3:	The children are playing on the swings at the park.

Words Write the _ng spelling as a unit as you write the words.

Line 2 introduces the spelling *nk* at the ends of words. Ask the children what they notice in this word line. (All the words rhyme.)

In line 3, the words have neither a true short *a* or long *a* sound. The children can blend the words with either vowel sound and then adjust their pronunciation accordingly.

In line 4, have the children blend the base word, then add the *-ing* ending.

To review the words, use them in oral sentences, emphasizing the word from the word lines. Ask the children to find, say, and erase the word each time.

- I am *singing* in the shower.
- *Thank* you for the birthday present.
- Father washed our clothes carefully so they didn't *shrink*.
- When the bell *rang* it was time for recess.

Point to one line of words and invite a child to choose a word and give a sentence clue for it.

Sentences Help the children blend and read the sentences.

➤ Reading/Writing Connection, pages 126–127, reinforce the /ng/ sound spelled _ng. Have the children blend and copy the words and sentences on page 126. They can complete the top part of page 127 by copying the sentence that matches each picture. For the bottom half of this page, help the children read all the words before giving the following clues for them to mark the target words.

Box 1: Mark the word *hang*. Will you hang curtains in the window?
Box 2: A scaly reptile with a long body and no legs.
Box 3: A word that rhymes with *thing*.
Box 4: A word that means the opposite of sour.
Box 5: A word that rhymes with *store*.
Box 6: Mark the word *cries*. The baby cries when she is hungry.

✴ READING THE BIG BOOK

Machines in Our Garden
pages 2–13

Activating Prior Knowledge

Ask the children to share what they have learned about machines during previous lessons.

Recommendations for Reading

Tell the children that today they can help you reread the first half of *Machines in Our Garden.* Reread pages 2–13, including the picture captions. Encourage the children to read along any words they know. Among the words that the children should be able to read are *garden, clean, way, lift, easily.*

Reading/Writing Connection, page 126

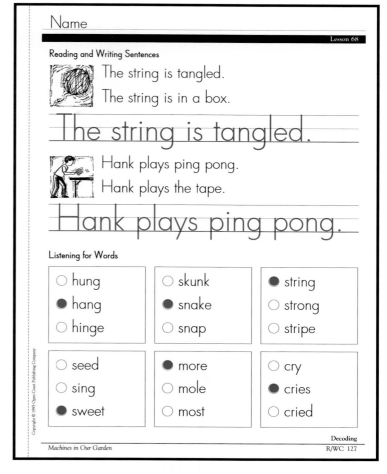

Reading/Writing Connection, page 127

Responding

- Invite a volunteer to come to the front of the class and point out his or her favorite word in the Big Book. Have the children use their words in new sentences.
- Ask the children to discuss what they like about this part of the story. Allow them to point out favorite pictures and to tell why they like the pictures.

✷ READING ALOUD

You may want to share one or both of the following books with the class:

If I Drove a Tractor by Miriam Burt Young
Trucks by Anne Rockwell

Remember to ask the children what new ideas these and other books about machines have given them. See **Learning Framework Card 5** for suggestions for reading aloud.

TEACHING TIP

Have the children do partner reading daily. Using previously read Phonics Minibooks and Step-by-Step Practice Stories for this purpose will help the children review and solidify their knowledge of the sounds and spellings they have learned. This is a good opportunity to read with children individually and to record their progress. Reading Assessment Sheets for Phonics Minibooks are available in *Assessment Masters, Grade 1.*

2 WRITING

✳ DICTATION AND SPELLING

Word-Building Game Have the children use their own paper for the Word-Building game. Write each word on the chalkboard or an overhead transparency. Before you write, allow a few moments for them to write the word on their own. Use the following word list:

dry

drying

crying

cried

cry

try

tried

Proofread each word as usual. Ask the children to explain when to use *y* and when to use *ie* to make the long *i* sound.

INDEPENDENT AND COLLABORATIVE WRITING

Have the children continue working on their recipes. If some children have finished, remind them to reread their recipes to be sure they have included everything. Since these will be part of a class book, children need to proofread their recipes and be sure they are clearly written. Remind children to put their names on their recipes and put them in their folders.

Hold Seminar, having children share some of the different recipes they have been working on.

You may want to share some books that tell about some inventive recipes. Suggested titles include

Mean Soup by Betsy Everitt

Monkey Soup by Lois Sacher

Thunder Cake by Patricia Polacco

TEACHING TIP

When writing words with long vowels, remind the children to check the card for possible spellings. If they are still unsure after checking, encourage them to ask for the correct vowel spelling.

3 GUIDED AND INDEPENDENT EXPLORATION

W O R K S H O P

Remind children that they may use this time to work on projects on their own or with small groups. Be sure that each child knows what projects he or she may choose and how to complete any independent work. Suggestions for teacher-guided, collaborative, and independent projects are provided below.

Work with the Teacher

- Review Sound/Spelling Card 38 and today's Blending lesson with children who are having trouble with the sound and spelling of /ng/.
- Introduce Step-by-Step Practice Story 40 to those children who may need extra help with -*ing* and _*nk* endings.
- Play the Word-Building game with children who need to work on their spelling. Repeat today's game or prepare another word list, according to the childen's needs.

Independent Work

- Activity Sheet 68 provides practice with words ending in _*ng* and _*nk*. Tell the children to choose the word that completes the sentence and to write that word on the line provided.
- Challenge children to add the -*ing* ending to each word in line 2 of the Blending exercise, then write and illustrate a sentence using one or more of the new words.
- Some children may want to continue working on their recipes.

Student Collaboration

- The children can work in pairs to review outlaw words with flashcards. Encourage peer tuturing by pairing independent readers with less confident readers.
- Pairs of children may read together books of their choice.
- Working with a partner, children may want to make a list of machines they find in the classroom.

TEACHING TIP

Encourage the children to read to each other. You, too, should choose children to read with. As you read with each child, note his or her progress.

Home/School Connection

- Send home Step-by-Step Practice Story 39, "Why, Bly?" for children to read aloud to their families.

Name

1. Can you hear the ladies __sing__ ?

    sing   sink

2. When I am sick it is hard to __think__ .

    thing   think

3. __Bring__ the baby her blanket.

    Bring   Brink

4. The bird's right __wing__ is hurt.

    wing   wink

5. I lost the __ring__ from my finger.

    ring   rink

6. The monkey can __cling__ to the vine.

    cling   clink

Machines in Our Garden

Activity Sheet 68

LESSON
69

Lesson Overview

New Learning

- Adding -*ing* endings
- /nk/ spelled *nk*

Materials

- *Machines in Our Garden*, pages 14–31
- "Cranky Hank," Step-by-Step Practice Story 40
- Learning Framework Cards 3, 4, 5
- Reading/Writing Connection, pages 128–129
- Activity Sheet 69
- Home/School Connection 13

GETTING STARTED

Choose one or more of the following activities to focus the children's attention and to review some of the concepts they have been learning.

Riddle Me This Explain that you can make a riddle from sounds on the Sound/Spelling Cards. Tell the children that you are thinking of a word that has the sounds on the cards you will point to. Point to Popcorn, Long A, Lion, saying the name of each picture as you point, and ask the children to guess your riddle (pail). Repeat the process for other words:

- Sausages, Nose, Long A, Camera (snake)
- Popcorn, Long O, Nose, Long E (pony)
- Timer, Long I, Gopher, Bird (tiger)
- Monkey, Lamb, Popcorn (map)

After the children become familiar with the game, say the riddle without pointing to the Sound/Spelling Cards.

Long Sound/Short Sound Spellings Write one word on the chalkboard at a time. Have the children read the word quietly to themselves.

Tell them that if the word contains /ī/, they should hold their arms out from their sides. If the word contains /i/, they should hold their hands close together in front of them. After the children have done this, ask them to read the word aloud together. You might want to use some of the following words:

cry

slip

mild

flight

slim

slime

fry

1 READING

PHONICS

✳ **Blending** Have the children blend the following words and sentences. For reference and additional suggestions for blending, see **Learning Framework Card 3.**

✏ **Line 1:** shake shaking smile smiling

Line 2: sit sitting stop stopping

Line 3: hopping hoping tapping taping

Line 4: raining hurrying thinking staying

Sentence 1: Penny is running quickly to get to the bank on time.

Sentence 2: We are making vanilla pudding for the family.

Sentence 3: Paige went shopping at the grocery store.

Words In line 1, compare the words *shake* and *shaking*, then *smile* and *smiling*. Point out that when words end with *e*, you drop the *e* before adding the *-ing* ending.

In line 2, ask the children what happens to the base word *sit* or *stop* when the *-ing* ending is added. Summarize by reminding the children that for words with short vowels, you double the consonant before adding the ending.

In line 3, ask the children what difference they notice between the words in each pair. Help them see that *hopping* has the short vowel sound while *hoping* has the long vowel sound by blending the words as follows: *hop—ping, hopping* and *hō—ping, hoping*. Repeat with *tapping* and *taping*.

Line 4 demonstrates that for many words you simply add *-ing* to the base word.

Review the words by giving the children oral sentences and asking them to fill in the blanks using words from the word lines. Have the children point to and read the words. For example:

- I'm _____ to catch the bus because I'm late.
- I'm _____ that it will stop raining soon.
- How long will you be _____ at my house?
- Your face is happy when you are _____.

Have the children give each other sentence clues to review other words in the lines.

Sentences The children may need extra help blending some of the words in sentence 2, such as *vanilla* and *pudding*. With *vanilla*, remind the children that the *ll* spelling makes only one sound, as does the *dd* spelling in *pudding*. Also point out that the *u* in *pudding* makes the same sound as the *u* in *put*.

➤ Reading/Writing Connection, pages 128–129, provide practice with the *-ing* ending. Help the children find the words at the top of the page that rhyme with each of the words given at the bottom. They should then write the rhyming word in the blank, adding the *-ing* ending to make a new word, then use the new words to complete the sentences on the top part of page 129.

Reading/Writing Connection, page 128

Reading/Writing Connection, page 129

Machines in Our Garden
pages 14–31

Activating Prior Knowledge

Ask the children to discuss anything they remember from the first reading of *Machines in Our Garden.*

Recommendations for Reading

Tell the children that once again, they will be helping you to read the Big Book by joining in whenever you come to a word they know. Reread the second half (pages 14–31) of Big Book 4, including the picture captions. Encourage the children to chime in on the words they can read. Move your hand under the words as you read. Examples of words they might read are *stuck, stones, skate, faster, wheelchair.*

Responding

- Invite the children to share any favorite words from the second half of the selection. If they are able to read the words, have volunteers come forward and point out their favorite words in the Big Book. Have the children use their words in new sentences.
- Ask the children to share and discuss their favorite parts of the second half of the story. Invite them to point out their favorite pictures and to tell why they liked the pictures.
- Call on children to **sum up** the story. Ask them to tell only what happened to Olga, Ignatz, and their friends. Select additional volunteers to sum up what they learned about each machine in the book. Direct them to the Machines Chart for assistance.
- Explain to the children that tomorrow they will have a machine fair to celebrate their completion of the Big Book, *Machines in Our Garden,* and that they should bring in examples of simple machines from home. Discuss some items they might bring in such as any toys with wheels, tools with levers such as pliers, scissors, nut crackers, nail clippers, bottle openers, screws of different shapes and sizes, plastic bottles or jars with screw tops, a screw-type clamp, a tape dispenser, even a comb. Encourage the children to discuss with an adult at home how the machines they find help make work easier and faster.

"Cranky Hank"
Story 40

Getting Ready to Read

Have the children put together Step-by-Step Practice Story 40. Ask a student to read the title of the story. Ask the children what they think the title means. You might also ask them what they think might happen in this story.

Recommendations

Have all the children read each page to themselves. Then call on a child to read the page aloud. If a child has difficulty with a word, help him or her sound it out by referring to the Sound/Spelling Cards. Call on different children for the two rereadings of the story.

Responding

- Have the children discuss any hard words they came across in their reading and ask them to explain how they figured out these words.
- To determine whether the children are focusing on the words in the story, ask the following questions, having the children point to the word in the story that answers each question:

  Why is Hank called cranky?

  What does the farmer think it is time to do to Hank?

  Where did the farmer stop on her way to the market?

  What did Hank do to the robber?

  Who thanked Hank?

Have the children reread the story with a partner.

✳ READING ALOUD

You may want to share one or both of the following books with the class:

Molly's New Washing Machine by Laura Geringer

Telephones, Televisions, and Toilets: How They Work and What Can Go Wrong by Adelaide Holl

See **Learning Framework Card 5** for suggestions for reading aloud.

TEACHING TIP

Remind the children to read each book twice. When they finish today's book, they should get one from a previous lesson. Reading Assessment Sheets for Phonics Minibooks are available in *Assessment Masters, Grade 1*.

2 WRITING

✳ DICTATION AND SPELLING

Have the children turn to page 129 of their Reading/Writing Connection book. Dictate the following words and sentence, using the suggestions for dictation that appear on **Learning Framework Card 4.**

Line 1: dry   fries

Line 2: bring   strong

Sentence: Mike tried to sing a song.

Help the children proofread each line.

INDEPENDENT AND COLLABORATIVE WRITING

List all the different recipes the children have been working on. Discuss how to organize the recipes. For example, you may want to group all the sandwich recipes together or all the cookie recipes together. Talk with the children about what kind of cover they would like and what title they would like to use for the book.

Have children finish their recipes and illustrate them if they like. If necessary, have children recopy recipes so they are clear. If a number of students are asking for the spelling of frequently used words, put them on the board. Otherwise, remind children to use the Sound/Spelling Cards to help them with spelling or to ask another student for help.

TEACHING TIP

You may want to make copies of the recipe book so each child in the class can have a copy to take home.

3 GUIDED AND INDEPENDENT EXPLORATION

W O R K S H O P

Remind the children that they may use this time to work on projects on their own or in small groups. Be sure that each child knows what projects he or she may choose and how to complete any independent work. Suggestions for teacher-guided, collaborative, and independent work are provided below.

Work with the Teacher

- Listen to pairs or individuals reread Step-by-Step Practice Story 40.
- Hold a Reading Relay between two teams of children. Prepare some new cards that include the spellings the children have learned recently.
- Review the -ing ending with a small group of children. Place the following words on the board. Have one child at a time come to the board, read a word from the list, add -ing to the word, read the new word, and use the new word in a sentence.

string	stop	play
thank	cope	study
load	scare	

Independent Work

- Activity Sheet 69 has the children complete sentences by writing the correct spelling on the blank.
- Challenge the children to copy a word from Blending, then make as many new words as they can by changing one sound at a time.

Student Collaboration

- The children may enjoy following a simple recipe. Write the following recipe on a chart and post it by a table where the children can work. Have the

ingredients, measuring cups, a large bowl and spoon, and a supply of resealable plastic bags available. Groups of four children can make a bowl of snacks, then each child can place some in his or her own bag.

2 cups honey-nut oat cereal
1/2 cup banana chips
1/2 cup raisins

Mix together for a quick snack.

- Ask pairs of children to look through Step-by-Step Practice Story 40 for words that use the -ing or nk spellings. Have them use some of these words in sentences.

TEACHING TIP

Encourage the children to read to each other. You, too, should choose children to read with. As you read with each child, note his or her progress.

Home/School Connection

- Distribute Home/School Connection 13, which tells families about the completion of *Machines in Our Garden* and encourages the families to help their child locate one or more simple machines around the house to bring to class to share.

Name

1. The lady __rode__ in her car.

| rod |
| rode |

2. The little __baby__ began to cry.

| bab |
| baby |

3. I hear the duck __quack__ in the pond.

| qack |
| quack |

4. She will __judge__ the contest.

| jug |
| judge |

5. A snail is not __speedy__.

| spedy |
| speedy |

Machines in Our Garden   Activity Sheet 69

Activity Sheet 69

LESSON
70

Lesson Overview

Materials

- *Machines in Our Garden*
- Phonics Minibook 12, *Mail Train*
- Learning Framework Cards 3, 5
- Reading/Writing Connection, pages 130–131
- Outlaw Word Flash Cards
- Activity Sheet 70

Prepare Ahead

- Magazines, catalogs, and other sources containing pictures of machines; paper; scissors; glue; markers (see page 364)

GETTING STARTED

Choose one or more of the following activities to focus the children's attention and to review some of the concepts they have been learning.

Keep the Card Game In a paper bag, place Outlaw Word Flash Cards and/or index cards with words containing spellings you want to review. Divide the class into teams of five students each. Explain that a player on each team will draw a card out of the paper bag and look at it. (The player's team members will also see the card.) If the player says the word correctly, he or she may put the card on the table in front of his or her team. If the player misses, the card will go back in the bag. The teams take turns. The team with the most cards at the end of about five minutes wins the game.

Almost the Same Write the words that follow on the chalkboard:

tiny	keep	large
funny	start	sleepy
sneak	close	giggle

Say one of the words that follow and ask children to find and read a word on the chalkboard that has almost the same meaning as the word you say. Use these words:

begin	little	creep
big	laugh	shut
silly	save	tired

1 READING

✳ Blending Have the children blend the following words and sentences. For reference and additional suggestions for blending, see **Learning Framework Card 3.**

Line 1: child wide sky pie bright

Line 2: me here greedy teacher chief

Line 3: crazy frame spray grain

Line 4: excuse unicorn open spoke

Sentence 1: Mules and horses stay in the stable.

Sentence 2: Martin likes to play basketball every Saturday.

Sentence 3: Giants and dragons were in the fairy tale we read yesterday.

Words This blending exercise reviews all the long vowel spellings that have been introduced. Before doing each line, review the spellings on the Sound/Spelling Cards.

   Have the children blend the words and identify the long vowel spelling in each word.

   Review the words by naming a long vowel spelling and having children find and read the word that contains that spelling.

   The children point to and read the word.

Sentences In sentence 3, some of the children may blend *read* with the /ē/ sound, while others may blend it with the /e/ sound. Encourage the children to read the whole sentence, then decide which pronunciation of *read* makes sense in this sentence. Suggest that they use *yesterday* as a clue.

❯ Have the children turn to pages 130–131 of their Reading/Writing Connection book. They can complete page 130 by writing the correct word in each sentence. For the top part of page 131, help them add *-ed* and *-ing* to each word. For the bottom part of the page, the children should choose the word that means almost the same as each given word, and write that word in the blank.

Name

Lesson 70

Completing Sentences

1. I ___think___ I'll play a tape.

think thing

2. Fred put on his ___socks___.

soaks socks

3. That's a big ___stack___ of paper.

stack stake

4. This is a ___cute___ cat.

cut cute

5. We ___sing___ with the music.

sing song

6. Tom has ___muddy___ feet.

muddy many

Blending

130 R/WC

Machines in Our Garden

Reading/Writing Connection, page 130

Name

Lesson 70

Adding -ed and -ing

paint	painted	painting
bake	baked	baking
slip	slipped	slipping
rule	ruled	ruling

Writing Synonyms

| song | nice | road | cute |

| pretty | cute | kind | nice |
| music | song | highway | road |

Machines in Our Garden

Spelling/Decoding

R/WC 131

Reading/Writing Connection, page 131

✳ READING THE BIG BOOK

Machines in Our Garden

Recommendations for Reading

Allow the children to choose one of the following activities:

- Have them go through magazines and other sources that can be cut up, to find examples of machines. Help them label the machines or parts of them, referring to the Machine Chart as necessary. Some children might prefer to draw their own machine. Help them label the simple machine or machines within the more complex one.

- Invite the children to think about what they would like a machine to help them do. Encourage them to think of inventions that could help make some job easier. Discuss with the children how they might use one or more of the simple machines they read about as part of their inventions. Will a lever help them push or pull something in a new way? Can they use a wheel to help them move an object more easily? Encourage the children to read or browse through books in the literacy center to give them ideas. Have them sketch some of their ideas on paper to share during the machine fair.

Responding

- Conduct the machine fair. Have the children share the examples of machines they found in magazines, drew on their own, and brought in from home. Have them tell how the machine is used and ask them to identify any simple machine parts that they can.

✱ READING A PHONICS MINIBOOK

Mail Train
Phonics Minibook 12

Getting Ready to Read

Reading the Title   Call on two or three children to read the title aloud.

Browsing the Story   Invite the children to page through the story, commenting on the illustrations and telling what they think the story will be about.

Recommendations

- Call on a different child to read each page of the story aloud. Clarify any difficulties on each page, then have a different child reread the page before going on.
- Reread the story at least twice, calling on different children to read.

car-whacker — someone who checks trains

hotbox — a wheel part that gets too hot

OPEN COURT and ✱ are registered trademarks of Open Court Publishing Company.

COLLECTIONS FOR YOUNG SCHOLARS is a trademark of Open Court Publishing Company.

Copyright û 1995 Open Court Publishing Company

Printed in the United States of America

ISBN 0-8126-1282-5

10 9 8 7 6 5 4 3 2 1

2

3

This is Mrs. Frank
sending a letter
to her grandson Hank.

4

This is the bag
that holds the letter
that Mrs. Frank
sent to her grandson Hank.

5

This is the train
that carries the bag
that holds the letter
that Mrs. Frank
sent to her grandson Hank.

6

This is the mail car
on the train
that carries the bag
that holds the letter
that Mrs. Frank
sent to her grandson Hank.

7

This is the mail clerk
in the mail car
on the train
that carries the bag
that holds the letter
that Mrs. Frank
sent to her grandson Hank.

8

9

This is a car-whacker
checking the mail car
on the train
that carries the bag
that holds the letter
that Mrs. Frank
sent to her grandson Hank.

10

"Stop the train!"
cries the car-whacker.
"We've got a hotbox!"

11

This is a car-whacker
fixing the mail car
on the train
that carries the bag
that holds the letter
that Mrs. Frank
sent to her grandson Hank.

12

13

This is the platform
where the mail clerk
tosses the bag
that holds the letter
that Mrs. Frank
sent to her grandson Hank.

14

This is the mail carrier
delivering the letter
that Mrs. Frank
sent to her grandson Hank.

15

Responding to the Selection

- Ask the children to talk about any hard words they came across in their reading and to tell how they figured out those words.
- Have the children explain what the story is about and share what they like best about it.
- To check that the children are focusing on the words in the story, ask the following questions, having children point to the word in the story that answers each question:

  Where does the mail clerk toss the bag?

  Who cries, "Stop the train!" and "We've got a hotbox!"?

  What is Mrs. Frank's grandson's name?

  What did Grandma Frank send in her letter to Hank?

Have the children reread the story with a partner.

✶ READING ALOUD

You might share with the children one or more of the following books about trains, yet another kind of machine that the children read about today:

Freight Train by Donald Crews

Trains by Gail Gibbons

Train Whistles by Helen Sattler

TEACHING TIP

Set aside ten minutes for partner reading every day. During this time, you should read with individuals, recording their progress. Reading Assessment Sheets for Phonics Minibooks are available in *Assessment Masters, Grade 1.*

Ask the children in what ways trains are similar to other the machines they have read about. See **Learning Framework Card 5** for suggestions for reading aloud.

2 WRITING

✱ DICTATION AND SPELLING

Word-Building Game Have the children use a sheet of paper for the Word-Building game. Follow the established procedure for the activity. Use the following word list:

hop
hope
hoping
hopping
shopping
shaping
shape
tape
tap

Proofread each word and have the children make any corrections before writing the next word. Call attention to the changes in the base words when the -*ing* ending is added.

INDEPENDENT AND COLLABORATIVE WRITING

If you have finished your class recipe book, children may enjoy writing simple how-to books. These are similar in nature to recipes, in that children need to think about clarity and sequence in order for someone to follow the steps. For example, children may want to write about how to tie their shoes, how to make their beds, how to set the table, how to make a kite. An example that you may wish to share with the children is "Putting on My Own Gloves" (*Ladybug,* January 1993).

Take some time for children to share their how-to pieces.

3 GUIDED AND INDEPENDENT EXPLORATION

WORKSHOP

Remind the children that they may use this time to work on projects on their own or in small groups. Be sure that each child knows what projects he or she may choose and how to complete any independent work. Suggestions for teacher-guided, collaborative, and independent activities are provided below.

Work with the Teacher

- To provide support or to assess their progress, listen to children reread Phonics Minibook 12.
- Work with children who are writing how-to books. Offer constructive criticism and provide any necessary assistance.
- Ask some of the advanced readers to read aloud to you. Invite other children to listen in.

Independent Work

- Activity Sheet 70 has the children classify words according to whether the word is a food, a person, or an animal.
- Children who are writing how-to books may continue their work at this time.
- Encourage the children to reread any Phonics Minibook story or Step-by-Step Practice Story that they have already read in class.

Student Collaboration

- Encourage pairs of children to reread Phonics Minibook 12, *Mail Train*, with a partner. Assign each pair a target spelling and have them list all the words with that spelling.

- If you have the student versions of the Big Book *Machines in Our Garden*, the children may want to read these in small groups.
- Have the children play the Stair Steps game in pairs or small groups. One student begins by writing a word on a piece of paper. The next student in turn must spell a word that begins with the last letter of the first student's word and write that word using the last letter of the first word and going down. The next child writes a new word going across from the last letter. For example:

s t a y
      e
      s e e d

TEACHING TIP

Encourage the children to read to each other. You, too, should choose children to read with. As you read with each child, note his or her progress.

Home/School Connection

Send home Step-by-Step Practice Story 40, "Cranky Hank," for children to read aloud to their parents.

Name

Lesson 70

meat   lion

sister   carrot

mule   rice

cake   lady

uncle   tiger

kitten   baby

meat

carrot

rice

cake

sister

lady

uncle

baby

lion

mule

tiger

kitten

Activity Sheet 70   Machines in Our Garden

Activity Sheet 70

Appendixes

Introduction of Sounds: Overview
Framework for Effective Teaching™
Thinking and Learning About Print, Parts A and B

LESSON	SOUNDS INTRODUCED	PRACTICE STORIES
1		
2		
3		
4		
5		
6		
7		
8		
9		A Table (SS 1)
10		The Egg (SS 2)
11	Monkey: /m/ spelled *m*	
12	Lamb: /a/ spelled *a*	The Cake (PM 1: *The Baby*)
13	Timer: /t/ spelled *t*	The Shirt (PM 1: *The Baby*)
14	Hound dog: /h/ spelled *h_*	The Hat (SS 3)
15	Popcorn: /p/ spelled *p*	
16	Nose: /n/ spelled *n*	Pam and the Man (SS 4)
17	Camera: /k/ spelled *c*	
18	Dinosaur: /d/ spelled *d*	The Cat (SS 5)
19	Sausages: /s/ spelled *s*	On the Mat (PM 2: *Nan's Family*)
20	Pig: /i/ spelled *i*	The Tin Man (SS 6)
21		The Pans (PM 2: *Nan's Family*)
22	Ball: /b/ spelled *b*	Tim Spins (SS 7)
23	Robot: /r/ spelled *r*	Nat's Nap (PM 3: *Nat the Crab*)
		Nat's Trip (PM 3: *Nat the Crab*)
24	Fan: /f/ spelled *f*	Brad's Ram (SS 8)
25	Gopher: /g/ spelled *g*	The Sand Pits (SS 9)
26		Sinbad Acts Fast (PM 4: *Sinbad the Pig*)
		Sinbad and Anna (PM 4: *Sinbad the Pig*)
27	Frog: /o/ spelled *o*	The Cot (SS 10)
28	Exiting X: /ks/ spelled □ *x*	A Fox and His Box (SS 11)
29		Amanda's Sax (PM 5: *Panda Band*)
		Amanda's Band (PM 5: *Panda Band*)
30	Armadillo: /ar/ spelled *ar*	Grab a Star (SS 12)
31	Camera: /k/ spelled □ *ck*	My Trip (SS 13)
32	Tugboat: /u/ spelled *u*	The Bug (SS 14)
33	Zipper: /z/ spelled *z*	Zip on the Run (SS 15)

LESSON	SOUNDS INTRODUCED	PRACTICE STORIES
34		Zack the One-Man Band (SS 16)
35	Lion: /l/ spelled *l*	PM 6: *In the Pond*
36	Hen: /e/ spelled *e*	Meg's Sled (SS 17)
37	/e/ spelled *ea*	Hen in a Pen (SS 18)
38	Yaks: /y/ spelled *y_*	The Stand (SS 19)
39	Washer: /w/ spelled *w*	Wendell Gets a Pig (PM 7: *Wendell's Pets*)
	Whales: /hw/ spelled *wh_*	Wendell's Pets (PM 7: *Wendell's Pets*)
40	Bird: /er/ spelled *er, ir, ur*	What Is It? (SS 20)
41		
42	Shark: /sh/ spelled *sh*	Jen's Web (SS 21)
43	Thongs: /th/ spelled *th*	Seth's Bath (SS 22)
44	Chipmunk: /ch/ spelled *ch*	
45	Chipmunk: /ch/ spelled □*tch*	Patch Gets the Ball (SS 23)
46		The Trash Stash (SS 24)
47	Camera: /k/ spelled *k*	Can I Help You? (PM 8: *The Market*)
		The Lamp (PM 8: *The Market*)
48	/ā/ spelled *a, a_e*	Gull and Crane (SS 25)
49	Jump rope: /j/ spelled *j,* □*dge,*	Jane and Jake (SS 26)
50	Jump rope: /j/ spelled *ge, gi_,*	Magic Pages (SS 27)
51	/ī/ spelled *i, i_e*	A Fine Parade (SS 28)
52	Sausages: /s/ spelled *ce, ci*	Spice Cake (SS 29)
53		PM 9: *The Spider Club*
54	/ō/ spelled *o, o_e*	The Cold Troll (SS 30)
55	Zipper: /z/ spelled *s*	The Surprise (SS 31)
56	Vacuum: /v/ spelled *v*	
57	/ū/ spelled *u, u_e*	Cupid the Mule (SS 32)
58	/ē/ spelled *e, e_e*	Steve's Secret (SS 33)
59		The Step Problem (PM 10: *Eva Uses Her Head*)
		The Bug Problem (PM 10: *Eva Uses Her Head*)
60	/ē/ spelled *ee, ea*	Dragons Don't Get Colds (SS 34)
61	Quacking ducks: /kw/ spelled *qu*	Queen Squid and Her Sea Pals (SS 35)
62	Long vowels + *r*	
63	/ē/ spelled *_y, ie_*	The Fancy Party (SS 36)
64		PM 11: *Dog Dreams*
65	/ā/ spelled *ai_,_ ay*	Sail Day (SS 37)
66	/ī/ spelled *igh*	The Opossum
67	/ī/ spelled *y, ie*	Why, Bly? (SS 39)
68	Gong: /ng/ spelled □*ng*	
69		Cranky Hank (SS 40)
70		PM 12: *Mail Train*

Framework for Effective Teaching™
Grade 1, Book 1

LESSON	SOUNDS INTRODUCED	PRACTICE STORIES
1	/ō/ spelled _oe	
2	/ō/ spelled _ow	
3	/ō/ spelled oa_	PM 13: *The Snow Game*
4	/ū/ spelled _ew, _ue	
5		
6		
7	Cow: /ow/ spelled ow	PM 14: *The Everybody Club*
8	Cow: /ow/ spelled ou_	
9		
10		
11		
12		PM 15: *Superhero to the Rescue*
13	Hawk: /aw/ spelled aw, au_	
14		
15	Hoot owl: /o͞o/ spelled oo, ue, u_e, u, ew	
16	Brook: /o͝o/ spelled oo	
17	Nose: /n/ spelled kn	PM 16: *Mr. Lee*
18		
19	Coil: /oi/ spelled oi, _oy	
20		
21		
22		
23		
24		
25	Robot: /r/ spelled wr_	PM 17: *Princess Julia*
26	Fan: /f/ spelled ph	
27		PM 18: *How the Rabbit Caught the Tiger*
28		
29		
30		

NOTE: Phonics instruction is reviewed and consolidated in *Framework for Effective Teaching,*™ Grade 1, Book 2.

Scope and Sequence

STRATEGIES AND SKILLS	LEVEL					
	1	2	3	4	5	6
Print Awareness						
Capitalization	▓					
Constancy of words	▓					
End punctuation	▓					
Follow left-to-right, top-to-bottom	▓					
Letter recognition and formation	▓					
Paragraph indention	▓					
Relationship between illustrations and print	▓					
Relationship between spoken and printed language	▓					
Word boundaries in text	▓					
READING STRATEGIES						
Setting Reading Goals and Expectations						
Activate prior knowledge.	▓	▓	▓	▓	▓	▓
Browse the text.	▓	▓	▓	▓	▓	▓
Consider why you are reading.	▓	▓	▓	▓	▓	▓
Decide what you expect from the text.	▓	▓	▓	▓	▓	▓
Responding to Text						
Make connections between what you are reading and what you already know.	▓	▓	▓	▓	▓	▓
Visualize, or picture, what is happening in the text.	▓	▓	▓	▓	▓	▓
Wonder freely as you read.	▓	▓	▓	▓	▓	▓
Predict what will happen next.	▓	▓	▓	▓	▓	▓
Think about how the text makes you feel.	▓	▓	▓	▓	▓	▓
Checking Understanding						
Interpret as you read.	▓	▓	▓	▓	▓	▓
Sum up to check your understanding as you read.	▓	▓	▓	▓	▓	▓
Ask questions to check your understanding as you read.		▓	▓	▓	▓	▓
Clarifying Unfamiliar Words and Passages						
Apply decoding skills if there are unknown words.	▓	▓	▓	▓	▓	▓
Determine what is unclear.		▓	▓	▓	▓	▓
Apply context clues if there are words whose meanings you don't know.	▓	▓	▓	▓	▓	▓

STRATEGIES AND SKILLS

	1	2	3	4	5	6
READING STRATEGIES						
Clarifying Unfamiliar Words and Passages *continued*						
Check the dictionary.		▓	▓	▓	▓	▓
Reread the passage that didn't make sense to you.	▓	▓	▓	▓	▓	▓
WRITING STRATEGIES						
Planning and Setting Writing Goals						
Use reading to improve your writing.	▓	▓	▓	▓	▓	▓
Record interesting and important topics to write about.	▓	▓	▓	▓	▓	▓
Note information you will need in order to write.		▓	▓	▓	▓	▓
Decide on the main goals of the writing.		▓	▓	▓	▓	▓
Revise your plans.		▓	▓	▓	▓	▓
Considering Readers						
Make your topic interesting.		▓	▓	▓	▓	▓
Decide what effect you want to have on your readers.		▓	▓	▓	▓	▓
Determine if readers will understand.		▓	▓	▓	▓	▓
Predict your readers' reactions, and then compare their reactions to what you expected.		▓	▓	▓	▓	▓
Summarize audience reactions.		▓	▓	▓	▓	▓
Revising Content						
Reread very carefully.	▓	▓	▓	▓	▓	▓
Pinpoint parts of your writing that can be made clearer.		▓	▓	▓	▓	▓
Identify information confusing to readers.		▓	▓	▓	▓	▓
Reorganize ideas or information.		▓	▓	▓	▓	▓
Use a story frame or plot line.		▓	▓	▓	▓	▓
Consider your own reactions and ideas.		▓	▓	▓	▓	▓
CONVENTIONS/SKILLS						
Writer's Craft/Reading						
Causal indicators	▓	▓	▓	▓	▓	▓
Characterization		▓	▓	▓	▓	▓
Choosing vivid verbs		▓	▓	▓	▓	▓
Dialogue	▓	▓	▓	▓	▓	▓
Elaboration through comparisons and contrasts		▓	▓	▓	▓	▓
Elaboration through forming questions and conjectures		▓	▓	▓	▓	▓
Elaboration through giving opinions		▓	▓	▓	▓	▓
Elaboration through giving reasons or causes	▓	▓	▓	▓	▓	▓

STRATEGIES AND SKILLS

Writer's Craft/Reading *continued*	1	2	3	4	5	6
Elaboration through including lists and examples		■	■	■	■	■
Elaboration through providing background				■	■	■
Elaboration through providing descriptions	■	■	■	■	■	■
Elaboration through providing explanations or definitions			■	■	■	■
Elaboration by providing opposing viewpoints			■	■	■	■
Elaboration through providing problems and solutions	■	■		■	■	■
Elaboration through providing specific facts	■	■	■	■	■	■
Exaggeration				■	■	■
Figurative language		■	■	■	■	■
Formal versus informal writing					■	■
Foreshadowing						■
Genre—adventure				■	■	■
Genre—biography and autobiography		■	■	■	■	■
Genre—expository text	■	■	■	■	■	■
Genre—fable	■	■	■	■	■	■
Genre—fairy tale	■	■	■			
Genre—fantasy	■	■	■	■	■	■
Genre—folk tale	■	■	■	■	■	■
Genre—historical fiction		■	■	■	■	■
Genre—legend	■	■	■	■	■	■
Genre—myth, tall tale	■		■	■	■	■
Genre—play/drama	■	■	■	■	■	■
Genre—poetry	■	■	■	■	■	■
Genre—realistic fiction	■	■	■	■	■	■
Genre—science fiction						■
Humor			■	■	■	
Indicators of additional information			■	■	■	■
Indicators of differing information			■	■	■	■
Indicators of place and location	■	■	■	■	■	■
Indicators of time and order	■	■	■	■	■	■
Irony						■
Persuasive writing		■	■	■	■	■
Plot		■	■	■	■	■
Point of view		■	■	■	■	■
Process description		■	■	■	■	■
Setting	■	■	■	■	■	■
Staying on subject			■	■	■	■
Strong topic sentences		■	■	■	■	■

STRATEGIES AND SKILLS	LEVEL					
Writer's Craft/Reading *continued*	1	2	3	4	5	6
Suspense and surprise		X	X	X	X	
Using headings and captions	X	X	X	X	X	X
Using quotations in writing				X	X	X
Variety in writing		X	X	X	X	X
Writing good beginnings		X	X	X	X	X
Writing paragraphs		X	X	X	X	X
Writing personal experiences		X	X	X	X	X
Grammar, Mechanics, and Usage						
Capitalization	X	X	X	X	X	X
Clauses and phrases			X	X	X	X
Comparing with adjectives and adverbs	X	X	X	X	X	X
Complete and incomplete sentences	X	X	X	X	X	X
Compound sentences		X	X	X	X	X
Compound subject and predicate				X	X	X
End punctuation	X	X	X	X	X	X
Kinds of sentences	X	X	X			
Parts of a sentence		X	X	X	X	X
Parts of speech		X	X	X	X	X
Pronoun/antecedent agreement		X	X	X	X	X
Punctuating titles of works (books, movies etc.)				X	X	X
Subject/verb agreement		X	X	X	X	X
Using adjectives and adverbs		X	X	X	X	X
Using colons and semicolons				X	X	X
Using commas in dates, addresses, and parts of a letter		X	X	X	X	X
Using commas in introductory phrases			X	X		
Using commas in a series		X	X	X	X	X
Using dashes and ellipses				X	X	X
Using gerund phrases				X	X	X
Using negatives correctly		X	X	X	X	X
Using parentheses				X	X	X
Using possessive nouns	X	X	X	X	X	X
Using possessive pronouns		X	X	X	X	X
Using prepositions and prepositional phrases		X	X	X		
Using and punctuating dialogue	X	X	X	X	X	X
Using reflexive pronouns				X	X	X
Verb tense		X	X	X	X	X

STRATEGIES AND SKILLS — LEVEL

Phonics/Decoding

Strategies and Skills	1	2	3	4	5	6
Blending sounds into words	▓	*	*			
Consonant clusters	▓	*	*			
Consonant digraphs	▓	*	*			
Consonant sounds and spellings	▓	*	*			
Outlaw words	▓	*	*			
Phonemic awareness	▓	*	*			
Syllables	▓	*	*			
Vowel diphthongs	▓	*	*			
Vowels: long sounds and spellings	▓	*	*			
Vowels: r-controlled	▓	*	*			
Vowels: short sounds and spellings	▓	*	*			

Spelling and Vocabulary

Strategies and Skills	1	2	3	4	5	6
Adding prefixes and suffixes		▓	▓	▓	▓	▓
Building vocabulary	▓	▓	▓	▓	▓	▓
Compound words	▓	▓	▓	▓	▓	▓
Frequently misspelled words		▓	▓	▓	▓	▓
Homophones	▓	▓	▓	▓	▓	▓
Inflectional endings	▓	▓	▓	▓	▓	▓
Long-vowel spelling patterns	▓	▓	▓	▓	▓	▓
Regular and irregular plurals	▓	▓	▓	▓	▓	▓
Short-vowel spelling patterns	▓	▓	▓	▓	▓	▓
Spelling generalizations		▓	▓	▓	▓	▓
Synonyms and antonyms	▓	▓	▓	▓	▓	▓
Unstressed vowel sounds (schwa)				▓	▓	▓
Using and punctuating contractions	▓	▓	▓	▓	▓	▓

Study and Research

Strategies and Skills	1	2	3	4	5	6
Alphabetical order	▓	▓	▓	▓		
Choosing sources		▓	▓	▓		
Comparing information across sources		▓		▓		
Formulating questions and conjectures		▓	▓	▓		
Interviewing		▓	▓	▓		
Making a bibliography					▓	▓
Making and using a time line		▓	▓	▓		
Note taking		▓	▓	▓		
Observing and recording details		▓	▓			

* Optional review at this level

Study and Research *continued*	1	2	3	4	5	6
Organizing information in a chart		■	■	■	■	■
Outlining				■	■	■
Parts of a book	■	■	■	■	■	■
Using a dictionary or glossary	■	■	■	■	■	■
Using a thesaurus				■	■	■
Using an encyclopedia		■	■	■	■	■
Using and understanding diagrams				■	■	■
Using maps, globes, and atlases		■	■	■	■	■
Using primary sources				■	■	■
Using the card catalog (including electronic cc)		■	■	■	■	■
Using the *Reader's Guide*			■	■	■	■

Acknowledgments

Photography

cover © Scott Coe

5 © Mush Emmons

6/7 © Boston Harbor/Steve Elmore, Tom Stack Associates

7 © Commitment/Mush Emmons

12 © Pilot whales/Doug Perrine, DRK Photo

13 © Bermuda/Roderick Beebe

16 © Street band/Mush Emmons

17 © Macaw/Leonard Lee Rue III, DRK Photo

17 © Rain forest/Michael Fogdei, DRK Photo

19 © Bill on radio/Bill Pinkney

20 © Commitment/Mush Emmons

21 © Lion/Jeremy Woodhouse, DRK Photo

21 © Rhinoceros/Kennan Ward, DRK Photo

21 © South African family/Bill Pinkney

23 © Storm/Bill Pinkney

24 © Tasmanian devil/Bill Pinkney

25 © Kangaroo/Stephen J. Krasemann, DRK Photo

25 © Koala/John Cancalosi, DRK Photo

25 © Kookaburra/Stephen J. Krasemann, DRK Photo

26 © Bird/Bill Pinkney

26 © Hawksbill turtle/Doug Perrine, DRK Photo

28 © Cape Horn/Wolfgang Kaehler

30 © Commitment/Scott Coe

30 © Bill Pinkney/Scott Coe

31 © Celebration/Scott Coe

Index